Geographic Literacy
Through Children's Literature

Linda K. Rogers

**Illustrations by
John L. Rogers**

1997
TEACHER IDEAS PRESS
A Division of
Libraries Unlimited, Inc.
Englewood, Colorado

For
my dad who piled us into the car for a ride
my mother who handed us the map
Karen Bromley who encouraged me to write
and, especially,
Jack, John, Sarah, and Hallie who willingly listened
and endured my many hours at the computer

TEACHER IDEAS PRESS
A Division of
Libraries Unlimited, Inc.
P.O. Box 6633
Englewood, CO 80155-6633
1-800-237-6124
www.lu.com/tip

Production Editor: Stephen Haenel
Copy Editor: Jan Krygier
Proofreader: Ann Marie Damian
Indexer: Christine J. Smith
Layout and Design: Michael Florman

Library of Congress Cataloging-in-Publication Data

Rogers, Linda K., 1947-
    Geographic literacy through children's literature / Linda K.
Rogers ; illustrations by John L. Rogers.
    ix, 161 p. 22x28 cm.
    Includes bibliographical references and index.
    ISBN 1-56308-439-2
    1. Geography--Study and teaching (Elementary) 2. Children's
literature--Study and teaching (Elementary) I. Title.
G73.R76 1997
372.89'1044--dc21   97-12081
                                               CIP

Contents

1 Geographic Literacy in Curriculum 1

2 Location 7

3 Place 25

4 Human-Environmental Relations 41

5 Movement 59

6 Regions 75

Figures

Preface

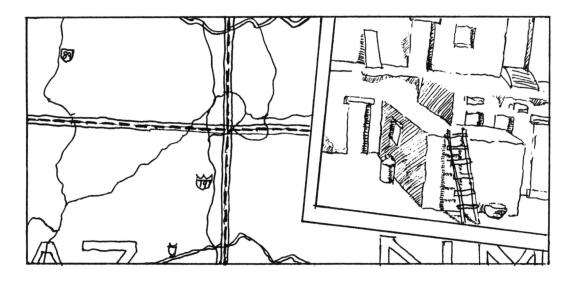

I have always been interested in maps. My dad would say, particularly on a summer evening, "Let's go for a ride." We would all (eventually, seven of us) pile into the car and ride and ride and ride. In central Illinois the roads are basically set on a grid, with few of the curves and none of the mountains of northeastern Pennsylvania. We would ride through the countryside, viewing fields in various stages of growth, and making distinct 90-degree turns at intersections. I learned from an early age that if you were going south, a right turn headed you west and a left turn headed you east. And, if you were heading east, a right turn sent you south and a left turn sent you north. And, if you were heading north . . . you get the picture. My parents would give directions using north, south, east, and west rather than landmarks. They would pass the map to the four or five of us in the backseat so that we could find our location and determine how long it would take us to reach the next intersection or town.

My dad was very interested in maps, and his road atlas would be heavily worn before its time because of the hours he spent poring over it. I think all five of his children have that same compulsion to scrutinize maps as if they were photographs of the places they locate. My own children have been handed maps and encouraged to trace our journeys.

I guess it is no surprise, then, that I feel strongly about promoting geographic literacy in elementary classrooms. So, when Karen Bromley asked me, as her graduate assistant, to begin finding children's books that could enhance the teaching of world geography, I was really interested and excited. As I gathered children's books and information about geographic education for an article we wrote together, I began to truly comprehend how little I actually knew about what geography encompasses. I also took a course in geographic theories, which further expanded my perceptions.

After Karen and I completed the article (1995), I found myself continuing to collect titles for the annotated bibliography we had begun, and I made several presentations at reading conferences in New York and Pennsylvania. This book is a result of my continued desire to encourage geographic literacy in elementary classrooms and the warm response I have had from teachers who attended my presentations and who want to incorporate geography into their curriculum. I hope this book inspires readers to use and expand on what I have presented.

Reference

Rogers, Linda, and Bromley, Karen. "Children's Literature: A Vehicle for Developing Geographic Literacy." *Social Studies and the Young Learner* 8 (November-December 1995): Pull-out feature II.

Chapter 1

GEOGRAPHIC LITERACY IN CURRICULUM

Important Background Information

The average person equates geographic literacy with place-name and location, yet that is only a small portion of the discipline (Salter 1991). Geographic literacy is actually achieved "when people understand why places are where they are, what these places are like, and how they relate to these people and to other places" (Jenness 1990, 231). Nonetheless, it is simplistic place-name ignorance that has led to public outcry. Students' poor performance on geography quizzes and tests has attracted the attention of the media and experts (Grosvenor 1985; Hill and LaPrairie 1989; Lawton 1995; Saveland 1993). In the June 1985 "President's Page" of *National Geographic,* Gilbert M. Grosvenor reviews distressing results of a 1984 questionnaire on geography given to 2,200 North Carolina college students. Comparing the 1984 results with an earlier questionnaire sponsored by the *New York Times* in 1950, Grosvenor

acknowledges the obvious: Students are not as geographically literate as they were in 1950. But he also points out that 71 percent of the students in the 1984 questionnaire said they had no geography courses at the elementary level, 65 percent had none in junior high school, and 73 percent had none in high school. Does this lack of geographic knowledge shift the problem of geographic illiteracy from the students to the teachers, or the schools? It is not that simple.

There are actually several problems within education that contribute to a lack of geographic literacy. First, academic geographers (university professors) have often chosen to separate themselves from "school geography"—geography taught in precollegiate settings (Salter 1987; Schmudde 1987). Second, students in elementary and secondary schools are usually taught geography as a discipline of only place-names and almost never as a subject separate from social studies or history (Abler 1987; Gardner 1986; Hill and LaPrairie 1989; Saveland 1993). Third, because the school curriculum is so full, it is often difficult to determine where geography can be fit in without eliminating something else. Finally, many teachers have taken no geography classes in their teacher preparation programs (Gardner 1986; Natoli 1994) and, as a result, don't feel confident teaching geography.

There has been an overt response to the issue of geographic illiteracy over the past decade. A joint committee of the National Council for Geographic Education (NCGE) and the Association of American Geographers (AAG) published guidelines for geographic education in both elementary and secondary schools. The favorable public response to this 1984 publication led to an effort by the NCGE and the AAG, along with the American Geographic Society

(AGS) and the National Geographic Society (NGS), to form the Geographic Education National Implementation Project (GENIP). GENIP is a national project designed to improve the status and quality of geographic education in the United States in grades K-12. In 1987 GENIP prepared a publication for elementary classroom teachers intended to aid them in planning and implementing geographic education titled *K-6 Geography: Themes, Key Ideas, and Learning Opportunities* (Kimball 1987). The publication identified five central themes in geography:

LOCATION: Position on the Earth's Surface;

PLACE: Physical and Human Characteristics;

HUMAN-ENVIRONMENTAL RELATIONS: Humans and Environments;

MOVEMENT: Humans Interacting on the Earth; and

REGIONS: How They Form and Change.

More recently, these themes have been elaborated (Boehm and Petersen 1994) to clarify both the physical and human aspects of geography.

The 5 Themes are the basis for chapters 2-6. Each theme will be discussed more fully at the beginning of each chapter. Various subthemes are also discussed; these subthemes are shown in italic type. The themes and subthemes are encapsulated in boxes at the end of the chapter introductions.

Geography for Life: National Geography Standards 1994 (Geography Education Standards Project 1994) was published in October 1994 through the National Geography Project. It arranges geographic knowledge into six essential elements and 18 Standards that define characteristics of geographically informed people.

- **Seeing the World in Spatial Terms**
  The geographically informed person knows and understands:
    1. how to use maps and other geographic representations, tools, and technologies to acquire, process, and report information from a spatial perspective.
    2. how to use mental maps to organize information about people, places, and environments in a spatial context.
    3. how to analyze the spatial organization of people, places, and environments on the Earth's surface.

- **Places and Regions**
  The geographically informed person knows and understands:
    4. the physical and human characteristics of places.
    5. that people create regions to interpret the Earth's complexity.
    6. how culture and experience influence people's perceptions of places and regions.

- **Physical Systems**
  The geographically informed person knows and understands:
    7. the physical processes that shape the patterns of the Earth's surface.
    8. the characteristics and spatial distribution of ecosystems on the Earth's surface.

- **Human Systems**
  The geographically informed person knows and understands:
    9. the characteristics, distribution, and migration of human populations on the Earth's surface.
    10. the characteristics, distribution, and complexity of the Earth's cultural mosaics.
    11. the patterns and networks of economic interdependence on the Earth's surface.
    12. the processes, patterns, and functions of human settlement.
    13. how the forces of cooperation and conflict among people influence the division and control of the Earth's surface.

- **Environment and Society**
  The geographically informed person knows and understands:
    14. how human actions modify the physical environment.
    15. how physical systems affect human systems.
    16. the changes that occur in the meaning, use, distribution, and importance of resources.

- **The Uses of Geography**
  The geographically informed person knows and understands:
    17. how to apply geography to interpret the past.
    18. how to apply geography to interpret the present and plan for the future.

The price of the 272-page *Geography for Life* is very reasonable ($9). It contains classroom strategies, skills articulation and application, and short essays on the meaning and significance of the 18 Standards. An 11-page booklet, *Key to the National Geography Standards,* has been published as a link between the 5 Fundamental Themes and the 18 Standards. You may want to consider purchasing either or both of these publications.

Geographic Alliances exist in each of the 50 states. Each summer, alliance-sponsored workshops provide geographic education and effective teaching methods for classroom teachers. Refer to Appendix B, "Teacher Resources," to find the address of the one in your state. Membership in the alliance includes a newsletter and access to a network of teachers and professional geographers who can support your classroom work.

How to Use This Book

If classroom teachers become thoroughly familiar with the 5 Themes, they will become aware of the occasions when they can successfully integrate geography into an already full curriculum. The social studies curriculum is a natural place to connect the geographic themes because it is where we have traditionally taught geography and because specific map skills and maps are included in most social studies texts. Most of us think about map skills and place location when we hear the word *geography,* but the interaction of humans with their environment and with one another is just as important in geography. In addition to social studies, many other parts of the elementary curriculum provide opportunities for the teacher to make connections with geographic themes. For example, many concepts explored in science are embedded in geographic concepts. Weather patterns in the United States move from west to east, climate determines the type of clothing and shelter needed for survival, and your position on the Earth and its relationship to the sun determine what time of day and season you are experiencing. In reading and language arts, teachers can help students discover that the setting of a story often has a direct impact on the actions of the characters or the mood of the story. Peter, in *A Snowy Day* by Ezra Jack Keats, could not have played in the snow if he lived near the equator. Alaska was the only place Jean Craighead George could set *Julie of the Wolves* to tell this special story of an Eskimo girl who interacts with her environment to survive.

The picture books presented in this book can be used to introduce or expand concepts already in the curriculum. Before you read the book to your class, be sure to read the jacket and the information on the copyright page. The publisher's description of the book, the author's and illustrator's biographical information, and even the dedication offer a wealth of information to bring to the reading of the book. *Remember, the books are, first and foremost, picture books to be enjoyed, so begin by reading them to your students for sheer enjoyment.* Savor the rich language and the illustrations, drawings, or paintings they contain. Then revisit them to explore the concepts they can enhance.

Each of the following chapters discusses a specific geographic theme. Although the 5 Themes and the 18 Standards look at the same thing, Kit and Cathy Salter (1995) point out that the themes represent an instructional approach. Because the themes made up the organizational framework I used as I began collecting the bibliography and ideas, they are the framework I am using in this book. If you examine the 18 Standards presented above you will find that they integrate the 5 Themes. As you read the ideas contained in this book and, especially, the annotated bibliography in Appendix A, you will discover that many of the books contain more than one theme. I am not rejecting the 18 Standards framework; rather, I find that using the 5 Themes makes it easier for me to present the books and ideas.

Chapters 2-6 offer specific ideas and "book talks" to demonstrate how picture books can be used to enhance children's understanding of the five specific geographic themes identified by the Geographic Education National Implementation Project (GENIP) in the mid-1980s. Appendix A, an annotated bibliography, includes a brief description of all the books mentioned in the chapters plus a few others that I found to be appropriate. Appendix B includes professional resources available to classroom teachers who wish to expand their geographic knowledge.

Review Appendix A, "Annotated Bibliography," first. You will find it helpful to scan, if not carefully read, it before you read Chapters 2-6. Collecting these books marked my original interaction with geographic literacy, and I began this book with the writing of the bibliography. References to the books within each chapter are usually brief. I wrote the chapters with the belief that you would be able to quickly refer to the annotations and make notes in the margins.

Ideas for using specific children's literature are provided in Chapters 2-6. Although these are complete in my mind, they are not "set in stone." Because only you know your students and curriculum, only you can make choices that best suit your classroom. Adopt the ideas as they are written or adapt them to fit your situation. I have undoubtedly missed other wonderful books that are available. (Each time I visit the children's section of my local library I find another book . . . or two . . . or three.) Look at children's literature with the geographic themes in mind and integrate them into all aspects of your curriculum.

Picture books are often deceptive. Although they appear to be "easy," and are even classified as such in most libraries, many of them contain very sophisticated concepts and are written at a higher than expected reading level with conceptually difficult vocabulary. Some are quite provocative, introducing complicated issues in a more simplistic format. For example, *Sami and the Time of the Troubles* (Heide and Gilliland 1992) illustrates the extraordinary life lived by children in war-torn cities (in this case, Beirut). Sami must live in a basement to remain safe from the bombings that frequently occur in his city. Yet he is able to enjoy doing family chores and helping neighbors when the streets are safe. Or, in *Smoky Night* (Bunting 1994) a small boy whose apartment is located in the midst of the Los Angeles riots is nonetheless able to watch the activity from the safety of the home environment he has with his mother.

You may need to check your library's online catalog to find how the books have been classified. For example, I have found Knight's *Talking Walls* on the shelves under a Dewey Decimal number in both of my local libraries, but Cherry's *A River Ran Wild* is found among the Easy books in one library and under the Dewey Decimal system in the other.

The annotated bibliography in Appendix A is divided into two parts: "Children's Literature" and "Geography Reference Books for Children." Each entry contains a summary and suggestions for the book's use within grade-level parameters and the appropriate geographic theme(s). Cross-references direct the reader to other books that can complement a particular study. I did not include any books I did not personally examine. In some instances I borrowed books through interlibrary loan, but most were in my small community library.

P.S.: Another Thought . . .

I strongly believe you should always teach with maps and a globe to help your students put whatever you are teaching in spatial context and in relation to where you and your students are in space. At some point during the 444 days that 52 Americans were held hostage in the U.S. embassy in Iran, a small group of my Chapter I reading students and I had a wonderful discussion I still remember vividly after many years. Danny, a fourth-grader, had obviously been listening to television reports and possibly to discussions at home. He asked, "Why don't we just fly in there and get them out?" Instead of getting out our work for that day, we put the globe in the middle of the table and located the United States and Iran. We used a piece of string and a ruler to estimate the distance between the two countries. After we determined the distance our planes would have to travel, we looked for countries who were our allies and would allow us to land and refuel. When the group left, I realized we hadn't completed the day's lesson, but I was quite pleased by our interaction and with myself for having seized a "teachable moment." As I think about the Iranian hostage crisis or the Gulf War or the conflict in the former Yugoslavia, I think I understand why many children and adults are uninformed and confused. Television news reports almost always feature maps. During the Gulf War we even saw reports of troop movements demonstrated on maps and models. But seldom are we shown where the place under discussion is located in relation to the United States. Good teachers know that students learn best when new information is connected to previous knowledge. So, I encourage you to be ready for those teachable moments and remember to build on your students' prior knowledge.

Resources

Geography for Life: National Geography Standards 1994. To order, send a check and a written request with your name, institution, address, and product number [#01775-12160] to National Geographic Society, P.O. Box 1640, Washington, DC 20013-1640. Single copy: $9.00. Discount for multiple copies.

K-6 Geography: Themes, Key Ideas, and Learning Opportunities. To order, send a check and a written request with your name, institution, and address to National Council for Geographic Education, Western Illinois University, Macomb, IL 61455. Single copy: approx. $6.

Key to the National Geography Standards. To order, send a check with your name, institution, and address to Ms. Connie McCardle, National Council for Geographic Education, NCGE Central Office, Indiana University of Pennsylvania, Indiana, PA 15705. (412) 357-6290; (412) 357-7708 (fax). Single copy: approx. $3.

References

Abler, R. F. 1987. "What Shall We Say? To Whom Shall We Speak?" *Annals of the Association of American Geographers* 77: 511-24.

Boehm, R. G., and Petersen, J. F. 1994. "An Elaboration of the Fundamental Themes in Geography." *Social Education* 58, no. 4: 211-18.

Gardner, D. P. 1986. "Geography in the School Curriculum." *Annals of the Association of American Geographers* 76: 1-4.

Geography Education Standards Project. 1994. *Geography for Life: National Geography Standards 1994.* Washington, D.C.: National Geographic Society.

Grosvenor, G. M. 1985. "Geographic Ignorance: Time for a Turnaround." *National Geographic* 167, no. 6.

Hill, A. D., and LaPrairie, L. A. 1989. "Geography in American Education." In *Geography in America,* edited by G. L. Gaile and C. J. Willmott, 1-26. Columbus, Ohio: Merrill.

Jenness, D. 1990. *Making Sense of Social Studies.* New York: Macmillan.

Kimball, W. 1987. *K-6 Geography: Themes, Key Ideas, and Learning Opportunities.* New York: American Geographical Society.

Lawton, M. 1995. "Students Fall Short in NAEP Geography Test." *Education Week* 15, no. 8: 1, 23.

Natoli, S. J. 1994. "Guidelands for Geographic Education and the Fundamental Themes in Geography." *Journal of Geography* 93, no. 1: 2-6.

Salter, C., Hobbs, G., and Salter, K. 1995. *Key to the National Geography Standards.* Washington, D.C.: National Geographic Society.

Salter, C. L. 1987. "The Nature and Potential of a Geographic Alliance." *Journal of Geography* 86, no. 5: 211-15

Salter, K. 1991. "The University and the Alliance: A Study in Contradictions." *Journal of Geography* 90, no. 2: 55-59.

Salter, K., and Salter, C. 1995. "Significant New Materials for the Geography Classroom." *Journal of Geography* 94, no. 4: 444-52.

Saveland, R. N. 1993. "School Geography." In *Teaching Social Studies,* edited by V. S. Wilson, J. A. Litle, and G. L. Wilson, 131-46. Westport, Conn.: Greenwood Press.

Schmudde, T. H. 1987. "The Image of Geography Equals the Structure of Its Curriculum and Courses." *Journal of Geography* 86, no. 2: 46-47.

Chapter 2

LOCATION

"Absolute and relative location are two ways of describing the positions of people and places on the earth's surface."

—W. Kimball, *K-6 Geography*, 3

This chapter deals with what many people consider to be geography: place-name and location. Reports of students' geographic illiteracy relate to the apparent place-name ignorance that exists in this country. Obviously, Location is not all of geography, but it is important. The basic skills we teach students provide a foundation for the other geographic themes discussed in this book and allow students to look at the world with open eyes. From my point of view, Location is integral to all of the geographic themes.

Absolute Location

Every site on Earth has a global address. We use many systems to establish this address: grids, maps, globes, map projections, and Earth-sun relations (Boehm and Petersen 1994). Students are taught to recognize and use these systems. The age and maturity of the child usually determine when and what systems are taught.

Grids provide location in relation to references such as longitude and latitude, found on world maps and globes, or alphanumeric grids, found on state and local maps.

Maps and Globes are used to find location. They are also used to show geographic elements such as pattern and process. Boehm and Petersen (1994) note that maps and globes can provide the location and distribution of factors such as population, climate zones, and political divisions as well as routes for travel.

Map Projections are the result of moving the three-dimensional representation of Earth (the globe) onto a two-dimensional map. Projecting a sphere on a page inevitably leads to distortions.

Earth-Sun Relations involve Earth's movement and its position relative to the sun. This relationship determines climate, seasons, and time zones.

Relative Location

Relative location is the way in which we describe one location in relation to another. For example, my hometown is located in central Illinois, and I attended a small college 45 miles southwest of my hometown. The Mississippi River is the border between Illinois and the states to its west.

Locations Have Geographic Explanations that tell us why certain features and places are located where they are (Boehm and Petersen 1994). These explanations may be factors of history, economics, or other physical or human considerations. When we look at the early settlements in this country (both Native American and European), we find them located near bodies of water because they provided immediate access to food, drinking water, and easy transportation. Castles and forts were built with defense in mind. They were often located on high ground to provide a better view of who was approaching. Many times they were located against mountains, rivers, or lakes to provide protection on at least one side.

In addition, *The Importance of a Location Can Change with History*. We can see this within the United States. Communities were established around the discovery of natural resources. For example, many communities were formed in California during the Gold Rush but were either abandoned or greatly reduced in population as the quantity of gold being recovered declined. The same is true in many regions dependent on the mining of coal. As either the coal deposits ran out or the demand for coal diminished, the importance of the location changed.

LOCATION

Absolute Location

- Grids
- Maps and Globes
- Map Projections
- Earth-Sun Relations

Relative Location

- Locations Have Geographic Explanations
- The Importance of a Location Can Change with History

Teaching Ideas

Many books are available that teach the basic skills. They are of varying difficulty and style. Although most of the books I'll refer to in this chapter appear in the "Geography Reference Books" section of the bibliography, several are found in the "Children's Literature" section.

Introductory Activities

All About Where (Hoban 1991) is a book with colorful photographs and relational words (such as *above, behind, under,* and *through*) that invite the younger reader to tell about the contents of each picture. These words help students describe where objects exist in space—an important part of Location. The book is designed for very young children. In the preschool and kindergarten classroom the teacher can provide children with the opportunity to physically illustrate the relational words found in such statements as "Stand next to the red cabinet"; "Sit behind the big desk"; or "Put the book under the puzzle."

Another way of introducing map skills with younger students is to make body maps. Creating such maps calls for students to locate body parts. In the middle of her unit of study on the human body, student teacher Val and her kindergartners created a body map. First, Val pulled down the map of the United States and pointed out the various elements of it. She noted where various states, rivers, and lakes were located. Next, Val's cooperating teacher laid down on a large sheet of butcher paper and Val traced around her. She included individual toes and fingers, but that was the extent of the detail. Lastly, the students took turns pointing to body parts that Val labeled. The terms used by the children included *eye, nose, mouth, ear, chin, hand, arm, elbow, knee, ankle, toes, fingers, belly button, leg,* and *shin.* Such an activity provides children with an authentic setting to practice the relational terms. The children used phrases such as "The nose is *above* the mouth" or " The ears are on the *side* of the head."

Yet another way to introduce maps, particularly to intermediate students, is to have a "Maps Day." Encourage every student to come to class with a map. Be very general. Don't offer any specifics or suggestions. Your responsibility before class is to collect a variety of maps, particularly the ones you believe your students will not bring to class. Among these might be local, regional, and state topographical maps; road and world atlases; specific road maps such as those produced by toll-road authorities; subway, train, or bus routes; and geographical or geological surveys. The state department of agriculture may have maps available that show where agricultural products are produced in your state. Check with your local chamber of commerce to see if it has brochures that show various population factors in a map format. Let your imagination guide you. Place all the maps the students have brought from home on a table and gather the students around it. (Or, sit in a circle on the floor and put all the maps in the center where they can be seen by everyone.) First, have the class identify the maps by type. This is a good opportunity for you to assess the breadth and depth of your students' understanding of maps. At this point you should introduce any type of maps you have brought in that the students have not and with which you feel they

should be familiar. Now, have the students look at the collection of maps and determine what categories could be used to group them. For example, you probably have two major groups: road maps and landform, or topographical, maps. Consider other ways to categorize: What are they used for? Who uses them? Who produced them? How are they presented? Examine them for similarities and differences: size, shape, colors, keys, use. Have the students vote for the one they think is the most interesting, most unusual, most common. Display an example of each type of map and make as many of the maps available as you can. Allow students to spend time examining them over a week or two. Encourage them to discuss their observations and to record them in their journals. If they aren't writing regularly in journals, establish a journal-writing routine for this activity.

Expanding Concepts

We teach and reteach the "basics." The cardinal directions can be introduced as early as preschool. The book *North, South, East, and West* (Fowler 1993) provides a very elementary beginning place. The author, through the use of photographs and text, explains the four main directions and explains how to use the sun to determine directions. You can take your class outside on a sunny day and reproduce the activities in the book. This can also lead children to notice the connection between natural phenomena and our representation of the world around us. The sun moves from east to west in our sky, so we can judge directions based on the position of the sun. When students study Native Americans and early explorers, they can examine how natural phenomena were used to guide travel and how they influenced their lives.

Consider involving your students in the following activity on a sunny day. Find a safe, paved surface on your school's property like the playground, sidewalk, or parking lot where the students can draw on the pavement over a period of hours without the drawings being disturbed. Begin by pairing the students. One student will be the "statue" and the other the "marker." Each pair of students will need a piece of chalk. Early in the day (around 9:00-9:30 A.M.), go outside to the designated area. Have each "statue" find a place on the pavement at least four feet away from another "statue." The statues should face the same way, standing straight with feet slightly apart and arms against their bodies. Consider having students face north. The markers should first trace the statues' feet, then the shadow cast by the statue. This shadow should be marked with the time. Have the statues move out of the chalk marks so that the markers can write the names of the partners in the foot tracings. Return to class. Two to three hours later (near noon), return to the marked shadows. Reposition the statues in their foot tracings. Be certain everyone is standing in exactly the same spot and facing the same way. Have the markers trace the new shadow. Return to class. In the afternoon (2:00-2:30 P.M.), repeat the process a third time. After each tracing, have the student pairs record their drawings and reflect on what they have learned. Use the "Making Shadows" worksheet provided in figure 2.1. When all three drawings are completed, and students have had a chance to record the information on the worksheet, gather the class for a discussion. Have students consider the following: How were the shadows they recorded alike? How were they different? What do they think created the shadows? What caused differences? Would this activity be possible on a rainy day? Would the shadows be different if the activity was completed during a different season? What connection do the students see between shadows and time?

Statue: _____   Marker: _____

Making Shadows

First Drawing
Time:

Second Drawing
Time:

Third Drawing
Time:

First draw the footprints, then draw the shadow.

First draw the footprints, then draw the shadow.

First draw the footprints, then draw the shadow.

What shape is the shadow?

Are the shadows in the first and second drawings alike or different? How?

Are the shadows in the first and second drawings alike or different? How?

Where is the sun?

Where is the sun?

Where is the sun?

Fig. 2.1. Making shadows.

I recently supervised a student teacher, Michelle, in a second-grade classroom, who taught a social studies unit that reviewed cardinal directions and the terms *urban*, *suburban*, and *rural*. She began by rearranging the students' desks and hanging signs from the ceiling. Each group of eight or nine students was arranged in double lines with the desks facing. The group nearest the classroom door was the urban group, the next group was suburban, and the group farthest from the door was the rural group. When Michelle referred to the urban and rural groups, she used the terms *urban/city* and *rural/country* interchangeably so that the students connected the unknown terms with the known terms. The placement of the suburban group between the other two was calculated to simulate their positions in reality.

One of Michelle's bulletin boards was a grid created by vertical and horizontal lengths of yarn placed at five-inch intervals. North, south, east, and west were indicated with word cards. Then, five paper pictures were placed in five of the grid's squares. Each day Michelle asked students to move the pictures, for example, "Move the squirrel three spaces north" or "Move the acorn five spaces east."

Michelle also created a quick daily activity that actively involved the students in using cardinal directions. The four main directions were on each of the four classroom walls. Michelle had the students stand up behind their desks. She then gave commands: "Face west," "Now, east." After five minutes or so, they moved to another activity. Later, Michelle and I considered some other possible ways to use this idea. We thought students would enjoy playing a "Simon Says" or "Mother May I" type of game in the gymnasium or on the playground, which would allow greater movement. With unlimited time (Michelle was only in the classroom eight weeks), the teacher could move to the intermediate directions (northeast, northwest, southeast, and southwest).

Of course, as children mature, we need to deal with the subtlety of the sun's position in the sky. When you live in the Northern Hemisphere, especially in the northern part of North America, the winter sun never rises as high in the sky as it does in the summer. Thus, positioning ourselves using the sun is more difficult. (A more complete discussion of the Earth-sun relationship appears later in this chapter.)

The Whole World in Your Hands: Looking at Maps (Berger and Berger 1993) contains a series of activities that move from the very local, very personal creation of a map of the child's bedroom to the preparation of a world map. This book offers some easy ways to lead students through mapmaking.

You can make simple room/building maps in a variety of ways. I visited a primary classroom in a private, ungraded school (with each classroom given a color designation, rather than a grade level) where the students, ages four to seven, used large wooden building blocks to create a map of the ground floor of their school. They began with a "field trip" outside during which they walked around the building, paying close attention to its sides and corners. When they returned, they discussed the shape of the building (a rectangle) and, using blocks, established the outside walls. Through further discussion with the teacher, they determined what was located in each corner of the ground floor. Eventually, they were able to produce a map of the ground floor with a single layer of blocks. (See fig. 2.2.)

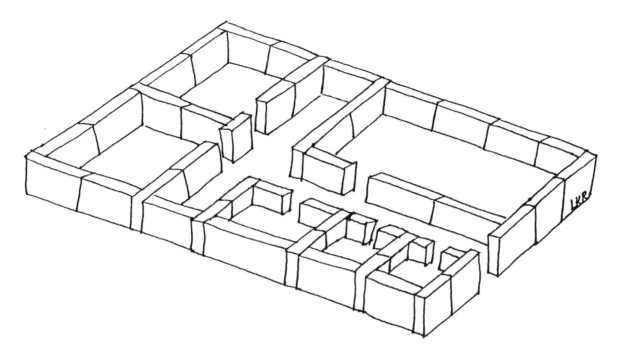

Fig. 2.2. Building block map of the ground floor.

We often consider mapmaking as a paper-and-pencil project, but the above activity certainly stretches our thinking. In the fall, when I was an elementary student, my brothers and sisters and I would rake a clearing in our yard. Then we would create a "blueprint" of a house using "lines" of leaves. It had lots of bedrooms and soft, leaf-pile furniture. There were doorways, which we were very careful to use as we played in the house. Consider some of the unique ways you might involve your students in mapmaking. A few ordinary materials come to mind: small and large blocks; a sandbox; sugar cubes or toothpicks glued to construction paper; strips of construction paper of varying lengths to define the boundaries while other shapes become specific features; salt dough formed into the appropriate shape and, possibly, presenting unique features. Chalk works very well on blacktop. Or, consider using ribbon or yarn lengths connecting sticks pushed into the ground. If you have bleachers on the side of the field you use, you can create the image and then observe it from the top of the bleachers (or from a second-story window?) to get a bird's-eye view. First attempts at mapmaking do not have to produce permanent maps.

Before I move into more discussions of student-generated maps, we have to stop and consider scale. When a map is created, the designer must decide what scale to use. Scale is the relationship between the actual size of the object being depicted and the size of its symbol on the map. If the relationship is represented incorrectly, we say the result is a distortion of the original. The Bergers offer an easy way to create scale in their book. In developing a map of their bedroom, students are advised to use graph paper. Then, the Bergers direct the students to use their own foot length as the unit of measure. For each foot length, the students draw along one section of the graph paper. This provides an easy introduction to establishing a formal scale.

When we reconsider the block map of the ground floor depicted in figure 2.2, we can see that first attempts at mapmaking can use relative scale. The teacher and students did not measure the length and width of the whole building, or the individual rooms. Rather, they considered relative size. Were the rooms all the same size and shape? Was the "Purple's" room larger or smaller than their own, "Yellow's," room? What shape was the hallway (L-shaped) and how long was it? How did the teachers' lounge compare in size and shape with the classrooms? In the same way, in your classroom, you can foster student thought about scale by inviting them to consider these questions: Is the wall with the windows longer, shorter, or the same length as the wall with the chalkboard? Is the doorway into the hall in the middle of the wall or to one end or the other?

When you take a field trip onto the playground, you can help students observe the relative location of such landmarks as sidewalks, playground equipment, and bus line marks. When you return to the classroom, guide the students through a visualized visit to the playground. Have them imagine they are in a particular location. Ask: What do you see in front of you? . . . behind you? What is on your right? . . . your left? Have them imagine that they are walking to another spot. Again, ask questions that require students to visualize where the objects are in relationship to the students and the other objects. As students gain more experience, you can introduce formal scale measuring. You can also add cardinal directions.

In the Woods: Who's Been Here? (George 1995) and *In the Snow: Who's Been Here?* (George 1995) take the reader on a trip through the woods with two children as they discover the easily overlooked clues of animals' habitats. A map drawn by the children is at the beginning of each book. It models the kind of map your students can devise. They just need you to encourage them to carefully observe their surroundings as you take them on field trips around the school or neighborhood.

Gail Hartman's books *As the Crow Flies: A First Book of Maps* (1991) and *As the Roadrunner Runs: A First Book of Maps* (1994) can also be used with young students just beginning to explore the representation of their world, as well as with older students. Hartman shows the reader five mini-maps, illustrated from the perspective of one animal in a particular environment. At the end of the book, a full map connects the previously viewed five mini-maps, providing the reader with a view of the entire area. In *As the Crow Flies* the area connects the mountains to the sea through the meandering of a river. The desert is the focus of *As the Roadrunner Runs*.

Students can create maps to represent part of the school building, part of the school grounds, or (for older students) their own home and neighborhood. Then, just as Hartman joined the mini-maps together, you and your students can create one large map that combines everyone's contribution. After the class has put together its large map of the community, compare it with a professionally prepared community map. I find that local real estate offices provide wonderful, inexpensive maps. Students can explore the reasons for the differences between their map and the professional one. If possible, have an outside speaker come in to share professional mapmaking techniques and, perhaps, advise students how to improve their own mapmaking techniques.

When our daughter, Hallie, was in seventh grade, her five-week computer unit was a more sophisticated version of the Bergers' activities discussed above. Using a software program, the students each produced a floor plan of their own bedroom. Hallie used a large tape measure to determine the length of the walls in her room. She also designated the placement of windows, doors, and closet. The program allowed her to set furniture into place. You can see the room dimensions reflected in the arrows on the plan in figure 2.3.

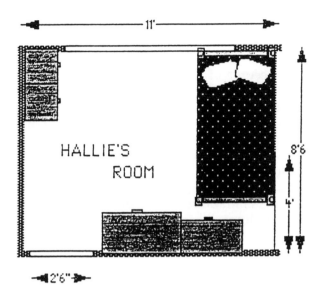

Fig. 2.3. Hallie's bedroom.

The second part of the unit was more complicated. Hallie spent two afternoons measuring each room on the main floor of our house. When she inserted her measurements into the program, she produced a floor plan of our house, shown in figure 2.4. The arrangement of the rooms is quite accurate, including the placement of windows, doors, closets, bathtubs, and cabinet. The actual outside shape of the house is not correct. It should be a rectangle with a "bump" off the back to represent the second bathroom the original owners added. At this point the teacher can guide the student through the analysis of how accurate the map is. Hallie could have remeasured the rooms where the inaccuracies occurred. Such an activity helps to introduce the skills required of cartographers.

Although the major focus of *Follow the Dream: The Story of Christopher Columbus* (Sis 1991) is the life of Christopher Columbus, Sis provides wonderful fifteenth-century maps throughout the book. He points out how the maps reflect the view of the world at that time. *Maps and Globes* (Knowlton 1985), *The Student's Activity Atlas* (Morris 1993), and *Maps and Mapping* (Taylor 1993) can be used to expand a study of mapmaking.

If your students have access to a computer, consider using programs that move them from the geographic reference books, yet require them to apply the skills they have acquired. The one Hallie used requires students to use mathematical skills. Recently I visited a fifth-grade classroom in which students could use their free time to "drive" on the computer screen. The program provided a bird's-eye view of a city map with buildings, street names, and landmarks. The students travel from one point to another. As they "drive" with Jenny, they view the city through the windshield of a car, turning appropriately. At any time they can return to the map to check their progress. I thoroughly enjoyed watching two girls maneuver themselves through the city, leaning left and right, thinking through which turn would send them in the correct direction.

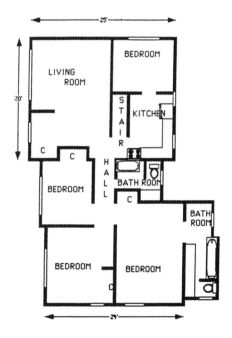

Fig. 2.4. Hallie's house plan.

Susan, who is student teaching in a departmentalized sixth grade, is responsible for teaching a unit study of regions of the United States. While the class is currently focusing on the Southwest, Susan has created an interactive bulletin board that encourages students to be aware of the whole country. A large political map of the United States, approximately 24 inches by 36 inches, is mounted in the center of a bulletin board. Students are encouraged to read the local newspaper, paying close attention to the origin of the story. The news story is to be summarized on a three-by-five-inch note card, carefully including the who, what, when, where, why, and how of the story. The card is then brought to class and placed on the bulletin board outside the borders of the United States. A piece of yarn is used to connect the card with the exact location of the story's origin. Susan has provided some incentives for the students: an ice cream party if they find a story from each of the 50 states before her time in the classroom is over; a Jolly Rancher candy for any contributor of a story located in a state capital; and, once five stories from the same state are identified, a Jolly Rancher for each of the story contributors. This is a wonderful example of how you can cross curricular lines. Susan's bulletin board allows her to teach reading and writing skills at the same time as she is building location skills and meeting curricular requirements in social studies.

Rotation and Revolution

As I stated in Chapter 1, I advocate using maps and globes continuously. But you must make sure the globe properly represents the tilt of the Earth. The tilt is extremely important to our understanding of how the relationship of the Earth and sun affects day and night as well as seasons and climate. Knowlton's *Maps and Globes* (1985) and Sipiera's *Globes* (1991) provide important reference information about globes.

Gibbons and Kandoian both address the issue of the Earth's rotation and revolution, which, of course, create our days and nights and the seasons. *The Reasons for Seasons* (Gibbons 1995) is really a reference book rather than a storybook, but its content is presented in a clear and whimsical style. It provides wonderful diagrams to demonstrate the tilt of the Earth, its daily rotation, and its yearly revolution around the sun. *What Makes Day and Night* (Branley 1986), another reference book, is intended for an even younger reader, while *Anno's Sundial* (Anno 1987) is for older readers. Kandoian deals with the seasons in the fictional *Molly's Seasons* (1992) and with day and night in *Under the Sun* (1987), in which Molly asks where the sun goes when she goes to sleep. Both books can be used to introduce the relationship between the Earth and sun. I have used a globe and flashlight to re-create the text in *Under the Sun*. Using tiny balls of poster tack, intended to hold posters on walls, I secured flags at the locations named in the book. The one-inch flags were made from toothpicks and construction paper. I held the flashlight as I rotated the globe, creating day and night around the world.

There are several books you might use to initiate discussions about seasons and climate. I think it's worthy to note two things here: First, weather is the short-term effect of the sun's radiation on the Earth from day to day, while climate is the long-term effect; and, second, we often forget that children (and some adults) assume the way seasons occur where they live is the norm. Consider using the books as a means to compare and contrast climate and seasons.

Those of us who live in those parts of North America where there are four distinct seasons sometimes forget that the holiday season in November and December isn't one of cold and snow for everyone in the world. *How Many Days to America? A Thanksgiving Story* (Bunting 1990) is set on a small boat in the Caribbean, not in a sled going "over the river and through the woods" as we so often see depicted in paintings and commercials.

Christmas at Long Pond (George 1992), *My Prairie Christmas* (Harvey 1990), *Christmastime in New York City* (Munro 1994), and *Christmas on the Prairie* (Anderson 1985) all are set in a winter climate, in contrast with *An Island Christmas* (Joseph 1992), set in Trinidad. In this book, Rosie introduces the reader to the preparation of the special foods as well as the sights and sounds of an island Christmas.

Two books that represent the climate and customs of people in the Arctic region are *The Seasons and Someone* (Kroll 1994) and *Nessa's Fish* (Luenn 1990). The continuous cold of this region contrasts with the type of climate most of us experience. These simple books introduce the need for humans to adapt to their environment—yes, another theme! (See Chapter 4 for more discussion and examples related to this topic.)

Layers of History

As I have collected books for the bibliography, I have been intrigued by the ones I felt demonstrated the "layers of history" that exist at any given locale. We don't always think about who might have lived, what might have happened, and what structures might have existed in one particular spot at various times through history. There are quite a few picture books that demonstrate this phenomenon. John Goodall has created three wordless picture books that document the history of one place: *The Story of a Farm* (1989), *The Story of a Main Street* (1987), and *The Story of the Seashore* (1990). In each book Goodall documents the changes in buildings, clothing, and customs over several centuries. All three are set in England, but are universal in appeal and concept. *New Providence* (vonTscharner and Fleming 1992) chronicles 80 years of changes in a fictitious, but typical, American city. Sorensen (1995) has also told the story of one community's growth in *New Hope*. Each time young Jimmy visits his grandfather, he asks about the statue in the park. The story his grandfather tells is about the role Jimmy's great-great-great-grandfather played in the birth of New Hope. The accompanying paintings show the transitions that a community undergoes as it grows and changes. The story is so realistic that I searched the book to determine whether Sorensen was documenting a family story, but found no evidence to support my theory.

Lyon's *Who Came Down That Road?* (1992) and *Dreamplace* (1993) also consider the past and present inhabitants of a particular location. Both books feature children who wonder about the people who had previously lived where they are now standing. *Dreamplace* is specifically about the Anasazi Indians. It might be especially useful in the beginning of a unit study of Native Americans because it introduces the question of how we know about past civilizations, especially those that didn't leave written records. Three other books can contribute to this study: *Forest, Village, Town, City* (Beekman

1982), *Talking Walls* (Knight 1992), and *Let's Go Traveling* (Krupp 1992). Beekman's book chronicles the evolution of cities from the first simple Indian villages to today's largest metropolises. The other two books take the reader to famous ancient wonders of the world, including the Great Wall of China, the Pyramids, and the Mayan Temples, and speculate about who lived there in the past.

All of these books can lead students to look at the layers of history of their own community. Our local newspaper prints "Then and Now" photographs on Sundays. As a relative newcomer to the area I really enjoy this glimpse into history. Your students could collect photographs of your own community from family members or friends. The local newspaper might be willing to loan or donate copies of old photographs for the students to examine. Children can conduct interviews with older citizens and conduct research about the community.

One of the "facts" we teach children in social studies classes is that settlements are located on bodies of water because of the need for access to fresh drinking water and a source of transportation. Other communities are established because of the availability of natural resources. Students can explore the reasons their own community was established and whether those reasons continue to be significant.

Vocabulary

Among the "basics" we need to teach is the vocabulary that carries the important concepts. Rosenthal's *Where on Earth: A Geografunny Guide to the Globe* (1992) is geared to older students while *Geography from A to Z: A Picture Glossary* (Knowlton 1988) as well as most of the books in "Geographic Reference Books" section of Appendix A provide essential vocabulary and concepts. *Maps and Mazes* (Chapman and Robson 1993) offers projects for mid-elementary-age students to complete independently as they learn about important concepts and vocabulary.

When Hallie was in fourth grade she came home with a cut-and-paste worksheet from social studies. The purpose was to connect vocabulary with illustrations. The vocabulary included words such as *island, peninsula, isthmus,* and *mountain*. At that point my husband and I were team teaching a methods course entitled "Integrating Art in the Elementary School." The worksheet's content seemed to be a perfect fit with what I call "cootie catchers." Your children have undoubtedly played with them, but not for learning. (You'll find the specific game and directions on pages 20-22; they provide an exciting vehicle for reviewing content information.)

Diptych Art Project

In that same fourth-grade year, Hallie came home with a wonderful diptych art project. My husband and I quickly included it in our art method's course curriculum. The purpose of the project was to present two pictures at the same time. Two pictures are drawn, then cut into one-inch strips. The strips are mounted on a "canvas" created from oaktag that has been folded, fanlike, and attached to a piece of cardboard. When it's completed, viewers see one picture if they're standing to the canvas's right and the other picture if they're standing to the canvas's left.

As we presented the activity to the class, we discussed the subject matter possibilities but left the choice to the individual students. The most successful ones demonstrated strong contrasts such as near/far and summer/winter, which fit here. Young Janie in Yolen's *All Those Secrets of the World* (1991) learns about near and far. You might demonstrate this project using Janie's observations. Consider using this project with your students to help them demonstrate contrasts in relational terms, seasons, or landforms. If the students are going to assemble the parts, it will be appropriate only for grades four and above. If younger students have help with the assembly of their pictures (or someone older completes this step for them), they can do this activity. (Some of the college students struggled with the assembly, and their final products were less exact than Hallie's fourth-grade effort!) Specific directions for a diptych art project are included on page 23.

Location never goes away. It undergirds all aspects of our interactions with our environment. Thus, it should be incorporated in every discussion of every book you read with your students. In fact, in my opinion, location should automatically enter into daily conversations with children. From basic relational words to precise descriptions using cardinal directions, children need to practice the skills involved in determining location. Use the books and activities in this chapter as a beginning place for yourself and your students.

Reference

Boehm, R. G., and Petersen, J. F. 1994. "An Elaboration of the Fundamental Themes in Geography." *Social Education* 58, no. 4: 211-18.

Construction of Cootie Catchers

1. Using the pattern in figure 2.5, on an 8 ½ " x 11" page, construct an 8" x 10" rectangle (¼" side borders and ½" end borders). Draw a line 2" from the bottom to divide the rectangle into an 8" x 8" square and an 8" x 2" rectangle.

2. Draw dotted lines within the square from corner to corner. Also draw dotted lines 2", 4", and 6" from the sides. The result should be 16 2" squares formed by the intersecting dotted lines.

3. Draw a dotted line diagonally from the center top to the center left side of the 8" square. Continue drawing dotted lines diagonally to connect the center left side to the center bottom, the center bottom to the center right side, and from the center right side to the center top. The result should be a diamond shape. The cootie catcher should now look like figure 2.5.

4. Complete the cootie catcher by drawing pictures in the triangles formed above the corners of the smaller, inner square and words and clues in the other spaces. (See fig. 2.6.)

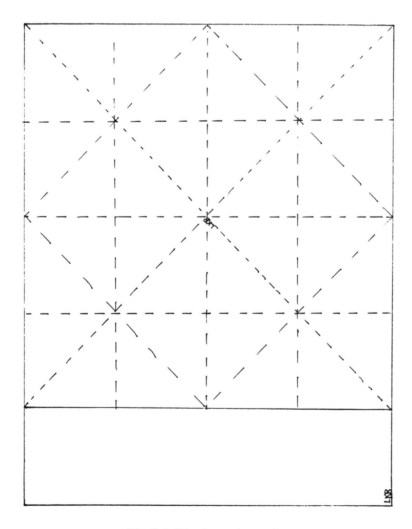

Fig. 2.5. Blank cootie catcher.

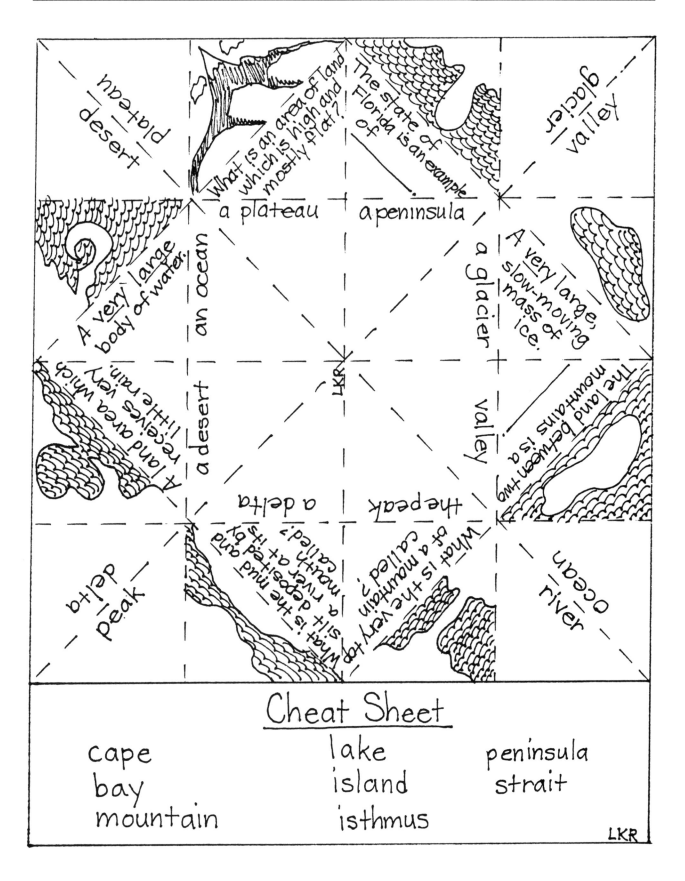

Fig. 2.6. Landforms vocabulary cootie catcher.

Preparing the Cootie Catcher

1. Cut on solid lines producing a square cootie catcher and a rectangular "cheat sheet."

2. Crease all dotted lines.

3. Fold the "cootie catcher" according to the following steps:
   a. with written-side up, fold under the four corners
   b. with picture-side down and word-side up, fold the four corners forward—you should only see pictures
   c. fold in half, once each direction to make it more flexible—the pictures should be hidden

4. Insert index finger and thumb in each pocket. The words should show.

Rules for Playing with a Cootie Catcher

1. Pair students.

2. One student manipulates the cootie catcher while the other takes a turn (the player).

3. The player selects one of the words and spells it while the manipulator opens and closes the cootie catcher, alternating directions.

4. The player now selects one of the pictures and spells the vocabulary word it represents (can use the cheat sheet) while the manipulator again opens and closes the cootie catcher.

5. The player selects one of the pictures, then the manipulator lifts the picture and asks the question under the picture.

6. If the player answers correctly, he or she receives one point.

7. Students switch roles and play again.

8. The winner is the one with the most points.

Tempera Diptych Relief Project

Materials:

12" x 18" drawing paper   tempera paints and brushes
12" x 18" oaktag   scissors/paper cutter
12" x 14" cardboard   glue
12" x 14" construction paper   ruler

Procedure:

1. Fold drawing paper in half, creating two 9" x 12" sides.

2. Draw two pictures. They should have the same horizon line, as shown in figure 2.7.

3. Paint the pictures. Allow them to dry.

4. Cut the painting in half on the fold line.

5. Cut each picture into 1" strips. Think of one picture as "A" and the other as "B."

6. Fold the piece of oaktag in 1" fanlike folds, as shown in figure 2.8.

7. Glue a neutrally colored piece of construction paper to the cardboard. Attach the folded oaktag to the construction paper and cardboard using a stapler.

8. Glue picture strips onto the folded oaktag. "A" strips are glued in order on the left side of the ^ and the "B" strips are glued in order on the right side of the ^ , as shown in figure 2.9.

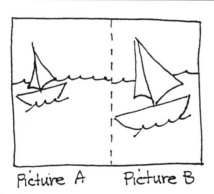

Fig. 2.7. Sample pictures with same horizon.

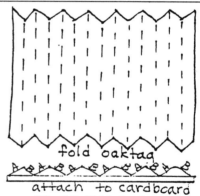

Fig. 2.8. Folded oaktag.

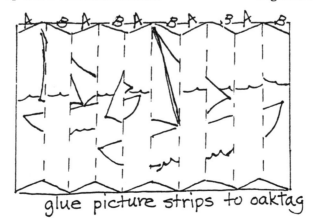

Fig. 2.9. Diptych art project showing near and far.

Chapter 3

"All places on the earth have distinctive tangible and intangible characteristics that give them meaning and character and distinguish them from other places. Geographers generally describe places by their physical or human characteristics."
—W. Kimball, *K-6 Geography,* 3

This chapter considers Place, the aspect of geography that deals with the characteristics of a particular location. Just as every site on Earth has a location, it has a sense of place. Geographers divide these characteristics into physical and human phenomena that can be mapped. But there are also intangible (by-products of the physical and human?) characteristics that draw some people to particular places and repel others.

Physical Characteristics

The physical characteristics of a place include landforms, climate, soils, natural vegetation (flora), animal life (fauna), and water. Although these characteristics are somewhat self-explanatory, they do merit some comment. It is difficult to isolate the natural vegetation, animal life, water, and climate of a particular place. The interrelationships among them are very strong.

Landforms do not include just the landforms themselves but the processes that shape them, such as wind and water erosion.

More than temperature and precipitation variance result from climatic differences. Landform processes, soils, water availability, vegetation, and animal life are all affected by *Climate*.

Natural Vegetation varies according to the type of environment: desert, tropical rain forest, tundra, or savanna. The *Animal Life* in a given place is related to the environment, climate, soils, and vegetation.

The availability of fresh *Water* and whether there is a deficit or surplus is another physical characteristic of a place. Unique, specific bodies of water also contribute to place.

Human Characteristics

The human characteristics of *Religions* (human belief systems) and *Languages* leave their imprint on

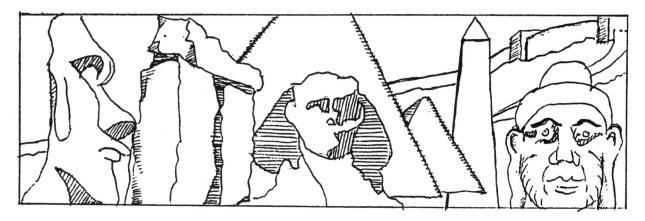

25

a place. The translated names of places and their features are often geographically descriptive: Mesa Verde (Spanish for "green table"), Himalayan Mountains (sanskrit for "abode of snow"), and Lake Winnipeg (Cree for "murky waters").

Population Factors include distribution, density, ethnicity, nationality, gender, age, and economic structures.

Other aspects are rates of birth, death, and population growth.

Urban, rural, suburban, and wilderness areas and the form of settlements are included in *Settlement Patterns*.

Economic Activities include how people make a living (e.g., through agriculture, industry, forestry, fishing, and providing services).

PLACE

Physical Characteristics

- Landforms
- Climate
- Natural Vegetation
- Animal Life
- Water

Human Characteristics

- Religions
- Languages
- Population Factors
- Settlement Patterns
- Economic Activities

Teaching Ideas

The sense of place has intrigued me since I began considering it. I currently live in an area located on the edge of the Pocono Mountains, but I was raised in central Illinois and had lived in the Chicago area for nearly 15 years before our move east. There is a marked contrast between the land-forms and even the flora. I had always thought Illinois had lots of trees—especially after I made a trip to Lincoln, Nebraska. Little did I know how few trees Illinois had compared to Pennsylvania. The most obvious physical difference is the elevation. Our area is very hilly. Both Chicago and north-eastern Pennsylvania are on about the same line of latitude, so winters are quite similar. Driving is not! When we first arrived in late summer, we explored the area, noting, "We won't go there when it snows!" After 10 years, we're much braver, but we are still most aware of the contrast.

Another physical aspect that we have compared across the country has been how much sky we can see. In Illinois you can watch the weather systems come in from the west. When I was a child, we often stood in the backyard with Mother, watching the progress of a thunderstorm as it neared our house. The horizon line in the Midwest appears lower, and there is an abundance of sky. Here in northeastern Pennsylvania, the mountains rise up around us, raising the horizon line and hiding the movement of weather fronts from our eyes.

As I was listening to a book on tape recently, I was struck by a phrase the author used: "mud-colored hair." That certainly could raise a variety of images in readers' minds. I've lived in three distinct areas of the United States, and believe me, the color of mud varies greatly. In central Illinois the soil is dark black with few, if any, stones. My husband and I lived in Atlanta, Georgia, for nearly a year and found the soil to be quite a contrast to our Illinois experience. The soil was red with a claylike consistency . . . and it stained your shoes and clothes! In Pennsylvania we have found the soil to be absolutely full of rocks. When we first dug in our new yard to begin a garden, we found it to be a difficult task because we were constantly hitting rocks, large and small, with the shovel. My parents were visiting, and my mother said, "Linda, they must have used fill in this yard." Not only is the soil rocky, it's brown, not black. When I ordered a half load of topsoil I quizzed the delivery man because it certainly didn't look like my (Illinois) idea of topsoil!

Young children recognize the unique physical characteristics of a locale, although they may not verbalize it. When our son, John, was three, we took a three-week car trip from our home in the Chicago area to Virginia. We visited several sets of friends and as many Civil War battlefields as we could. On our return, as we drove down the main street of our hometown, John exclaimed, "You know, *my* town has a street like this!" What does this mean? *I* think it means we need to talk with our children from a very early age about the physical and human characteristics they see around them. I cannot emphasize enough our responsibility to help children become keen observers of the world around them.

As I prepared for this chapter's discussion I struggled with how to limit what was to be included. The problem exists because a sense of place can, and should, be included in a discussion of every book. Another problem arises from the integrative nature of the geographic themes. I will be earmarking books because I think they exemplify a sense of place or can be part of a study to create a sense of place, but many of these books could just as easily be part of a study of regions or movement or human-environmental relationships, so don't be surprised when you find books cited in more than one chapter.

This book really began with Chris Van Allsburg's *Ben's Dream* (1982). It was the first book Karen and I identified in our search for books to enhance teaching world geography. What a wonderful example of how landmarks, whether natural or human-made, contribute to the sense of place! Although I have not indicated the name of the illustrator in any of the books, I want to note how important I believe the illustrations can be, especially as they aid the author in conveying a sense of place. Two books about the seashore, *The Summer Sands* (Garland 1995) and *The Seashore Book* (Zolotow 1992), evoke special feelings in me each time I look through them. As a landlocked person who didn't see the ocean until her late twenties, I find that the illustrations (and Zolotow's words) quickly return me to the sights and sounds of the Atlantic shore.

Several books examine the flora and fauna of particular places. Specifically, Gibbons and the Weirs provide considerable information about the rain forest. Gibbons's work, *Nature's Green Umbrella: Tropical Rain Forest* (1994), is more reference-like, providing generic rain forest information. It makes little reference to human characteristics. The Weirs, however, in *Panther Dream: A Story of the African Rain Forest* (1991), use the rain forest as the context for a story about a young boy who lives on the edge of the African rain forest. Two other books about the rain forest are more lyrical and simplistic, appropriate for introducing the topic: *The Great Kapok Tree: A Tale of the Amazon Rain Forest* (Cherry 1990) and *Welcome to the Green House* (Yolen 1993). A study of the rain forest is particularly important at all ages now because the effect of its destruction is being felt globally. Children are very interested in environmental issues and deserve the opportunity to explore this topic in depth. Our local middle school has an Ecology Club that has raised more than $10,000 to purchase acres of rain forest in Central America. It is then protected from destruction just as our national parks protect wildlife and wilderness areas in our own country. Fortunately, for us, one of our seventh-grade science teachers is the Ecology Club's advisor and an expert on the rain forest. He has made several visits to rain forests in Central America and shares his personal experiences and slides with groups throughout the area. To find out how your class can buy an acre of rain forest to protect from destruction, write: The Children's Rainforest, P.O. Box 936, Lewiston, ME 04240. You can also contact the local Sierra Club or other environmental groups to find an outside speaker who can offer information and resources to expand your students' understanding of rain forests.

Annemarie, a student teacher in second grade, taught a thematic unit about the rain forest over a three-week period. Students became experts on specific rain forest animals. They presented the results of their information on half-sheet forms that asked about the physical characteristics, their food source, and the layer of the rain forest in which they lived. When the animals were part of class discussions, Annemarie always deferred to the "expert" to provide the necessary information. One of the art activities, which also served as an assessment tool, was the creation of booklets illustrating the four layers of the rain forest. The source of Annemarie's art project was an article in *The Mailbox* (Audet, Gibson, and Flag 1995). The booklets were formed by using two 9-by-12-inch sheets of white construction paper. Stack the two sheets, then, holding them vertically, slide the top sheet upward approximately two inches. Then fold both paper thicknesses forward in such a way that you create four graduated layers or pages. Staple the fold. (See fig. 3.1.)

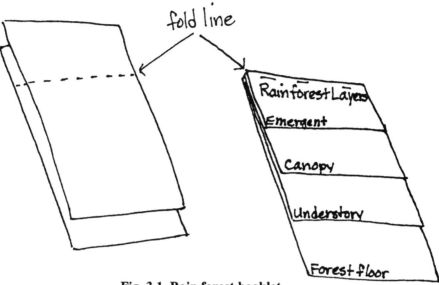

Fig. 3.1. Rain forest booklet.

Please note the way in which I moved from looking at the four books as a means of acquiring a sense of place about the rain forest to human-environmental relationships. Sorry, but it was a teachable moment.

Water

Another aspect of the rain forest that students studied was the water cycle and its unique characteristics in a rain forest. Water, in both its presence and absence, adds to the sense of place. Eleonore Schmid has written a book that provides a simple explanation of the water cycle. The softly colored illustrations in *The Water's Journey* (1994) strongly connect the water cycle with landforms and the important role water plays in supporting life on Earth. The book is really aimed at the young reader, but it does provide a way to begin a discussion about the water cycle in your community.

- Just how much precipitation does your community have each year?
- What type of environment does your yearly amount of precipitation create: a desert, tropical rain forest, tundra, or savanna?
- How is the industry in your community affected by your yearly rainfall or snowfall?

I live in an area where farmers need a certain amount of rainfall from April through August or September to ensure a successful harvest. Too little rainfall and the crops may never grow. Too much rainfall and they may be washed away. In the winter, the ski resorts near us need snow and cold temperatures to allow them to produce artificial snow, if needed. If the condition of the ski slopes is not attractive to skiers, local hotels and restaurants, as well as the ski resorts themselves, feel the effects. The water cycle is taught in the primary grades and repeated throughout the curriculum. The three terms students encounter are *evaporation*, *condensation*, and *precipitation*. These terms are defined in figure 3.2, and the continuous nature of the water cycle is illustrated.

Water Cycle

1. Cut on dotted lines.
2. Fold rectangle on fold line.
3. Place wheel within folded rectangle.
4. Insert brad through all 3 thicknesses at dark dot.

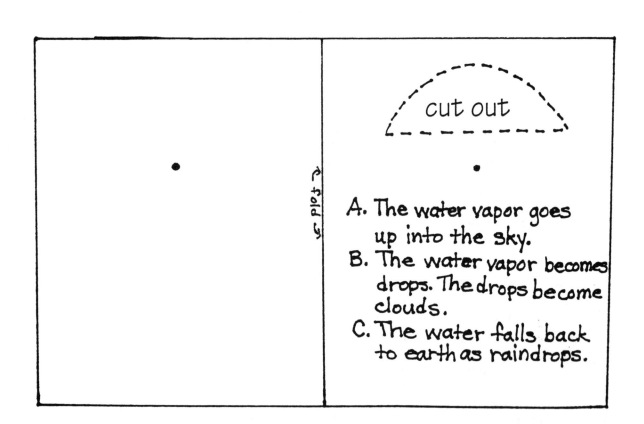

A. The water vapor goes up into the sky.
B. The water vapor becomes drops. The drops become clouds.
C. The water falls back to earth as raindrops.

Fig. 3.2. The water cycle.

The four Long Pond books by William George and his wife's two books, *In the Woods: Who's Been Here?* (1995) and *In the Snow: Who's Been Here?* (1995), are set in the woods around an actual place in the Poconos: Long Pond, Pennsylvania. The books all take a close look at the natural flora and fauna around a pond in a wilderness forest. They model children learning to be observant of their surroundings and treating the environment with respect. These books are lovely, with richly painted illustrations. Although all elementary school-aged children will enjoy them, they offer anyone who cannot physically visit the forest a chance to visit through words and pictures and develop a sense of place. Students can learn more about the flora and fauna in their own community. They can compare and contrast what they learn with the information in the books. The realistic paintings illustrating the books may inspire some students to present their information in some sort of art form.

Another natural body of water, the river, is important because it contributes to other aspects of place: soils, economic patterns, and population factors. *A River Ran Wild* (Cherry 1992) relates the environmental history of the Nashua River from its discovery by the Native Americans through the polluting years caused by industrial dumping to its revitalization by means of an ambitious cleanup. This book provides another opportunity for students to consider what their role might be in preserving the environment. There may be a local story about misuse or revitalization of water sources that students can learn about through library research or a guest speaker. The "Fred the Fish" activity at the end of this chapter was designed by Pat Chilton for Michigan's Kalamazoo Soil Conservation District in July 1979. It was brought to my attention several years ago by one of my undergraduate students in a language arts methods course. The class of young adults thoroughly enjoyed participating in this activity. I used it later in a vacation church school group. All of the children, from the youngest to the oldest (ages 3-12), eagerly participated in the brainstorming at the conclusion of the activity! Try it with your class, whatever the age. It seems a natural introduction or addition to the study of rivers, environmental conservation, and pollution.

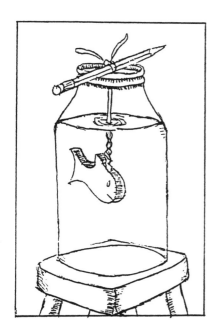

Voices of the River: Adventures on the Delaware (Cheripko 1993) and *Where the River Begins* (Locker 1993) describe, in fact and fiction, a trip from the source of a river to its end. Jan Cheripko and a 14-year-old family friend travel 215 miles down the Delaware River from its source in Hancock, New York, to Philadelphia. Over the course of the 10-day trip, the two visit historic spots along the river, camping out on some nights and staying in more traditional lodging on others. The trip is documented by photographs. One of the interesting aspects of this book is a series of honest remarks by the 14-year-old, Matt Smith, who says he probably wouldn't have agreed to the trip if he had known what to expect. On the other hand, he's proud of having completed something he began despite its difficulty.

The two fictional boys and their grandfather in *Where the River Begins* take a camping trip to the source of the river that flows by their home. This book asks and answers a question children may never consider: Where does the river begin? Many times we take a river for granted, never thinking about where it has been before it gets to our location or, for that matter, where it goes next. The Mississippi River is a "mighty" river (as much as a mile across at its widest point) during most of its journey to the Gulf of Mexico. But its source is a small, 12-foot-wide river from Lake Itasca in Minnesota. It is joined by more than 250 tributaries before it empties into the Gulf.

Take your students on a trip along a river or stream in or near your community. Find a local expert to help you plan the trip and, perhaps, accompany you. It would be wonderful to be able to discover its source, but considering how unlikely that is, find some good local maps that can provide you with information about the route the waterway takes and where you are along its course. With your students, find the answers to the following questions and others you generate.

- Where does this waterway begin and end? Are you near the source or the end?
- What impact does this waterway have on your community?
- Is it large enough to supply a means of transportation to move goods from factories? Is it used as a source of drinking water?
- Is it associated with the production of hydroelectric power?
- What is the natural flora and fauna living in and near the water?
- What bridges cross the waterway?
- Is the waterway used as a recreational resource?

Keep Jan Cheripko and Matt Smith in mind. Make your field trip a photojournalistic occasion. Designate a photographer and document your discoveries. Collect examples of plants to be examined back in the classroom. Although it's unlikely that you'll formally publish a book, create a class journal of the trip to share with parents and other classes in your school. Include the photos taken during the trip as well as any examples from nature that will enhance the text. Let me suggest a couple of ways you might share the journal in an organized fashion. Invite parents or other visitors to visit your classroom at a designated time. While they are visiting, present the class's discoveries either formally in a whole group presentation or informally at centers with a few children who act as the spokespersons at each center. Or share the activity with parents by sending the research results home with each child. You will need to create a document of some sort that is easily transported and can withstand the trip from school to home. Consider sending home some type of record sheet to allow parents to comment. You can use similar strategies as you share with other classrooms within your school.

Peter Spier's *The Erie Canal* (1990) offers an interesting way to begin looking at the system of canals built throughout the United States to support the movement of goods and people from one place to another. Spier accompanies the words of the song "The Erie Canal" with whimsical drawings of people and goods journeying "from Albany to Buffalo." A more recent, sophisticated, and detailed account of the building of the Erie Canal is *The Amazing Impossible ERIE CANAL* (Harness 1995). This book is appropriate for a study of canals. The Erie Canal, which was completed in 1825 and covers more than 350 miles, was not the only canal built in the early days of the United States. Although some canals are no longer in use, the intercoastal waterways are. First, learn the song with your class. If possible, visit a canal. Discover as many canal systems as possible. Find out what purpose each serves (served). Create a sandbox for your classroom and use it to demonstrate how canal systems work. Model specific canal systems using salt dough and watercolors. (Fig. 3.3 is a salt dough recipe.)

Salt Dough Recipe

Ingredients:

    1 cup flour
    1 cup salt
    1 cup water

Materials:

mixing bowl	plastic knives
measuring cup	rolling pin (optional)
spoons	polymer medium (optional)
waxed paper	

In the mixing bowl, mix the flour and salt. Gradually add water until the appropriate consistency is reached. Knead the dough 7 to 10 minutes until it is smooth and puttylike.

Once the dough is the right consistency (does not stick to the student's hands), roll it out to about ¼" thick on waxed paper or shaped as desired. Then place it in a safe place in the classroom to dry (approximately two days).

The dried dough can be painted with watercolor or tempera paint. It can be sealed with a polymer medium.

Fig. 3.3. Salt dough recipe.

Letting Swift River Go (Yolen 1992) and *Shaker Lane* (Provensen and Provensen 1987) both look at communities that are affected by the creation of a reservoir. In Yolen's book, based on her personal experience, the reservoir was created to provide drinking water for nearby Boston. The Provensens describe a fictional community as it develops and is then covered by the water of a reservoir. Students can determine the source of their community's drinking water, whether there are any reservoirs in the community, and what purpose they serve.

A Specific Country: Vietnam

I debated about where to include the following books. There are at least four well-written books about Vietnam that I believe are worthy of use in the classroom. They could be included in a study of Regions, when you get to Southeast Asia. They could also be included in a study of wars, which I believe are part of Movement (human interactions). But I finally decided to include them here as another example of how children's books can help establish a sense of place.

A couple of years ago I read an interesting account on the KidLit listserv of a fifth-grade class that responded rather dramatically to the reading of *The Wall* (Bunting 1990) by their teacher. The students wanted to know about the Vietnam War and began to gather information, mostly through interviews with family and friends who had served in Vietnam. What had begun as an attempt to share a simple, yet moving, picture book ended in a unit of study initiated by the students themselves. This story came to mind as I came across the following three books: *The Lotus Seed* (Garland 1993), *Grandfather's Dream* (Keller 1994), and *Ba-Nam* (Lee 1987). The first two tell stories that are directly connected to the war. In *The Lotus Seed*, a young girl driven from her homeland because of the war carries a lotus seed to remind herself of the culture and traditions from which she is separated. *Grandfather's Dream* relates the story of the environmental work needed to restore the wetlands of the Mekong Delta to attract the Sarus cranes, who were driven from the area during the war. The third, *Ba-Nam*, takes the reader with a Vietnamese

family to the graveyard to celebrate Thanh-Minh Day, a day to visit the graves of ancestors and present offerings. Young Nan has a frightening adventure that involves the old gravekeeper, Ba-Nam. The story provides a peek into Vietnamese customs.

Depending on the age and sophistication of your class, consider opening a discussion and investigation of Vietnam. The illustrations in *Grandfather's Dream* are true to the simplicity of oriental art. Locate photographs of the Mekong Delta before and after the war, if possible. Have your students compare the photographs to Keller's paintings. The author's note and description indicate that she is very interested in involving students in projects such as this one. It may be possible to contact her through the publisher and establish a dialogue in which your students can question her about Vietnam and the restoration project she participated in and documented in this book. Lee's story, *Ba-Nam*, is based on her childhood experiences in Vietnam. She may also be willing to communicate with your class. Also, consider having a guest speaker visit your classroom. Any local veterans' group should be able to put you in touch with a local veteran of the Vietnam War if your students do not have personal contacts. Because of the sensitive nature of this topic, however, be sure to set the parameters of the interaction.

City and Country

Numerous books can be used to compare and contrast the physical and human characteristics of the city and the country. The Provensens present the contrasts rather cleverly in *Town and Country* (1994). As they describe the town, the words are in narrow columns that remind us of the tall buildings in this bustling locale. In the country section, the words are arranged horizontally under the pastoral landscapes. Rius and Parramon provide very elementary descriptions of the city and country in *Let's Discover the City* (1986) and *Let's Discover the Countryside* (1986). *Delivery Van: Words for Town and Country* (1990) and *Taxi: A Book of City Words* (1990), both by Betsy and Guilio Maestro, can be used to develop vocabulary while comparing and contrasting the two areas. Create a chart such as the one in figure 3.4 to record the similarities and differences found in the books. Have your students add other characteristics from their own experiences.

Have students determine where they live. Is it clearly town or country, or is it more difficult to determine? Perhaps students will want to add a third column to the chart to compare their community to the town and country designations. From this beginning—town and country—go on to contemplate with your students the terms *urban*, *suburban*, and *rural*, as Michelle did with her second-grade students (see Chapter 2) and determine if the addition of the term *suburban* helps them define the settlement pattern of their own community.

Several books contribute to a look at specific characteristics of big cities. *Urban Roosts* (Bash 1990) takes a unique look at housing in cities—that is, the housing of birds! The watercolor illustrations and text describe the ways finches, pigeons, and other birds have found to survive in the city. *Big City Port* (Maestro and DelVecchio 1991) describes the activities at a busy seaport. Although it is generic, it provides background information that can be applied to large coastal cities throughout the world. *New Providence* (vonTscharner and Fleming 1992) documents the physical changes that take place in a typical American city over an 80-year time span. Students in your class may be able to find photographs that document a specific location in your community over a number of years. Consider creating a display that helps the students compare and contrast these photographs. Bunting's *Smoky Night* (1994), while focusing on the relationships of humans in an emergency (the riots in Los Angeles), also provides a peek at living in an apartment in the inner city. In *Left Behind* (1988),

Let's Compare Town and Country

	Town	Country
Buildings		
Jobs		
People		
Roads		
Other		

Fig. 3.4. A town and country comparison.

Carol Carrick relates the frightening misadventure of Christopher as he becomes separated from his class in a big-city subway. For children who live in smaller towns, or suburban or rural areas, Christopher's scare is very real. The book is also a delightful way to introduce the importance of following teacher directions when on a field trip.

A Specific City: New York City

As I bring this chapter to an end, I want to offer another type of study that I believe fits comfortably within Place. That is the study of a specific city. It could also be the subject of a Regional study, but I am choosing to include it here. As you look through the children's literature offerings in Appendix A, you will find several books that highlight actual cities: *The Inside-Outside Book of London* (Munro 1989), *The Inside-Outside Book of Washington, D.C.* (Munro 1993), *A Visit to Washington, D.C.* (Krementz 1989), *Our Home Is the Sea* (Levinson 1992), *The Day of Ahmed's Secret* (Heide and Gilliland 1990), *Sami and the Time of the Troubles* (Heide and Gilliland 1992), and *The Moon Was the Best* (Zolotow 1993). Others, like *Piero Ventura's Book of Cities* (Ventura 1975) and two of Peter Spier's, *People* (1988) and *The Star-Spangled Banner* (1992), provide some information about several particular cities.

My research has found that New York City is the subject of more picture books than any other city. From the simple to the complex, New York has been described over and over. Roxie Munro takes an unorthodox look at the city in two books, *Christmastime in New York City* (1994) and *The Inside-Outside Book of New York City* (1994). In the first, the reader looks at the Thanksgiving Day parade, decorative window displays along Fifth Avenue, and New Year's Eve in Times Square, among other "Christmasy" spots. In the second, the reader visits famous tourist spots from the inside and outside. This book and Munro's other inside-outside books could also be included in the basic skills section of Chapter 2 when you and your children work with relational words such as *inside* and *outside* . . . and *above* and *near* and *behind* and. . . .

Levinson's *I Go with My Family to Grandma's* (1992) is a whimsical introduction to the five boroughs of New York City. The alliterative text provides some delightful models for younger children's writing. The diversity of transportation used by the cousins can be another area of discussion and examination. Both older and younger students can compare and contrast the transportation means available to the cousins with those in their own community. Do all of the ways the cousins get to Grandma's currently exist? Did they ever exist in your community? How many of them have your students ever ridden on or in? Consider creating a survey with the students and then, depending on the age level, collect data to be placed on a graph of some sort. The data collecting can take place in small groups within the classroom or be expanded to include other classes. Figure 3.5 presents a transportation survey form you can use.

Older students can locate the boroughs on a map of the city. Even though the book is set at the turn of the century, students can explore how long ago and for what purpose the borough structure was created. What political structure exists in their own community? What effect does that structure have on the students and their families?

The Maestros (*The Story of the Statue of Liberty* 1989) tell the story of the conception, construction, and reconstruction of the Statue of Liberty, an internationally recognized symbol of New York City. This book provides the basis for a more complete study of the statue itself. It also offers a beginning look at what New York City, the Statue of Liberty, and the United States

Transportation Survey

Form of Transportation	Number Who Have Used It	Where It Was Used
Subway		
Ferry		
Bicycle		
Car		
Other		
Other		

Fig. 3.5. A sample transportation survey.

have meant to immigrants arriving in New York Harbor. *An Ellis Island Christmas* (Leighton 1992) tells the story of a young girl arriving from Poland with her family to meet her father, who has already immigrated. Her fears and joys are poignantly expressed in the text and illustrations. A similar story is told in *Watch the Stars Come Out* (Levinson 1995). In this story, the children are sent across the Atlantic alone. Students can estimate the distance the ship traveled each day (Levinson tells us it took 23 days) as it crossed the Atlantic. Both books are set in the past. Although Ellis Island no longer serves an immigration purpose, books are available in your library that can be used as reference sources as your class discovers more about Ellis Island.

Pop! Goes the Weasel and Yankee Doodle (Quackenbush 1976) illustrates two popular songs of the Revolutionary era. Drawings showing historical sites in New York City in 1776 and 1976 accompany the text. A map at the end of the book locates the sites, and short paragraphs describe them. Spier's *The Legend of New Amsterdam* (1979) portrays the city life of Manhattan Island in the 1600s, when it was called New Amsterdam. A map shows the location of important businesses and homeowners. Both of these books contribute to a look at the "layers of history" (see Chapter 2 for other books with "layers") in New York City. A wonderful contrast is *My New York* (Jakobsen 1993), in which a young New Yorker tells her Midwestern friend about her favorite places in Manhattan. This book also includes a detailed map of Manhattan and informative paragraphs about the locations cited. Students can compare and contrast the locations highlighted in each of these books.

Just as Becky, the young New Yorker in *My New York*, tells her friend about her favorite places, your students can write a letter or create a brochure about favorite places in their community. Remind them that the intent of a brochure is to encourage its readers to visit the place it describes. It will need photographs or drawings to enhance the text.

A combination of all of these books plus any you may find, along with maps and travel brochures, can serve to create a real sense of New York City as a place. You can learn about some of its landforms (Manhattan Island, New York Harbor), the climate and flora, some aspects of its settlement, some population factors, and the many ways in which the people make a living.

Reference

Audet, T. I., Gibson, K., and Flag, A. 1995. "A Treasure Chest of Life." *The Mailbox* 17, no. 2: 26-30.

Fred the Fish

This activity was adapted from "A Fish Story," designed by Pat Chilton for Michigan's Kalamazoo Soil Conservation District in July 1979.

Materials:

a large glass jar	pancake syrup
cold tap water	salt
a white sponge	punched paper dots
a heavy binder clip	liquid detergent
string	hot tap water
a pencil	red food coloring
6 small paper cups	green food coloring
soil	script cards (made in step 6, below)
plant fertilizer (powder)	9 index cards

Procedure:

1. Fill the jar ¾ full of cold tap water.

2. Cut a fish out of the sponge.

3. Attach the binder clip to the bottom of the sponge as a weight and suspend the fish in the jar by tying it to a pencil positioned across the jar's mouth.

4. Place soil in cup #1, fertilizer in cup #2, pancake syrup in cup #3, salt in cup #4, paper dots in cup #5, and hot water and detergent in cup #6.

5. Distribute the cups and food coloring to eight students.

6. Distribute the script cards to nine more students; you may want to glue them to the index cards first. (See the "Script Cards" section on the next page for the text of the cards.)

7. Ask the remaining students to number their papers from 1-9.

8. As the students with the scripts read, those with the cups should dump their ingredients into the jar on cue. The recorders should write a different adjective each time the question "HOW DOES FRED FEEL?" is asked.

9. At the end of the activity, lift Fred out of the jar. Discuss his change in appearance and that of the water's. (Someone will probably remark "Fred is dead!") Share the lists of adjectives. Ask students to draw cartoons depicting Fred's adventure.

10. Brainstorm as many ways to dispose of this water as you can. Then evaluate the environmental consequences of each alternative. When someone suggests filtering the water, ask students to design and use their own filtration system and dispose of some of the water in the jar.

Script Cards

Card #1. Imagine a clean river as it meanders through a protected wilderness area. In this river lives Fred the Fish. HOW DOES FRED FEEL? Fred has lived in this stretch of the river all his life. But now he decides to go on an adventure and explore the area downstream.

Card #2. Fred swims into farm country. He passes a freshly plowed riverbank. It begins to rain, and some soil erodes into the river. *Cup #1.* HOW DOES FRED FEEL?

Card #3. Fred nears a suburban housing development. Some fertilizer from the farms and the lawns washed into the river a while back. *Cup #2.* The fertilizer made the plants in the river grow very fast and thick. Eventually the river couldn't furnish them with all the nutrients they needed. They died and are starting to decay. Their decomposition is using up some of Fred's oxygen. HOW DOES FRED FEEL?

Card #4. Fred swims under a highway bridge. Some cars traveling across it are leaking oil. The rain is washing the oil into the river below. *Cup #3.* HOW DOES FRED FEEL?

Card #5. During a recent cold spell, ice formed on the bridge. County trucks spread salt on the road to prevent accidents. The rain is now washing salty slush into the river. *Cup #4.* HOW DOES FRED FEEL?

Card #6. Fred swims past the city park. Some picnickers didn't throw their trash into the garbage can. The wind is blowing it into the river. *Cup #5.* HOW DOES FRED FEEL?

Card #7. Several factories are located downriver from the city. Although regulations limit the amount of pollution the factories are allowed to dump into the river, the factory owners don't always abide by them. *Cup #6.* HOW DOES FRED FEEL?

Card #8. The city's wastewater treatment plant is also located along this stretch of the river. The pollution regulations aren't as strict as they should be and a section of the plant has broken down. *(Squirt two drops of red food coloring into jar.)* HOW DOES FRED FEEL?

Card #9. Finally, Fred swims past the hazardous waste dump located on the bank next to the river. Rusty barrels of toxic chemicals are leaking. The rain is washing these poisons into the river. *(Squeeze one drop of green food coloring into the jar for every leaking barrel.)* HOW DOES FRED FEEL?

From *Geographic Literacy Through Children's Literature.* © 1997 Linda K. Rogers. Teacher Ideas Press. (800) 237-6124

Chapter 4

HUMAN-ENVIRONMENTAL RELATIONS

"All places on the earth have advantages and disadvantages for human settlement. High population densities have developed on flood plains, for example, where people could take advantage of fertile soils, water resources, and opportunities for river transpiration. By comparison, population densities are usually low in deserts. Yet flood plains are periodically subjected to severe damage, and some desert areas, such as Israel, have been modified to support large population concentrations."

—W. Kimball, *K-6 Geography*, 3

This chapter discusses the interrelationship of humans and their environment. Geographers offer a number of subthemes that expand this major theme (Boehm and Petersen 1994). Two of these involve ethical considerations for the environment. In the early history of human exploration of the Earth, we rarely considered what kinds of environmental problems we were creating. We in the Western world (Europeans and Americans) acted as if natural resources were unlimited, and we often exploited the environment in ways that clashed with the cultural attitudes of the indigenous peoples. In the more recent past, the technology that has created synthetic materials, which have made our lives easier and provided economic support, has also created problems such as those of disposal. Our children are much more aware of the ethical issues involved in human-environmental relationships than we were at their age. We can and should provide opportunities for our students to encounter these issues, discuss them,

and expand their knowledge. Most of the children's literature discussed in this chapter does not address directly the ethical issues, but that doesn't mean you can't raise them. As you look at the subthemes, think about where they can be integrated into your classroom curriculum.

The Earth as an Environmental System

Interrelationships Between Humans and Environments result because the physical and human environments are interconnected. Change in one usually brings change in the other.

The Role of Technology is integral to the relationship as humans have learned to modify their environment through the application of technology. Modification occurs in all aspects of human life. But the use of technology does not come without problems. Among *The Problems of Technology* are air and water pollution, waste disposal, and toxic materials.

Humans must cope with *Environmental Hazards.* Some hazards are a result of nature while others are caused by humans themselves. Among natural environmental hazards are earthquakes, volcanoes, and floods. Examples of hazards caused by humans include nuclear disasters and oil spills.

All places have *Environmental Limits,* such as the availability of water, land, and other natural resources, yet humans have learned to cope through *adaptation.* Humans have discovered ways to adapt to their environment. People live differently in different environments. Their ways of making a living and the types of houses they build are among the variations affected by the environment.

Ethics and Values

Issues Relating to Management and Protection of Environmental Resources: Environmental stewardship and economic development are often in conflict. How will we balance the two?

Different Cultural Attitudes About the Environment and Its Resources: Cultures often have different attitudes concerning the use and conservation of the environment.

HUMAN-ENVIRONMENTAL RELATIONS

The Earth as an Environmental System

- Interrelationships Between Humans and Environments
- The Role of Technology
- The Problems of Technology
- Environmental Hazards
- Environmental Limits
- Adaptation

Ethics and Values

- Issues Relating to Management and Protection of Environmental Resources
- Different Cultural Attitudes About the Environment and Its Resources

Teaching  Ideas

Ben's Dream (Van Allsburg 1982) shows us several examples of Human-Environmental Relations with regard to human constructions. The Great Wall of China, conforming to the mountains and valleys in its path, follows the path of rivers. Mount Rushmore, the enormous man-made relief of four U.S. presidents, was carved from the granite side of a mountain in South Dakota. The builders of the Tower of Pisa were forced to suspended construction in the twelfth century when they noticed the problems a shallow foundation in soft soil were causing. The construction was completed 200 years later, and we can observe the results of the combination of shallow foundation and soft soil—the tower leans about 10 degrees!

You and your students can learn more about the construction of the Great Wall in *The Great Wall of China* (Fisher 1986). Its construction took 10 years and cost many lives. In addition to learning about the Wall, students can learn about the Chinese characters used to write the author's "chops" (signature) throughout the book. Students might want to find other well-known construction projects that took many years to complete and still remain centuries later. They may also look for local examples. I find the building of highways through Pennsylvania mountains absolutely fascinating. Not only do the designers have to determine route directions and the placement of entrance and exit ramps, but they have to anticipate blasting through and cutting away giant parts of the mountain. When you travel through these passes, you can see the grooved places in the rock surface where blasts were located and rock was cut away.

The interrelationship of humans and environment, which brings change, is ongoing. The discussion in Chapter 2 about the books that depict what I've called "layers of history" also leads us to note the way in which change is really never ending. Change is often a reflection of new technology. Goodall's books, *The Story of a Farm* (1989) and *The Story of a Main Street* (1987), certainly reflect that. Farming changed with the invention of new machinery, just as the size and style of buildings in cities changed with improved building materials and techniques. Changes we make to the environment to improve our own living impact flora and fauna. *Urban Roosts* (Bash 1990) is a particularly good example of how the environment adapts to changes made by humans. Despite the fact that humans have built large structures that take the place of the natural habitats the birds in this book usually live in, they, like humans, have learned to adapt to their environment. What evidence of the interrelationship between humans and the environment do your students observe in your community, county, or state?

The problems brought about by technology are evident in both *A River Ran Wild* (Cherry 1992) and *Grandfather's Dream* (Keller 1994). The obvious problem in the first book is industrial pollution. The problem in the second book is less apparent. In *Grandfather's Dream* the Sarus cranes have been driven from the Mekong Delta because the war in Vietnam destroyed the wetlands, which were their natural habitat. The destruction of the wetlands (also called marshes and estuaries) is a concern in many areas of the world as many populations wrestle with the ethical question of whether to allow wetlands to be filled to allow building or farming to take place. *Heron Street* (Turner 1989) tells, in rather vague verse, of how the herons were driven from their natural habitat once humans began settling the area. This picture

book can be used to initiate discussion about the destruction of certain regions of the world. A reference-type book, *Everglades: Buffalo Tiger and the River of Grass* (Lourie 1994), takes the reader on a tour of the Everglades conducted by a Native American who shares historical and ecological information about this endangered area in Florida. Students can learn more about areas of the world that have been classified as endangered. They can locate information about their own community. The local chapter of the Sierra Club is a good place to begin. Students can gather information through formal research methods or through interviews with community experts. Students can also learn what role they may play in preventing community ecological destruction.

Modification and Adaptation: An Integrative Unit Plan

I wrote the following integrative unit plan because I was interested in examining the feasibility of integrating the geographic themes into the required curriculum. I chose the third-grade level for two practical reasons: First, I had taught third grade for several years, so I was familiar with ability levels; and second, I have a comfortable working relationship with one of the third-grade teachers in my neighborhood elementary school. She was willing to provide me with the district's textbooks and guides.

As I looked through the texts I decided that the best theme to use as the focus was Human-Environmental Relations, considering the Human-Environmental Relations. More specifically, I worked with this organizing statement: *People modify and adapt to natural settings.* I hoped the unit would serve to introduce students to these concepts:

1. People live in many places;
2. Places have advantages and disadvantages; and
3. People adapt to and are influenced by places (land and climate). These adaptations are accomplished through specially designed clothing and buildings. In addition, the methods of food production or gathering and transportation are determined by the land and climate.

The unit included in this chapter is an *introductory unit* designed to cover 10-15 days of classwork at the beginning of the year. The length of the unit depends on how your classroom time is structured. The basic understandings established in this unit can then be continuously integrated into the social studies, reading, and science concepts taught throughout the year.

Skills from several curricular subjects are integrated within this introductory unit:

English: Students will participate in oral language activities through small- and whole-group discussions, through formal and informal interviews with family and friends, and through a formal interview with an outside speaker. They will also write sentences. These activities are consistent with curricular requirements in third grade.

Math: Students will gather survey information as an out-of-class activity. Based on the teacher's choice, graphs may be constructed, which is skill within the curriculum.

Social studies: Students will be presented with the introductory information about communities that is usually given in a social studies textbook. Specific vocabulary and study questions will be included throughout the unit. Basic map skills will be an important part of this unit.

Reading: Many supplemental picture books will be provided by the teacher to enhance this unit of study. The books will be made available to the students for individual use. Some of the books will be read to the whole class to help introduce concepts and motivate the students. Many books will be included in learning centers.

Fine arts: Students will be encouraged to express their understanding of concepts through the fine arts. One activity included within the unit involves creating and dressing human figures.

As the teacher and students continue their work throughout the year, the Human-Environmental Relations theme can be integrated into **social studies** as communities are studied, into **reading** as the particular settings of stories are examined and discussed, and into **science** as various aspects of the environment, and humans' impact on it, are explored.

── **Day 1**

Read *Ben's Dream* (Van Allsburg 1982) to your class. As you read the book, have the students identify the monuments Van Allsburg includes. Have photographs of the monuments available and be prepared to provide factual information about each of them. During the discussion about the monuments note (if the students don't) how some monuments are affected by the land (e.g., the Great Wall of China is built along the contours of the land; the London Bridge was built to help people adapt to an environmental feature—the Thames River).

Have the students look closely at photographs and drawings of specific places such as parks and city squares, found in most communities. Guide the inspection of the pictures with questions that require your students to analyze the content and make comparisons with their own community. *New Providence* (vonTscharner and Fleming 1992) looks at the main streets in a fictional town over a period of 80 years. It shows a main square in the city. My suburban community doesn't have such a place, but the nearby larger city, which is the county seat, has a "Courthouse Square." Ask students if or where members of their community can and do gather.

Use the following questions and answers to shape the content of information that you provide or lead students to discover.

Why do people live in communities?

People live in communities because they like each other's company. They like to belong to a group. A community is a place where people can belong. It is a place where they can carry on their lives. People often live in certain communities because of their work.

What places are in the business center of a community?

The business center is usually downtown. Most of the office buildings where people work and the stores where they shop are in the business center.

What are banks?

Banks are places where people keep money.

What do people do together in a community?

People in a community can do many enjoyable things together, such as participate in or watch sporting events. The places where people go to have fun are shared by all of the people in the community.

Have your students complete the survey sheet presented in figure 4.1, either individually or in small groups. If you send the survey home with the student, to be completed with the help of a parent, consider the possibility that some will not be returned. You may want to have the students predict what information they expect to gather. If you want to do this formally, consider using a transparency of figure 4.1 or a questionnaire you and the students construct. Then, make predictions about what your research will reveal. Record your predictions to be referred to later.

When this activity is completed, gather the information and record your findings next to the predictions, then have the students analyze them.

- Did you discover why people live in your community?
- What are the favorite activities of the students and their families?
- How well did you predict the outcome?
- Why do the students think they were correct or incorrect? You may want to include a brief history of the local community here.

Try to determine the answers to the following questions.

- Who settled in your community first?
- Did you consider Native Americans to be the first settlers?
- Why was it settled?
- How did your community get its name?
- Does anyone in your class have ancestors who were original settlers?

A local historical society might be willing to share pictures of the early days of your community's settlement. Perhaps someone would even visit to provide an oral history. Or, consider offering the research possibilities to interested students. Allow them to report their results to the class.

Day 2

The focus of this day's lesson is the basic needs all humans have: food, clothing, shelter, love, and safety. If you are using a textbook, read the section that tells about basic human needs. If not, use the following questions and answers to shape the content of your discussion.

What needs do people have?

People need *food* to make them strong and healthy. People need *clothing* for protection against the environment. When it is cold, people wear heavier clothing than when it is warm. People build *shelters*, such as homes, stores, and offices, to protect themselves from extreme weather. People in communities work together to help one another meet all these needs.

What people in a community help meet our need for safety?

Police officers, firefighters, doctors, and nurses are all people who help human beings meet their need for safety. Communities often have a hospital where hurt or sick people can go for special care.

Why are schools and libraries important to people in a community?

Schools are places where people can learn about things. Libraries keep books for people of the community to use. They are good places for people to go to learn things.

After the above discussion, ask the class, "How does where we live affect our basic needs?" and brainstorm the answers together. Record answers on a piece of poster board or a transparency to be saved and referred to later.

Why People Live in a Community

	My family is here.	Work found here.			
Why do you live here?					
	Sports	Scouts	Church	Parks	Other
What activities do you do here?					

Use the chart to tally answers in the columns. Present your findings below.

How many people live here because other family members do? _____

How many people live here because of the work they do? _____

How many people participate in sports activities? _____

scouting events? _____

church activities? _____

park activities? _____

What other community activities did people name? _____

_____

_____

From this informal survey, what can you conclude about why people live in this community?

_____

_____

_____

_____

_____

Fig. 4.1. Community survey sheet.

Read *Houses* (Siberell 1979) to the class. This book provides a history of the development of houses. If you are unable to find this particular book, ask the children's librarian for another title that offers similar content. Give students the "Homes Survey" form shown in figure 4.2. Students should complete the first part of the survey in class before taking it home to complete the second part. Arrange your class in groups of four or five students.

A word of caution: If you live in a community where there is a wide range of homes and economic conditions, you may not want to use the survey as it is prepared here. If revealing their housing situation would prove embarrassing to students, adjust this part of the plan, or consider eliminating the students' names altogether.

Day 3

The focus of today's class is the variety of houses found in your own community. Collect the data from the students' "Homes Survey" forms. Tally the number of housing types and consider why these dwellings are built in your community.

Because the region I live in experiences four seasons ranging from cold, snowy winters to hot, humid summers, homes are built to keep people safe and comfortable throughout the year. All businesses and homes have central heating of some sort. Most businesses and many homes have air conditioning for the hottest days of the year. Those of us who do not have air conditioning have screens for our windows to allow the air to flow through, but not the insects that live in our environment. We also have rainfall, especially in the spring and fall, so our roofs are usually slanted, and we have rain gutters to carry away the water. Many people have sump pumps to keep their basements dry during wet times of the year. Our children go to school from late August through early June. The schools must also have central heating, but only the newer schools have air conditioning.

Read *A Country Far Away* (Gray and Dupasquier 1991) to the class. The book takes a whimsical look at the similarities in the lives of two boys, one in a Western country, one in a rural African village. Although the boys' lives are shown to be basically similar, the background shows the contrast in the buildings and environment. Encourage the students to examine the illustrations closely for both the similarities and differences and the reasons for them.

Divide the class into two groups. Give one group *It's Fun Finding Out About People and Places* (Manley 1980) and the other group *People* (Spier 1988). Both books show the diversity of homes and clothing among populations. Provide students with enough time to read through the books. Have them decide what information about basic human needs they discover and would like to share with the other group.

When the class reassembles, be sure to discuss with the students the cause-and-effect relationship of climate and landforms on the houses built around the world. Invite students to identify climate and landform influences on the houses built in your community.

Day 4

The focus of this plan is the physical characteristics of communities. Note that this is also an aspect of the geographic theme, Place. If you are using a textbook, read the section that discusses landforms and the ways in which they contribute to the uniqueness of communities.

Ask the students what physical characteristics make their community special. You may have to supply some examples or clues to get the students started. Record their responses. Then add all the physical features students can think of that do not exist in their community. Be certain the list includes

HOUSES SURVEY   Part 1: In your small group, ask the following

questions:

<u>What kind of home do you live in?</u> Put a check mark in the correct column. Add

the number of checks in each column.

Name	Apartment	Condominium	Single Home	Other?
1.				
2.				
3.				
4.				
5.				
Totals				

<u>What kind of home was marked most often?</u>

Part 2:   Take this survey home with you. Look at the buildings on each

side of your home.

<u>What type of home are they?</u>

	Apartment	Condominium	Single Home	Other	Stories	1?	2?	3?
Right								
Left								

YOUR NAME_____

Fig. 4.2. Homes survey form.

From *Geographic Literacy Through Children's Literature*. © 1997 Linda K. Rogers. Teacher Ideas Press. (800) 237-6124.

river, lake, ocean, mountain, and desert. Provide magazines for students to examine for photographs and drawings of landforms. They can glue pictures to construction paper and include a definition, or students can work together to create a collage of pictures showing a particular landform.

In a class discussion, have students consider the following questions about their own community:

- What are the advantages of living here?
- What are the disadvantages?
- How have people adapted to the disadvantages?
- Is it possible that some of the disadvantages are also advantages?

The emphasis should be on the relationship of the physical characteristics and the advantages and disadvantages of human habitation.

Begin basic map skill instruction. Introduce the way in which we represent objects in reality with models and maps. Use a model railroad scene if you can find one. Or, create a small community scene with children's toy houses, model trees, and plants. Be sure to include a base, such as poster board, that shows roads and bodies of water. First, display the model on a table so that you and the students can talk about how the buildings, plants, roadways, waterways, and other natural landforms are positioned. Use relational terms like *next to*, *beside*, *near*, and *far*. Establish the cardinal directions and discuss relationships using phrases such as "north of," "to the south," and "on the west side." Move the model to the floor so that the students can stand above it and look straight down. Tell the students that this is a bird's-eye view of the model. Note how the houses, trees, roads, and waterways look. Draw a map based on the "bird's-eye view." Use the terms *symbols* and *map key* when you and the students compare the map to the model it represents.

The children in *In the Woods: Who's Been Here?* (George 1995) and *In the Snow: Who's Been Here?* (George 1995) take a walk through the woods near their home. A small map showing the area and the route they took is found in the front of each book. This can be useful in helping students see how symbols can be used.

Show the students a map of the United States. Locate your own state, then your community. Now, show the students a map of your state and locate your community on it. Lastly, show the students a map of your community. Locate important landmarks: the school the children attend, the middle (or junior) and senior high schools, a neighborhood shopping center, a well-known park, the public library, and the business center of your community.

See if a local realty office will supply free or reasonably priced maps of the community. Send the students home with a map and have them locate the site of their home on it. Encourage them to "read" the map with an adult or older sibling. Tell them to trace (with their finger) the route they take from their home to school when they travel in the family car. Have them trace the route their bus takes each day. Have them trace other routes, such as those to the store, church, piano lessons, or sports activities. They should bring the map back to school the following day.

Day 5

Use your copy of the community map to mark the home of every student in the class and the school. If you don't mind replacing your map next year, write directly on it. Give each student a number and put the student's number in a circle in the appropriate spot. Then put the student key on the map so that students can refer to it at other times. Another way to mark the map so that you can use it in the future is to mount it on a bulletin board and then use long pins (fitted with number flags) to mark the students' homes. This may also make it easier to locate several students who live along the same street if the map is relatively small. Consider color coding the students by flag or pinhead. You may want to make each group or row in the classroom a different color.

Read *The Armadillo from Amarillo* (Cherry 1994) to the class. The book, after following the armadillo's progress across Texas, puts the animal in place. He discovers he is in a city in a state which is one of 50 states in the United States which is on the continent of North America which is on the planet Earth. Return then, to the maps you looked at yesterday. Your students looked at three maps: community, state, and national. Now, look at a map of the Western Hemisphere and a globe to further "place" them. Vocabulary to be introduced should include *address, zip code, capital, borders, boundaries, continent, North America,* and *hemispheres.*

Other important vocabulary words that will help students work with maps are *distance scale, cardinal directions, North Pole, South Pole,* and *equator.* Find each of these on each of the maps and the globe. Be sure to refer to your community each time. Do not forget to use relational words to help students understand these terms in context. Use the following statements and questions to guide a discussion.

- "We live north of or above the equator."
- "What country is south of us?"
- "What states are next to us?"
- "Which direction should we travel from our state to get to the Pacific Ocean?"

Please note: The word *above* works only if your map places "north" at the top of your map, and even then, I'm reluctant to use it! There are maps available that put Antarctica at the top, rendering the world as we have traditionally perceived it as upside down. Consider sharing such a map with your students and discussing how it changes the familiar.

Provide several locations within your classroom, each with a map, for students to gather around in small groups. Vary the type of map at each location. Include a country map, a state map, and a community map. Have three or four questions for the group to answer with each map. The questions should be similar to the ones you answered earlier. After each group has had a chance to answer the questions, gather the whole class and discuss the answers. Be sure to refer to the maps for the answers. Remember that these are skills that students need to use to refine and retain. Use maps as much as you can to help students develop map skills and build mental maps of their world. If you have enough time, or if you wish to extend this lesson into another day, rotate the groups so that all students have an opportunity to interact with a variety of maps.

───────────────────────────────**Day 6**

The focus of this lesson is the means by which buildings are erected in your community. Most of us don't give much thought to building. As I was growing up, my dad built houses as a source of extra income. The result was that I learned how houses in central Illinois are constructed. In fact, because my mother and dad did almost all of the construction, I had a fairly intimate knowledge of the subject. Although the basic steps in home construction are the same here in northeastern Pennsylvania, the preparation of the land on which the home, or any building, will stand can be quite different. Several

years ago a local developer began to clear an area in my community for a small shopping center. In the Midwest, a large bulldozer would level the ground and digging would begin for the foundation and/or basement. Before any leveling could begin here, huge blocks of stone had to be systematically cut out of the tract of land and hauled away. The remaining "wall" on the back side of the cleared space rises at least 30 or 40 feet above the parking lot of the shopping center. Once the space was created, construction began and followed the basic order I had observed in Illinois.

Ask your students what kinds of preparations are made to prepare for building in your community.

- Is the land cleared, leveled, cut into, or in some other way restructured?
- What landforms in your community influence construction?
- Is your water table so close to ground level that your homes cannot have basements? For example, few homes along our southeastern coast have basements because the ocean influences the level of the water table on the land.
- Have the students ever had experience with construction? You may find that someone's dad or grandfather or uncle is a contractor and could be called on as an outside resource.

Discuss how buildings are put into place in your community. With the students, determine what landforms around your homes and school influenced their construction. Be ready to provide some examples that model what the students should consider. Include a discussion about what materials are used in your community, region, and state. Does your region have an abundance or absence of a particular building material that influences building choices?

At this point, provide the students with information about making introductions and the appropriate way to participate in formal conversations. Our district includes this in an English textbook. You may want to spend a class period role-playing introductions and conversations. These oral language skills will be used when your class interviews a guest speaker.

Prepare class interview questions for a visitor who is involved in some aspect of construction in your community. Your choice of speaker will depend on what information you seek and who is available to you. Consider one of the following: an architect, a structural engineer, a builder, or a representative from the state department of transportation. As you and the class prepare for the interview, consider these questions:

- What do we want to know?
- Who in the class will ask the questions? Should one child be the interviewer or should several ask the questions?
- How will we record what we learn?
- What will we do with the information we receive?

Day 7

Interview the guest. After the guest has departed, discuss what you learned and if there is further information students want to pursue. If so, you can choose to arrange for another guest speaker, tailoring the questions to the guest's area of expertise.

—Day 8

This day's focus is the varying size of communities. The terms *suburb* and *rural* are introduced. The social studies text my school district uses profiles New York City as a large city; Washington, D.C., as a medium-sized city; Cape Canaveral, Florida, and Sun City, Arizona, as unique small cities; Spring, Texas, as a suburb of Houston; and Boonesboro, Kentucky, as a small town. Remarkably, this textbook, which provides opportunities to develop and expand mapping skills, does not locate these six communities on a U.S. map! Don't make the same mistake. If you are going to present real communities, be sure to locate them on a map with your students as well as provide information that describes the physical and human characteristics that define them as unique places.

Consider communities of various sizes in your home state. As I currently live in Pennsylvania, I would focus on Philadelphia as a large city, Scranton or Wilkes-Barre as a small city, my home community as a suburban community, and State College as a unique community because it is home to Pennsylvania State University. There are many small, rural communities nearby that I could identify for study.

The characteristics to highlight relate to the size of the community: the population, the number and sizes of the schools, the businesses, and types of recreational areas, to mention a few. Ask your students to determine what term would best describe their own community.

- Is it rural, a small town, a town, a small, medium, or large city?
- Is it a community that is a suburb of a city?
- Is your community famous for something?
- Is it the county seat or the state capital?

Read *Forest, Village, Town, City* (Beekman 1982) and *The Changing City* (Muller 1977) or *New Providence* (vonTscharner and Fleming 1992) to the students. Introduce the City and Country centers that you have prepared and set up in your classroom (see below). You can make these as simple or complex as you want. The centers should include as many of the books listed below as you can find, along with directions for using the center. Feel free to adapt the requirements. The work at the centers is fairly simple. The intent is to give students the opportunity to gather information and compare it to their own experience. Use the following directions with the students.

City and Country Centers

You must:

1. Read two books from each center.

2. Draw a picture of the most important fact you learned in each center.

3. Use at least three sentences to compare (your community) to what you learned about cities and the country.

Books Recommended for the Centers:

CITY CENTER

Bash, Barbara. *Urban Roosts*
Bunting, Eve. *Smoky Night*
Carrick, Carol. *Left Behind*
Goodall, John S. *The Story of a Main Street*

Heide, Florence Perry, and Judith Heide Gilliland. *The Day of Ahmed's Secret*
Jakobsen, Kathy. *My New York*
Krementz, Jill. *A Visit to Washington, D.C.*
Leighton, Maxinne Rhea. *An Ellis Island Christmas*
Levinson, Riki. *I Go with My Family to Grandma's*
Maestro, Betsy, and Ellen DelVecchio. *Big City Port*
Maestro, Betsy, and Guilio Maestro. *The Story of the Statue of Liberty*
Maestro, Betsy, and Guilio Maestro. *Taxi: A Book of City Words*
Munro, Roxie. *Christmastime in New York City*
Munro, Roxie. *The Inside-Outside Book of London*
Munro, Roxie. *The Inside-Outside Book of New York City*
Munro, Roxie. *The Inside-Outside Book of Washington, D.C.*
Quackenbush, Robert. *Pop! Goes the Weasel and Yankee Doodle*
Rius, Maria, and J. M. Parramon. *Let's Discover the City*
vonTscharner, Renata, and Ronald Lee Fleming. *New Providence*
Zolotow, Charlotte. *The Moon Was the Best*

COUNTRY CENTER

Bannatyne-Cugnet, Jo. *A Prairie Alphabet*
George, Lindsay Barrett. *In the Woods: Who's Been Here?*
George, William. *Beaver at Long Pond*
George, William. *Box Turtle at Long Pond*
George, William. *Christmas at Long Pond*
George, William. *Fishing at Long Pond*
Goodall, John S. *The Story of a Farm*
Locker, Thomas. *Where the River Begins*
Provensen, Alice, and Martin Provensen. *Shaker Lane*
Rius, Maria, and J. M. Parramon. *Let's Discover the Countryside*
Siebert, Diane. *Heartland*
Yolen, Jane. *Letting Swift River Go*

APPROPRIATE FOR BOTH CITY AND COUNTRY CENTERS

Beekman, Dan. *Forest, Village, Town, City*
Cherry, Lynne. *The Armadillo from Amarillo*
Maestro, Betsy, and Guilio Maestro. *Delivery Van: Words for Town and Country*
Provensen, Alice, and Martin Provensen. *Town and Country*
Robbins, Ken. *Bridges*
Ventura, Piero. *Piero Ventura's Book of Cities*

Day 9

Although you can schedule the students' time working in the centers in any way you want, my personal preference is to set aside at least one day as Center Time. Therefore, this day is for independent work.

Day 10

Many social studies textbooks provide a special section in each unit called CLOSE-UP. In this unit of my local district's text, Native Americans are highlighted. The food, shelter, clothing, geographic location, and traditions of American Indians, Eskimos, and Hawaiians are briefly discussed. If you do not already teach a unit on Native Americans, you may find this brief overview helpful. Locate the areas of the United States where these Native Americans were living when they were "discovered" by European explorers. Find your own community and compare its location. Discuss the influence that landforms, animals, plants, and climate had on the Native Americans as they sought the materials necessary to provide for basic needs: food, clothing, shelter, love, and safety. *Nessa's Fish* (Luenn 1990) and *The*

Seasons and Someone (Kroll 1994) look at life in the Arctic region, while *Dreamplace* (Lyon 1993) and Byrd Baylor's books about the desert can be used to expand students' understanding of Native Americans in the Southwest. I found two books that contrast the way in which Native Americans treated the environment with how other inhabitants treated it. Susan Jeffers has illustrated the often-quoted statement Chief Seattle made in the mid-1800s about how we should treat the Earth in *Brother Eagle, Sister Sky: A Message from Chief Seattle* (1991). Another book, *And Still the Turtle Watched* (MacGill-Callahan 1991), tells of how the Delaware River has been mistreated by humans since the Native Americans were pushed out of the area.

──**Day 11**

Today's lesson focuses on the way humans have developed clothing for themselves. Read parts of *Clothing* (Ventura 1993) to the students. Make your selection based on your students' maturity. Ventura makes the point that clothing is used for protection and "show." Ask your students what they believe this means. Ask them to think of examples of the types of clothing people wear for their jobs and leisure. Think about the type of clothing you would consider "normal" for your community. Why is it normal? What might someone wear in your community that would let you know they were not from your community?

Give the students the following homework assignment: Look at your clothes. Choose two of your favorite outfits—one meant for protection and one for "show"—and make sketches or take notes on them. Bring your notes or sketches to class tomorrow for a special project.

──**Day 12**

Today your students will be dressing oaktag figures with the two outfits they chose from their wardrobes. As you begin class, ask some of the students to tell about or show their sketches. Ask them why they chose these particular outfits. Also ask them why they believe they fit the criteria for the assignment.

Provide each student with two oaktag figures (see fig. 4.3) or create your own patterns. Using construction paper, scissors, crayons, markers, and glue, have the students make an outfit for each of the oaktag figures that resembles the sketches/notes of the two outfits they brought to school. Then have them glue the outfit onto the figure. You may need to take some time to demonstrate how your students can use the oaktag figures to establish the correct size for the parts of the outfit. For example, place the oaktag figure on a piece of scrap paper. Trace around the shoulders, arms, and torso down to the waist. Now show the students how the shape of a shirt, sweater, or coat will need to be at least this size. Point out where lines for the neckline, sleeve lengths, and bottom length should be marked. Ask the students to consider whether the clothing they plan to draw is snug fitting or more bulky than the figure itself. The answers to these questions will help the students create more realistic clothing. After the students have traced a prototype pattern, the next step is to place the pattern on the construction paper, then trace around it before adding details. If necessary, repeat the process with the waist-to-feet part of the figure. Remind the students to include headgear and footgear if they are part of the outfit.

Provide two 3-by-5-inch cards for each student to use to write a brief statement about each outfit's purpose. As students complete the project, have them share their figures and purpose statements. One means of displaying these figures is a bulletin board. They might also be arranged in a pictograph if you and the students categorize them by style, use, season, or some other characteristic.

Fig. 4.3. Oaktag figure pattern.

───────────────────────────────────Day 13

Conclusion: Return to the brainstorming list from Day 2 that was generated from the question "How does where we live affect our basic needs?" Review the listing and determine what might be added, deleted, or changed.

Means of Assessment for This Unit

There were a variety of activities in which students participated throughout this unit. Without using the more formal, traditional means of assessment, consider the following as a means by which you can determine how well your students understood the concepts you presented in the study.

- Completion of the "Homes Survey"
- Participation in the City and Country Centers
- Community map homework assignment
- Completion of the "dressed" oaktag figures project
- Class discussion/participation

Bibliography

The books included here are ones mentioned in this unit, or ones you may find useful. Note that they do not appear in the annotated bibliography in the back of this book. The asterisk (*) on three of these entries indicates that the books are no longer in print but can be found in libraries if you are willing to search for it.

Carlisle, Norman, and Carlisle, Madelyn. 1983. *Bridges*. Chicago: Childrens Press.
    This "new true book" of bridges discusses the first bridges, famous and unusual bridges, and bridge design and construction. The simple text is enhanced by photographs of bridges.

Macaulay, David. 1983. *Underground*. Boston: Houghton Mufflin.
    The text and intricate black-and-white drawings in this book describe the subways, sewers, building foundations, telephone and power systems, columns, cables, pipes, tunnels, and other underground elements of a large modern city. Other good titles by David Macaulay are *City, Cathedral,* and *Pyramid*.

*Manley, D. 1980. *It's Fun Finding Out About People and Places*. New York: Derrydale Books.
    Similar to, but less "busy" than Peter Spier's *People*, this book describes people and places throughout the world.

Muller, Jorg. 1977. *The Changing City*. New York: Atheneum.
    The author has used a unique portfolio approach to show the same section of a city, pictured at intervals of approximately three years from 1953 to 1976 as it slowly loses it character and purpose, either through neglect or lack of planning. The eight full-color, fold-out pictures can be laid out and compared.

*Russell, S. P. 1977. *The Big Ditch Waterways*. New York: Parents' Magazine Press.

This book discusses man-made canals used throughout the world for irrigation, transportation, and drainage. Maps indicate the location of each waterway.

*Siberell, A. 1979. *Houses*. New York: Holt, Rinehart & Winston.

In brief text and attractive pictures, the author describes how houses have evolved through the ages. The reader sees not only the development of more and more sophisticated houses, but how the need, lifestyle, and available materials dictate the kind of houses we live in.

Ventura, P. 1993. *Clothing*. Boston: Houghton Mifflin.

Through detailed drawings the author traces the evolution of clothing styles, fabrics, and uses throughout history. He notes the two purposes for clothing: to protect ourselves and to display ourselves for admiration. (Caution: Some drawings show bare-breasted women.)

Reference

Boehm, R. G., and Petersen, J. F. 1994. "An Elaboration of the Fundamental Themes in Geography." *Social Education* 58, no. 4: 211-18.

Chapter 5

MOVEMENT

"Regions and places are connected by movement or human interactions. Humans are increasing their levels of interaction, in communication, travel, and foreign exchange. Technology has allowed us to shrink space and distance. People migrate and travel out of curiosity, economic or social need, as a response to environmental change, or because they have been forced to move for other reasons."

—W. Kimball, *K-6 Geography*, 3

Geographers separate the characteristics of Movement into three divisions: Its Form and Stimulus, Global Interdependence, and Models of Human Interaction. This chapter will focus on the first two characteristics; the third is too sophisticated for geographic literacy at the elementary level.

Movement: Its Form and Stimulus

The social studies curriculum draws heavily on this division of the Movement theme at the elementary level. Most primary teachers include a unit of study on *Transportation Modes.* Within this subdivision are private, public, and freight transportation.

A part of this theme is *The Movement of Everyday Life,* which we either take for granted or do not recognize as a part of geographic literacy. Within this subdivision are individual travel behavior, networks of communication, spatial organization of society, and spatial efficiency within market areas.

The *History of Movement* is yet another subdivision of this theme. Movement is important in both history and geography. The History of Movement also includes migration, the history of settlements, and frontiers. Voyages and expeditions of discovery and exploration are also covered in this subdivision.

Economic Stimulus for Movements emphasizes that economic factors can stimulate or influence behavior. Also contained in this subdivision are issues of colonization, mercantilism, and current migrations.

The final subdivision of this division of Movement is that of *Energy and Mass-Induced Movements*. These are movements associated with the water cycle (such as weather, wind, and ocean currents), tectonic movements, movements associated with volcanism, mass movements such as landslides, and movements within ecosystems.

Global Interdependence

The world is connected by many means, communication, transportation, and economics among them. *The Movement of Goods, Services, and Ideas* considers where raw materials come from, where they are going to, and where particular products, technologies, services or ideas come from and why. As this movement takes place, there are issues of *Foreign Trade,* which include trade partner countries, tariffs, and production facilities, and those of the *Common Market,* which include shared labor, markets, and production facilities.

MOVEMENT

**Movement:
Its Form and Stimulus**

- Transportation Modes
- The Movement of Everyday Life
- History of Movement
- Economic Stimulus for Movements
- Energy and Mass-Induced

Global Interdependence

- The Movement of Goods, Services, and Ideas
- Foreign Trade
- Common Market

Teaching Ideas

As I collected books for the bibliography, keeping the five geographic themes in mind, I was surprised by the number of children's books that could be used to support the Movement theme. Originally, the books I was considering as examples of Movement were those concerned with history of movement, particularly the history of settlements and voyages of discovery and migration. Eventually, I began to look at books with a broader vision of movement—one that included transportation, immigration, and wars.

We read and hear that "the world is shrinking." Although I think we as adults believe this (and understand this) at some level, I do not think our children understand it. Their experiences, for the most part, occur within a technologically advanced and rich environment. For that matter, although I certainly remember the two-lane highways that made traveling a test of patience and endurance, most transportation experiences in my life have been activated by superhighways, tollways, rapid transit trains, and public airlines. My job requires a considerable amount of driving. This week was an exception: I drove 700 miles and was home for dinner and to sleep every night! Our family thinks nothing of jumping in the car and driving 350 miles round-trip to visit our son in college for a few hours. A few years ago, when a Ugandan friend was in our home, the nightly news was continually reporting the U.S. involvement in Somalia. I asked him how far Somalia was from where he has lived in southwestern Uganda all of his life. "Oh," he said, "it is very far. Five hundred miles." I was surprised because that was less than the distance to any of our family members' homes. Then I remembered that Charles's means of transportation was a bicycle. He regularly visited the eight parish churches under his leadership on a bicycle. Since his return to Uganda our parish has been able to provide him with the necessary funds to purchase a motorcycle. The 15 to 25 miles between his parish churches is certainly more easily traversed, but the roads are so rough that in the first few months of the motorcycle's use Charles had to replace several pistons. Yes, 500 miles *is* a long way if you do not have access to a vehicle, fuel, and good roads.

Transportation

Many children's books can be used in a study of transportation. Although many of the books mentioned on subsequent pages fit within the Movement theme directly, they can also be used in a study on Human-Environmental Relations because they demonstrate the variety of ways humans have devised to move themselves from place to place despite environmental conditions.

Several of the books that demonstrate the ways we have explored new and unknown areas on the Earth are also examples of early means of transportation. *Across the Wide Dark Sea* (Van Leeuwen 1995) is the most recent book I've seen that relates the story of the Pilgrims' journey across the Atlantic. The author chose to tell the story from the point of view of nine-year-old Love Brewster, son of William Brewster. Using primary sources for her research, Van Leeuwen's fictionalized account depicts the joys and struggles of this momentous undertaking. By using other nonfiction sources,

your students can discover just what this journey involved. Use a globe and yarn to mark the ship's movement. Note that the Pilgrims intended to end up in the Virginia colony earlier in the year, but the return to England with the leaky *Stillwell* and winds that blew them off course instead brought them to New England after the growing season. Some students might want to investigate the kinds of navigational instruments that were available to sailors in the 1600s. Use the globe or detailed world maps to determine the distance the *Mayflower* traveled. If you check the nonfiction sources closely, you can also calculate the average speed the ship traveled.

Another interesting book in which a young boy is the narrator of an ocean journey is *Bluewater Journal: The Voyage of the Sea Tiger* (Krupinski 1995). Twelve-year-old Benjamin Slocum travels with his family from Boston to Honolulu to Hong Kong in the clipper ship *Sea Tiger*. The story, told through Benjamin's journal entries, describes the adventures and hardships of the four-month journey in 1860. The book provides factual information through a map of the voyage included at the beginning of the book and a short summary of clipper ship history and a glossary included at the end. Again, you and your students can determine the length of the journey in miles and the average speed. Benjamin's journal entries discuss the ports of call, which supply dates and places to help you establish probable statistics. The book's short history of clipper ships is a great beginning point for further research into an interesting period in our country's history and the worldwide trade market.

Another way you can use *Bluewater Journal* is through an examination of the way it models journal writing. Many people keep journals as they travel. Other examples of books featuring journal writing appear in this book's bibliography: Jan Cheripko, in *Voices of the River: Adventures on the Delaware* (1993), kept a journal as he and Matt Smith canoed down the Delaware River; the fictional Rachel Rose (*Let's Go Traveling*, Krupp 1992) and Anni (*Anni's Diary of France*, Axworthy 1994) kept journals of their travels; and John Burningham used sketches, photographs, and tape recordings to remind him of his trek *Around the World in Eighty Days* (1972).

Stone and Steel (Billout 1980), *The Random House Book of How Things Are Built* (Brown 1992), and *Bridges* (Robbins 1991) all remind us that our means of transportation can be greatly influenced by the environment in which we operate them. Robbins provides us with a close look at 14 bridges. The other two books look at a mix of human constructions, several of which are connected with transportation. *The Random House Book of How Things Are Built* is divided into sections that reflect different periods in world history. This is helpful as you consider the development of transportation technology and the supporting construction. It even includes the Channel Tunnel between England and France (the "Chunnel"), which recently opened.

Consider the age of your students and then plan an activity that involves them in exploring local structures that support transportation. You may wish them to discover local bridges or tunnels or underpasses that make travel easier. The very youngest students can use building blocks to create these. Older students may want to first try making bridges or tunnels using blocks, then move to smaller scale and more permanent constructions. Using bass wood or flat toothpicks, a utility knife, and white glue, students can build such structures. They may want to use local structures as the models for their creations, or they may want to create their own design and construct it.

Flight (Burleigh 1991), *The Glorious Flight* (Provensen and Provensen 1983), and *Balloon Trip* (Scarry 1982) all deal with our desire to experience flight. Scarry's trip in a hot air balloon includes the history and techniques of ballooning. A close look at hot air ballooning can be connected with a

science unit on air. Students as young as kindergarten and first grade are introduced to the concept of wind, which is a basic part of understanding what makes ballooning possible. Older students build on this concept as they recognize the effect of varying air temperatures on the movement of the air. If you live in an area where there is a hot air ballooning club, you can invite a member into your classroom to share his or her experiences.

The Provensens' award-winning book, *The Glorious Flight*, tells the story of Frenchman Louis Bleriot's flight across the English Channel soon after the Wright brothers made their famous flight at Kitty Hawk, North Carolina. Bleriot's 1909 flight was the first made across the channel in a heavier-than-air vehicle. His factories produced 10,000 aircraft for the French and other Allies during World War I.

Flight is an interesting retelling of Lindbergh's transatlantic flight in 1927 from New York to Paris, based on his own account. Most of the illustrations are drawn from an unusual perspective, making the reader feel much more connected with the flight. Students may want to know more about Lindbergh, who was quite young when he began to fly and when he made this flight. Few of us know that Lindbergh actually made the solo flight across the Atlantic to win a contest and $25,000. That is a substantial amount of money. What would it have purchased in Lindbergh's day?

Use maps of Europe to estimate the length of Bleriot's flight across the English Channel. The Provensens provide the time it took him to complete the journey. Challenge students to determine the rate at which he traveled. Next, look at a world map that can be used to determine the length of Lindbergh's flight. If Burleigh's text doesn't provide enough information, assemble a variety of nonfiction books about the history of flight and Lindbergh or send students to the library to locate more information.

Older students can compare and contrast Lindbergh's and Bleriot's flights using the "Historic Flights" chart depicted in figure 5.1 or a chart of their own creation. Or, consider making this chart a transparency and complete it as a class.

The grandchildren travel to Grandma's on five different means of transportation available to Americans at the turn of the century in *I Go with My Family to Grandma's* (Levinson 1992). The five burroughs of New York are still political regions. Students can use maps to locate these burroughs and determine in what direction the cousins are heading as they go to Grandma's. Have students determine whether New Yorkers continue to use all of the means of transportation found in the book or whether some of them have been replaced. This is an opportune time for you and your students to explore the differences between public and private transportation. *Left Behind* (Carrick 1988) is a wonderful look at the subway system in a large city as seen from a small boy's point of view—a small, *lost* boy's point of view. When I first read this book, I had two reactions. The first was delight at seeing Carrick's main character, Christopher, in another setting; he's such an appealing little boy. The second was how wonderful this book would be in introducing the importance of staying with the class on a field trip. Surely, if Christopher's adventure were a true account, the poor teacher would have been absolutely distraught!

If you can obtain a map or schedule of a city subway system or other public transportation system, display it and determine, with your students, the various characteristics of the system. Compare and contrast the features of public and private transportation. Depending on where you live, your students may be more familiar with one type over another. Try to take your students on a field trip that includes public transportation. In Illinois, because of our proximity to Chicago, we could use the commuter trains to travel into the city for field trips. My husband accompanied our son's

Compare and Contrast the Historic Flights Depicted in *The Glorious Flight* and *Flight*

	The Glorious Flight	Flight
Type of aircraft		
Length of flight in miles		
Length of flight in hours		
Purpose of flight		
Origin of flight		
Destination of flight		
Pilot		

Fig. 5.1. Historic flights chart.

third-grade class on a field trip into Chicago that began with a ride on the commuter train. Then, using a city map, they visited important Chicago landmarks such as the Sears Tower, Navy Pier, and the Chicago Art Institute, as well as famous sculptures by Chagal, Picasso, and Caulder. Although the students walked throughout the field trip, they saw many types of public transportation: public buses, taxis, and the elevated trains.

Have your students collect data about the types of public transportation they have used. Collecting these data and organizing them into some type of graph provides students as young as kindergarten age with an authentic application of mathematics concepts. The "Public Transportation" chart depicted in figure 5.2 can be used to collect the data. Whether students work independently or in pairs to collect the data outside the classroom, or are grouped within the classroom and survey only within the classroom, the resulting information can be graphed.

Research your region's transportation history. When I taught in Illinois, I was able to take my class on a field trip to a trolley park. We would take a short ride on a restored trolley car and learn about how the trolley fit in the history of our area. Where I live currently is a large national park displaying steam-powered trains. In addition to being able to take short and long rides on a steam train, visitors can tour a museum featuring historic photographs, railroad memorabilia, and a working roundhouse. Other possible field trips might take you and your class to the "bus barns" of your local public bus company, the bus station, the airport, or the commuter train station.

Ferryboat (Maestro and Maestro 1986) fits nicely into this unit of study. In some parts of our country, people need to use a ferryboat daily to get to their jobs or conduct business. Encourage your students to discover where ferries are in use. Then, use maps to explore the areas of our country where ferryboats— like the one in Connecticut that inspired this picture book—are an everyday part of life. If you are near a ferry, perhaps you can take your class on a field trip to discover the "ins and outs" of ferry transportation. Or, consider asking someone from the ferry service to visit your class and provide information.

There are large ferries in the world that transport people from country to country. Before the new English Channel Tunnel opened in 1994, commuters traveling between the coasts of England and France had to use ferries or Hovercraft. Train ferries connect London and Paris. There are other major ferryboat services in the Baltic Sea, across the strait of Bosporus, between several Japanese islands, across Lake Michigan, and between Seattle, Washington, and Vancouver, British Columbia. Older students may want to research these services and share their information with the class.

History of Movement

Within this subdivision of the Movement theme are two areas of study that are the subject of several children's books: migration and exploration. Another subdivision that can be integrated into Movement is Economic Stimulus for Movements. The books discussed in this part of the chapter generally do not address directly the economy, but you, as the teacher, can insert the appropriate information. I am also including a section of books about wars because I feel there have often been aspects of Movement involved in wars. As you have read in earlier chapters, wars create environmental problems. Wars can also change political borders, affect trade, and halt the smooth movement of goods and services.

Public Transportation

Ask at least five people about the types of public transportation they have used. Put a tally mark next to the type. Remember that some people may have used more than one type.

 Taxi (Cab)

 Train

 Ship

 Airplane

  Hot Air Balloon

Fig. 5.2. Public transportation chart.

The exploration and westward movement in our own country are documented in a number of children's books. Van Leeuwen's (1995) *Across the Wide Dark Sea* tells the story of the *Mayflower* journey and the Pilgrims' first year. The difficulties involved in settling a new community are evident in this book and several others. In *Aurora Means Dawn*, Sanders (1989) tells, through the fictional adventures of a real family, the story of how a new settlement began in Aurora, Ohio, in 1800. *New Hope* (Sorensen 1995) also tells about the beginning of a fictional community through a serendipitous act and then describes the growth of the community to modern times. *Dandelions* (Bunting 1995), *Dakota Dugout* (Turner 1985), and *My Prairie Christmas* (Harvey 1990) provide a picture of living on the prairie in the early days of this country's settlement. These books contrast the settled, "civilized" life these pioneers left behind with the new hardships they encounter. *Christmas on the Prairie* (Anderson 1985) shows, in photographs, the typical Christmas celebration in a Midwestern settlement in 1836. Eventually, the Midwest became a "safe" place, and Americans began to move farther west, leaving their comfortable life behind. You and your students can find the specific locations discussed in these books and research the settlement of these areas.

Some students may want to learn about local history and discover who the earliest settlers were. Try to locate a community group involved in local research. Some historical societies feature museum-type buildings you can visit. They may also be able to provide a spokesperson to visit your class and provide useful information, interesting stories, and old documents and pictures reflecting your community's history. Perhaps the newspaper archives can supply historical photographs for class use.

Help your students determine what made people willing to leave the familiar and comfortable behind in exchange for the hardships and unknowns of building new settlements on the frontier. Another of Harvey's books, *Cassie's Journey: Going West in the 1860s* (1995), tells the story of one family traveling in the westward movement to California. The story is fictional, but it is based on the journal writing of many women who made the journey across the rugged country and encountered the dangers.

Take your children on a journey to California (in 1860). Start your class in an eastern city. Make preparations for the journey west. Decide what belongings your families will be able to carry along and what you'll have to leave behind. Consider what sorts of provisions you will need to complete your journey. Investigate the various routes (trails) used by the pioneers. Use maps to determine how long the entire journey will take, what landforms will cause particular problems, and what kinds of weather conditions you should expect. As you journey, document your adventure on a large class-created map of the United States as it looked in 1860. Mark the places along the way that are of particular interest. Find some journals of the journeys made by real travelers. Allow the students to create a fictional tale shaped by actual events recorded in the journals. There is a note at the end of *Aurora Means Dawn* in which Sanders tells how he created stories based on historical documents. His experiences may help your project.

Cowboy Country (Scott 1993) offers an interesting look at the life of today's cowboy, connecting life today with that of cowboys in the past. As people settled at various places across the western frontier, the job of the cowboy was important in the survival and growth of new communities. This book also reminds us that humans continue to use animals for transportation even in this age of technology.

Another aspect of this type of movement is that taken by people who are not exploring their own country but emigrating from their own country to another. *An Ellis Island Christmas* (Leighton 1992) and *Watch the Stars Come*

Out (Levinson 1995) tell about immigrants entering the United States during the time that Ellis Island was the major gateway to this country. You and your students will find the history of Ellis Island a rich study. There are a number of books with photographs documenting this story, although they are not included in this book as they are not children's books. Students may find that there are members of their own families who entered the United States through Ellis Island. Older students may wish to pursue a study of U.S. immigration policy over the past two centuries. The eighth-grade English students in our local school district participate in research leading to a debate on a topic selected by the teachers. In past years topics such as capital punishment and regulating violence on television have been chosen. The quota system attached to immigration since World War II might prove to be an exciting debate topic. Certainly there have been "waves" of immigration from particular countries resulting from unrest in the homeland. In the 1970s, for example, many refugees fleeing the conflict in Vietnam arrived on U.S. shores. Much disagreement was voiced about the "boat people," as they were often called, and their right to enter the country, especially in light of the fact that U.S. immigration policy involves quotas. *The Lotus Seed* (Garland 1993) tells about a girl who brings her Vietnamese culture with her symbolically in the lotus seed she carries. *The Whispering Cloth: A Refugee's Story* (Shea 1995) is set in a refugee camp in Thailand, one of the countries willing to accept Vietnamese refugees after the Laos Communist government drove them from Laos for fighting alongside American soldiers during the war in Vietnam and Laos. Use a world map to locate Vietnam, Laos, and Thailand. Likewise, *How Many Days to America? A Thanksgiving Story* (Bunting 1990) tells from a child's point of view an interesting story of a family that flees a Caribbean island country. There are many islands from which people attempt to escape to a better life, risking their lives in small boats on often rough seas. You and your students can identify the islands of the Caribbean, the political and economic atmosphere, and their distance from south Florida. Consult the newspaper for current activities involving people attempting to immigrate to the United States despite the difficulties they may encounter.

Several books describe historic explorations. *The Discovery of the Americas* (Maestro and Maestro 1991) is intended for intermediate students. It discusses hypothetical and historical voyages of discovery in the Western Hemisphere, including the possibility that humans passed over the Bering Strait from Asia to Alaska. An extremely helpful addition to the text is the informational tables included at the end of the book. Consider using this book with the introduction of the exploration of the Western Hemisphere.

The journeys of Marco Polo to China have been documented in several children's books. Ceserani's (1977) *Marco Polo* is a relatively simple version of the more than 20 years in the late thirteenth century that Polo spent in China with his father and uncle. Marco Polo published a book that became the basis for maps of the East and the inspiration of other expeditions, including Columbus's two nearly 100 years later. Use Ceserani's text as an introduction to a look at how exploration brings about the discovery of new products and ideas. The book discusses some of the foods and inventions Polo brought from China to Europe on his return.

Fisher (1990) has written a picture book, *Prince Henry the Navigator*, which is a biography of this fifteenth-century navigational visionary. The knowledge gained in Prince Henry's navigational school made it possible for explorers like Columbus to travel the seas. Obviously, Christopher Columbus will be included in a study of exploration. Two picture books may be useful: *Follow the Dream: The Story of Christopher Columbus* (Sis 1991) and *Encounter* (Yolen 1992). Sis's account is the more traditional, "pro-Columbus"

story we are used to reading. His detailed drawings, which include maps illustrated in the style of fifteenth-century cartography, are especially enlightening. He also includes comments in the author's note about fifteenth-century mapmakers' penchant for enclosing their world with walls. Encourage your students to consider Sis's reflections on walls, real and imaginary. Read Fisher's story of the building of *The Great Wall of China* (1986) which tells about how the emperor believed he could protect his subjects from the Mongols. If you want to extend a study of walls, use *Talking Walls* (Knight 1992).

Encounter provides a much less traditional look at Columbus's discovery of the New World. Told by an old man, who was a young boy when Columbus arrived, the story is unsettling. Rather than feeling pleased by the new visitors' arrival, the boy tried to warn his elders of the danger they represented. Now an old man, he takes no pleasure in being correct. This book provides an opportunity for you to introduce questions about who gains and who loses in the course of "discovery." Sis's (1993) book about Jan Welzl, *A Small Tall Tale from the Far Far North*, raises this issue more subtly as the narrator, Jan, expresses his concerns about the influx of Europeans into Alaska and the Eskimo culture. Your students will undoubtedly make the connection that European exploration of North America was a gain for the explorers but a loss for the Native Americans. Two picture books, *And Still the Turtle Watched* (MacGill-Callahan 1991) and *Brother Eagle, Sister Sky: A Message from Chief Seattle* (Jeffers 1991), look at how European exploration led to environmental problems we must now address.

More contemporary examples of exploration and travel are seen in *Around the World in Eighty Days* (Burningham 1972), *Let's Go Traveling* (Krupp 1992), *Anni's Diary of France* (Axworthy 1994), *Your Best Friend, Kate* (Brisson 1992), and *Komodo!* (Sis 1993). In each of them, the main character travels to another place and shares the information gleaned from the journey with the reader.

Burningham's book documents an actual journey. The author successfully re-created the journey "around the world in eighty days" that fictional character Phileas Fogg undertook in Jules Verne's nineteenth-century novel. The children's book records the author's impressions of his 44,000-mile trip through 24 countries. He used a tape recorder, sketchbook, and camera to help him remember the trip. This book provides a wonderful incentive for reading the original novel, tracking the journey, and comparing it to Burningham's efforts. If you are not able to get multiple copies for your students to read together, find a copy and read it to the class. Be sure to read the book ahead of time so that you can anticipate the kinds of research your students may be involved in during this study. Consider preparing a large bulletin board map of the world to focus the adventure. The names of the cities and countries that Verne cites may have changed over the past century. Be sure to indicate all of the names for each location if there have been changes. Create a chart that lists the place-name in Verne's novel, the current place-name, the controlling government, and any other pertinent information your students discover in their research. Determine how accurately Burningham was able to re-create the fictional journey. Calculate the distance between stops. Track the journey on a globe using string and some type of adhesive. Compare the journey on the globe and on a map. The novel was also made into a movie. It may be too long for a single viewing, but students may enjoy comparing and contrasting the novel with the movie and then with Burningham's journey.

The main character in three of the books mentioned above is a fictional preteen girl who documents her journey through diary entries, letters, or postcards. Rachel Rose travels to historic landmarks around the world in *Let's Go Traveling*. The book includes her preliminary plans and documents

the trip through photographs, drawings, diary entries, and postcards sent to friends and family at home. The book models various types of writing skills that young students are taught in primary classrooms. Again, you and your students can track Rachel Rose's journey on a globe and a world map. Because her journey, like Burningham's, crosses many borders, she needs a passport. The book presents a realistic setting in which the subject of travel between countries can be discussed. Some of your students may have traveled to other countries and can share their experiences. Discuss the significance of relationships between countries on travelers. What prohibitions might be in place that make travel to a foreign country difficult?

Kate and Anni are traveling with their families. Kate and her family are touring 11 states and Washington, D.C., in their car. The reader learns about the states and Kate's journey through the letters she writes to her friend, Lucy. These letters are also models for practicing writers. You and your students can expand the information provided about each state and its capital. Using an atlas, trace the probable routes that Kate's family took as they traveled from capital to capital. Calculate the distances between them. Consider the time the family spent in the car. Apply current gasoline prices to calculate the fuel cost for the trip. Attempt to obtain brochures or other materials that include photographs and descriptions of the landforms Kate's family encountered on their vacation.

Anni's trip is quite different from Kate's. She and her parents are traveling through a foreign country. The diary entries are a wonderful mix of information about the landscape, the food, and the people. Anni and her parents use various modes of transportation and travel at a much less hectic pace than Kate and her family. Use a good map of France to locate the specific places Anni's family visited and determine the type of landforms they encountered. Compare and contrast the two girls' family trips. Discuss the differences in preparation for a trip within the United States and to another country. Remind your students of the length of time each family was away from home. What effect might that time away have had on their preparations? Encourage your students to think about the challenges to travelers in both situations.

Komodo! is a more whimsical, less realistic account of a journey a young boy makes with his family to the Indonesian island of Komodo in hopes of seeing a real dragon. The text includes information about the Komodo dragon. You and your students can use reference materials to verify the information. Some students may wish to locate additional information about the Komodo dragon, which is the largest of the monitor lizards and related to the mosasaur, which lived 65 to 136 million years ago. Just as you discussed the preparations necessary for Kate and Anni to travel, consider with your class the preparations and precautions necessary for this trip.

These books describe pleasure trips for the travelers. Do not forget to encourage discussions about business travel conducted locally, regionally within the United States, and globally. Challenge students to discover what type of transportation people use to conduct business in other places. What kinds of exploration are currently undertaken? Are there areas in this country or in the world that remain unexplored? Why might we want to learn about them?

═══ War

The most logical place to discuss war seems to be within the theme of Movement. Certainly, in my mind, it is a negative but undeniable aspect of Movement. Wars are often the result of one group attempting to settle in an area already occupied by another group. The intersection of two cultures has also led to wars over beliefs. During wartime, troops from one group may occupy foreign territory. Occupation has several possible consequences. It may limit the flow of goods and ideas, change the daily activities of native inhabitants, establish cultural mixing, and force the flight of refugees. Surprisingly, there are a number of children's books that either touch on war or actually address the issue.

All of the books included here have a connection to a major conflict. I think what makes them interesting and useful are the ways in which they connect the reader to the human element of what we often think of as an impersonal event. Use these books where you feel they fit best within your curriculum. We do include the Civil War and World War II in our social studies texts; the Vietnam War may also come up.

How My Parents Learned to Eat (Friedman 1987), *The Bicycle Man* (Say 1989), *Grandfather's Journey* (Say 1993), *All those Secrets of the World* (Yolen 1991), *Randolph's Dream* (Mellecker 1991), *Let the Celebrations BEGIN!* (Wild 1991), *Rose Blanche* (Innocenti 1985), *Sadako* (Coerr 1993), and *The Bracelet* (Uchida 1993) all relate in some way to World War II. The first four books have an indirect link, while the final five are directly tied to it.

American servicemen stationed in Yokohama following World War II are important characters in *How My Parents Learned to Eat* and *The Bicycle Man*. In both stories, the American soldiers meet and develop a relationship with the Japanese. The focus of the first book is the courtship of an American soldier and a Japanese woman. He learns to eat with chopsticks and she learns to eat with a knife and fork to impress each other. This is a wonderful opportunity for you and your students to explore the diverse ways people eat. Students may want to research the development of eating utensils. Contact a local Japanese or Chinese restaurant and ask if they will donate a pair of chopsticks for each member of the class. Then, learn to use them. *The Bicycle Man* is a long, lanky American soldier who "steals the show" on Sportsday at a school on the mountain up from the Yokohama harbor. The soldier does a series of tricks on the bicycle and is presented with the grand prize. The story is autobiographical. Students may wish to learn more about Yokohama and author Allen Say. Say is a Japanese American whose book *Grandfather's Journey* tells of the ties the story's grandfather feels to both Japan and the United States. The war between the two countries eliminates his ability to return to the United States after his marriage in Japan. The grandson, who tells the story and travels between the two countries, says he understands how his grandfather can miss one place while in the other. How much of this book is autobiographical might be the focus of student research.

All Those Secrets of the World tells about four-year-old Janie, who moves with her mother and infant brother into her grandparents' home on Chesapeake Bay while her father goes off to war. The reason for the move is not safety as it was in Randolph's case (*Randolph's Dream*) but probably convenience for a new mother of two. As the book begins, the reader goes with Janie and her family to say good-bye to her father. As the setting is on the Chesapeake, it's quite likely that the ship Janie's father boards is leaving from Norfolk, Virginia. What other kinds of changes in American family life resulted from the war? You and your students can explore issues represented by topics such as "Rosie the Riveter," ration coupons, and steel pennies. Why would a naval base be located at Norfolk? Consider the locations of our nation's military bases.

Randolph's Dream is a story that mixes fact and fantasy. Seven-year-old Randolph lives in 1940 London, but because of the dangers of World War II, his mother sends him to live in the country. Once there, he begins to have dreams in which he flies. At first his flying is confined to local areas, but eventually his flight takes him from the English countryside to North Africa, where he saves his father, who is stationed there with the British forces. You and your students can locate some of the places named in this book. Determine what route Randolph probably took as he flew to North Africa, based on the illustrations. Compare and contrast the landforms, weather, and other pertinent information about England and North Africa. Students hear and read much more about the conflicts in the Pacific and Europe. Help them discover more about North Africa, a major "theatre" of the war.

Randolph's Dream provides a natural beginning point for a look at the effects war has on children. Randolph, like many English children, was separated from his family during the war. You might look at Goodall's books, particularly *The Story of a Farm* (1989) and *The Story of the Seashore* (1990), because they reflect the physical changes World War II caused in England. Further research can uncover other changes.

Emi, a young Japanese American second-grader, is sent with her mother to an internment camp in the United States during World War II in *The Bracelet*. The book focuses on Emi's concern about the lost bracelet her best friend gave her as she left and her personal discovery that she can remember the friendship without the bracelet. This book provides an opportunity to examine the hysteria connected with the war that greatly affected the lives of more than 100,000 Japanese Americans. Emi's story is just one of many. Based on the maturity of your students, research and discuss such internment camps. What happened to children like Emi and their families? In the past few years there has been an exhibition of artwork produced by inhabitants of these camps. The U.S. government has also attempted to make financial restitution. What do your students think about the internment? How did they develop their opinions?

Sadako tells the true story of a young girl who contracts leukemia in 1954 as a result of the atomic bomb dropped on Japan at the end of World War II. She attempts to fold 1,000 paper cranes to create a miracle that would allow her to live. But, even with the help of family and friends, she dies before her goal is reached. A monument to Sadako was established after her death. Students may wish to explore Sadako's life story more closely, or research President Harry Truman's decision to drop the bomb and the physical and psychological consequences that resulted. Some students may wish to learn how to fold paper cranes and learn more about how this art form became connected to creating miracles.

If appropriate, delve further into discussion about children and war. The unusual and somewhat disturbing *Let the Celebrations BEGIN!* is set in a concentration camp during World War II. Despite the seriousness of the setting and its emaciated characters, the story is truly celebratory. The women and Miriam, the young storyteller, work together to create toys for the very young children of the camp. The book is based on a reference to a small collection of stuffed toys made by Polish women in Belsen for the first children's party held after the liberation. Depending on the maturity of your students, use this book in a study of the Holocaust and World War II. Another book that deals with the confinement of children during the war is *Rose Blanche*. Roberto Innocenti, who was a small child in Europe during World War II, says he wrote this book to "illustrate how a child experiences war without really understanding it." This book is not celebratory as is Wild's book, but it is hopeful at the end as the German soldiers retreat and the Russian soldiers arrive. The story and its illustrations are disturbing as

they show the movement of soldiers into Rose's small German town and her discovery of hungry children in a prison camp in the woods nearby. Be sure you read the book carefully so that you realize fully what happens to Rose Blanche. I would be very cautious in using this book and choosing the audience.

I have found four books that I believe can contribute to a study of the Vietnam War. *The Lotus Seed* (Garland 1993) connects the conflict with the necessity to escape to a safer place—and the risk of losing one's culture. *The Whispering Cloth: A Refugee's Story* (Shea 1995) is also about innocent people forced to leave their homeland as a result of the conflict. Both of these books provide the reader with a look at the Vietnamese and Hmong cultures. Young Mai, who is living in a refugee camp with her grandmother, learns to tell stories with embroidery. Students may wish to duplicate Mai's handiwork through the creation of a picture story from their own lives. *The Wall* (Bunting 1990) and *Grandfather's Dream* (Keller 1994) both look at the results of the conflict. *The Wall* takes a young boy and his father to Washington, D.C., where they search for the boy's grandfather's name among the listings of the dead. It's a poignant look at how war touches the families of those who die and the way we memorialize the casualties of war. *Grandfather's Dream* looks at how war touches the flora and fauna. This book is discussed more fully in Chapter 4 as it relates to human-environmental relationships.

The Civil War is the setting for *Pink and Say* (Polacco 1994). Two young Union soldiers are brought together in Georgia when Say, a White Northerner is wounded and Pink, a Black Georgian, takes him home to nurse him. As they try to return to their own companies, they are captured by Confederate soldiers and sent to Andersonville prison, where Pink dies. This true story was passed down through several generations before the author wrote it down and dedicated it to the memory of Pink. Although the Civil War had many causes other than the slave issue, this book and two others, *Nettie's Trip South* (Turner 1987) and *Aunt Harriet's Underground Railroad in the Sky* (Ringgold 1992), offer many possible discussion topics about the conditions that contributed to the war. Turner's book takes a look at pre–Civil War Richmond, Virginia, through the eyes of a 10-year-old girl from Albany, New York. This story was inspired by the author's great-grandmother's diary of her trip South in 1859. Ringgold's book tells about Harriet Tubman and the underground railroad. You may live in an area where the underground railroad had stops. Contact a local historical society for information. A closer look at Harriet Tubman can contribute to a study of courageous Americans.

Energy and Mass-Induced Movements

As I began this chapter I realized that I did not have any book in the bibliography that discussed the issues involved in Energy and Mass-Induced Movements. During the time I have been working on this chapter I visited a second-grade classroom where one of my student teachers was placed. Annemarie and her cooperating teacher were teaching a three-week integrated unit on dinosaurs, which included social studies, science, math, and language arts skills. The major culminating activity for this unit was a parent's day in which parents were invited to "tour" the classroom during a designated hour while the students (wearing name tags) acted as guides to the displays. One display showed the continental drift theory. In one of her lessons, Annemarie had created a paper model of all of the continents connected together, with magnetic tape on the back and hung on the blackboard. The

combined continents were then separated and allowed to "drift" apart. Dinosaur stamps were used to show the location of specific dinosaur fossils on the now separate continents.

Although it was noted as early as the 1600s that the continents looked like pieces of a jigsaw puzzle, the theory of continental drift was not endorsed until the 1960s. It was at this time that proponents of the theory could provide a logical, accepted explanation for the movement of such large masses as the continents. The basic theory says that the continents were once joined, forming one large landmass. This continent is called *Pangaea*, "all lands," by scientists (Young 1976). The continental split happened very slowly over hundreds of millions of years—and continues. Gibbons (1995) points out that this continuation is one of the reasons we refer to Earth as a "living planet." Plate tectonics (this process) explains why earthquakes, volcanoes, and mountain ranges occur in specific places around the world. Tectonics (which means "construction"), the branch of geology that studies the planet's structure and the movement of the plates, has only been in existence since the mid-1960s. I was able personally to review three books, two for children, one for adults. *Planet Earth/Inside Out* (Gibbons 1995) is the simplest. In clearly worded text and full-color drawings and diagrams, it provides a considerable amount of information about the Earth from its formation to the present. *Earth in Motion: The Concept of Plate Tectonics* (Fodor 1978) and *Drifting Continents, Shifting Seas* (Young 1976) both focus on the continental drift theory. Fodor's intended audience is children, but it doesn't appear much easier to understand than Young's, which is intended for adults. They are good resources for you to use to build your own background.

While I have not offered a complete plan or a large number of books, I hope I have provided a glimpse at what you *can* teach to young children. Let's not underestimate their ability to learn.

Conclusion

Not only have our modes of transportation contributed to the shrinking of the world, mass communication links us with faraway places so quickly and easily that we almost take it for granted. A friend of mine tells about misdialing a phone number when he was investigating the history of a used car he was buying in upstate New York and discovering, much to his surprise, that he'd direct-dialed a number in Amsterdam! My husband and I were sitting on the floor in front of the television January 15, 1991, when, suddenly, the Gulf War began in our family room. With the advent of the "information highway" our students can converse with students anywhere in the world if they have access to a computer connected to the Internet.

The fact that we are now so closely tied with the whole world makes it especially important that our children know more about the world and the interrelationships of it at many levels. Events thousands of miles away from our own homes have repercussions for us. Our national leaders are continually involved in global issues. We must be knowledgeable—and so must our children. Help them become citizens of the world.

References

Fodor, R. V. 1978. *Earth in Motion: The Concept of Plate Tectonics*. New York: Morrow Junior Books.

Young, Patrick. 1976. *Drifting Continents, Shifting Seas*. New York: Franklin Watts.

Chapter 6

REGIONS

"The basic unit of geographic study is the region, an area that displays unity in terms of selected criteria."

—W. Kimball, *K-6 Geography,* 3

Regions exist only in our minds, that is to say, we determine their existence. We create regions with specific boundaries, such as countries or states within countries. We also create regions with indistinct boundaries, such as the Sahara Desert or the Great Plains. Our criteria may include physical features, ethnic distinctions, or language differences. The same location may belong in several regions, depending on the criteria used to describe it. For example, I currently live in northeastern Pennsylvania, in Lackawanna County, in the Wyoming Valley, in anthracite coal country. In terms of ethnic and religious regional distinctions, it is a largely Roman Catholic region with many European cultures clustered throughout the valley. Although the largest percentage of the population claims either Italian or Irish ancestry, the Welsh community is the largest concentration outside of Wales.

Geographers, in defining regions, first state the criteria, then draw the boundaries. They subdivide the theme into three areas: *Uniform Regions, Functional Regions,* and *Cultural Diversity.*

Uniform Regions

Uniform Regions are defined by some cultural or physical characteristic. These may include the product produced, as in the Wheat Belt; the common belief, as in the Bible Belt; or a political division, as with a country, county, parish, or township.

Functional Regions

Functional Regions have a focal point and are the organized space around a central location. Examples include metropolitan areas or market areas served by a particular store or the district around a school.

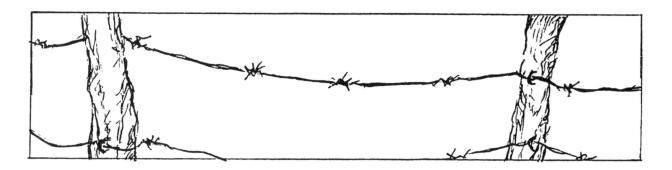

Cultural Diversity

Geographers remind us that understanding regions can lead to understanding *Cultural Diversity*.

Such study can help us understand the ways in which national, racial, or ethnic groups interact with each other.

REGIONS

Uniform Regions   **Functional Regions**

Cultural Diversity

Teaching Ideas

This chapter will look at the Regions theme in two ways. The first part of this chapter will present a more narrative discussion of children's books that can contribute to particular regional studies. The second part of this chapter will feature suggestions for a unit study of the continent of Africa.

Chapter 3 has a rather long discussion of New York City as part of a study to explore the sense of Place. Certainly, such a study is also a Regional study—a functional region. In the same way, there are less detailed discussions about rivers and other bodies of water, Vietnam, and city and country differentiations in Chapter 3. All of these discussions could apply to this chapter. Chapter 3 also discusses the rain forest in the context of flora and fauna, but I point out its importance in terms of environmental issues. From that point of view, it could be included in Chapter 4, "Human-Environmental Relations," or in this chapter as a uniform region study. I think you get the idea. Geographic themes are not easily taught separately. They are naturally integrated and thus can be integrated into an already set curriculum.

Unit Study Ideas

Walls

As I was in the first stage of collecting titles for this chapter, I came across a book, quite by accident, that continues to intrigue me. I have struggled with where to include it because it fits into so many categories, and yet, only pieces of it fit in those categories. After much thought I've decided to discuss the book here. *Talking Walls* (Knight 1992) describes walls located in different countries all around the world. Each wall is presented in the context of children interacting with it. Among the 14 walls included are the Great Wall of China, the Berlin Wall, and the prison walls that held Nelson Mandela. Informative paragraphs at the end of the book describe each wall, and a world map shows the walls' locations. The author and illustrator provide an interesting dedication that refers to the walls, real and imagined, that contain people around the world. Later in my search I came across *Follow the Dream: The Story of Christopher Columbus* (Sis 1991). Peter Sis was born and raised in Czechoslovakia during the Cold War era. His author's note points out the walls around the maps created in the fifteenth century and the way he used this historical fact in illustrating his book. He also indicates that invisible, political walls can hold people in one place. I think the dedication in *Talking Walls* and Sis's comments are the reasons I

decided to place this book in a chapter about Regions. Regions are mental constructs. Walls, real or imagined, are the means by which we define some regions. I highly recommend *Talking Walls*. It seems to me that it provides a whole study . . . walls. But it also looks at various landmarks around the world that are discussed in other books.

Begin a study of walls with a reading of *Talking Walls*. Decide, with your students, the categories these walls fit into. You may wish to use the walls chart included here as figure 6.1. Consider how the walls were created, when, and by whom. There are man-made walls and natural walls; there are walls that form boundaries and walls that create rooms or buildings. Brainstorm together, encouraging your students to think creatively.

Take your students on a walking or riding tour of your neighborhood, if possible. Discover significant local walls. Examine the purpose of these walls and compare and contrast them with the walls selected by Knight in *Talking Walls*. Your class may wish to create a class book of "talking walls."

Other subject areas can be integrated into this study. Measure the walls you find. Determine dimensions and calculate area. Examine the materials used to build them. Research the age of the structures and how building practices may have changed since their construction.

Specific Regions

Prairies

The prairies in North America are also called the Great Plains. They extend from Canada into the United States. An extensive area of flat or rolling, predominantly treeless, grassland, prairies are especially suited to producing grain and raising livestock. I have found two children's books that deal with contemporary images of the prairies. Both are beautiful books. *Heartland* (1992) by Diane Siebert is typical of her simple, lyrical texts enhanced by remarkable paintings. As a native Midwesterner, I find the paintings in this book perfect. They are my images of Illinois, especially the farmland. This book would be a wonderful way to look at the plains today and introduce a regional study. *A Prairie Alphabet* (Bannatyne-Cugnet 1992) provides detailed, full-page paintings accompanied by simple, alliterative text describing the Canadian prairies. The author includes a description of North American plains and prairies as the book begins and ends with detailed paragraphs describing the content of each painting. The alliterative text, descriptive paragraphs, and detailed paintings supply the reader with a tremendous amount of information about the land and the people living there. These two books can be used to compare the way the plains look now and during the time of the great westward movement earlier in our history.

Christmas on the Prairie (Anderson 1985), *Dandelions* (Bunting 1995), *Cassie's Journey: Going West in the 1860s* (Harvey 1995), *My Prairie Christmas* (Harvey 1990), *My Prairie Year* (Harvey 1993), and *Dakota Dugout* (Turner 1985) are all set in the ninteenth century. Cassie passes through the Great Plains on her trip from Illinois to California, but the action in the other stories is set on the prairie.

Christmas on the Prairie documents a re-creation of Christmas Eve and Christmas morning in 1836 in the fictional village of Prairietown, Indiana. The children and adults in the photographs participate in living history demonstrations at Connor Prairie Pioneer Settlement near Noblesville, Indiana. There are many living history sites throughout the United States. Some sites have living history continually, such as Plymouth Plantation and Appomattox Courthouse in Virginia, while others, such as New Salem in

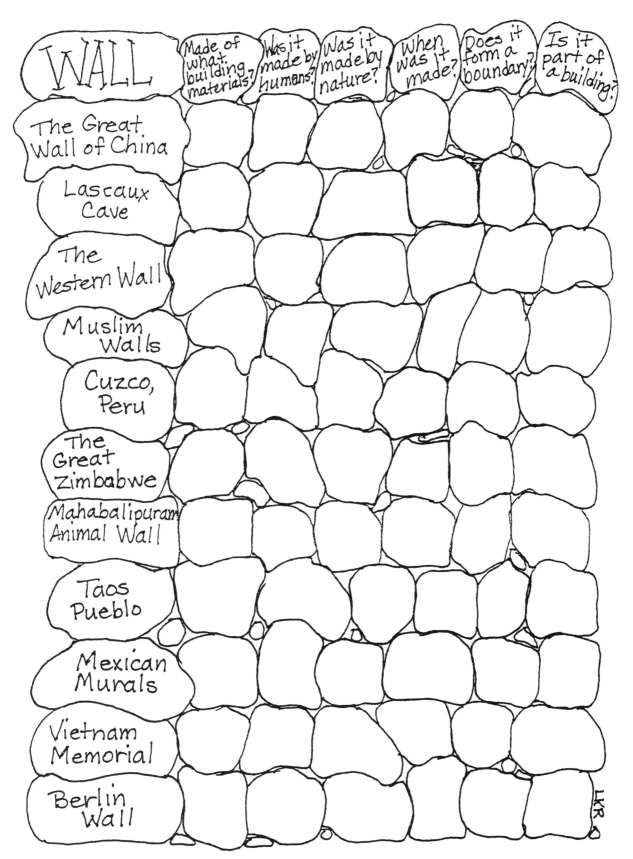

Fig. 6.1. Walls chart.

Illinois and Boonesboro in Kentucky, designate special dates. If you have a site near you, take advantage of it.

Now, back to the book: It provides you and your students with a close look at furniture, foods, utensils, and clothing used by people living on the prairie in the nineteenth century. The photographs document historically researched information. The attention to detail can model a living history event that your students can create in your classroom or school. The seventh-grade students in our middle school read *Johnny Tremain* in reading; conduct research on food, clothing, and games in English; and study the Revolutionary War in social studies for an entire quarter. The culminating activity is a Colonial Fair in which the students display the results of their research and provide expert information to the parents and other students who visit the Fair. Consider the way in which you might create such an event. It might be based on your study of life on the nineteenth-century prairie, or another time period you study.

The other books are more traditional children's books. Each includes the hardships of prairie life within the context of a realistic story. Harvey and Turner both used family diaries as reference points. Descriptions of the sea of grass, the loneliness, and the ruggedness of life are repeated throughout. The mother in *Dandelions* and the grandmother storyteller in *Dakota Dugout* both express their fears of and frustrations with the living conditions. Research sod homes with your students. If possible, build a wall of sod. After you and your students have conducted research on prairie life, encourage students to write entries describing their daily prairie life in a class or individual diary. *Little House on the Prairie* (Wilder 1975) and *Sarah, Plain and Tall* (MacLachlan 1985) are just two of many longer chapter books that you might read to your students to provide further background.

Use maps to locate the states that are considered part of the Great Plains. Discover what kinds of crops are grown and livestock raised. Take this opportunity to help students create their own maps showing the products and their location. If you have the time, compare the location and products in the United States with those produced on the prairies of Canadian provinces.

Pocono Mountains

William George has written four delightful books that tell about the outdoor adventures of a father and son in Long Pond, Pennsylvania, in the Pocono Mountains. *Christmas at Long Pond* (1992), *Box Turtle at Long Pond* (New York: Greenwillow Books, 1989), *Beaver at Long Pond* (New York: Greenwillow Books, 1988), and *Fishing at Long Pond* (New York: Greenwillow Books, 1991) provide a full picture of the flora and fauna in this particular location. The illustrator of these books is George's wife, Lindsay Barrett George, who recently wrote and illustrated two books of her own: *In the Woods: Who's Been Here?* (1995) and *In the Snow: Who's Been Here?* (1995). The focus of these books is the protective coloration that helps animals hide, but clearly the setting is the same as that of the Long Pond books. If your students are in an urban setting or the desert, these books can be useful in introducing rural and forested regions. The strong emphasis on respecting the environment also makes these books appropriate for science studies and for some aspects of the Human-Environmental Relationships theme. *In the Woods: Who's Been Here?* and *In the Snow: Who's Been Here?* are also wonderful models for creating a map after a class walk.

The Seashore

My first view of the ocean was in the mid-1970s when my husband and I lived in Georgia for 10 months. We visited Tybee Island, off the coast of Georgia and east of Savannah. I suppose my first reaction was surprise, because in many ways it looked like the shoreline of Lake Michigan. The smell was different, as were the tides and the jellyfish washed up on the beach, but the vast expanses of water and beach were similar. It took us nearly 10 years to get back to the Atlantic, when we began to vacation in the Outer Banks of North Carolina each summer with our children.

I have found a few children's books that focus on the seashore. The simplest is *Let's Discover the Seaside* (Rius and Parramon 1986), which provides a simple guide with background information and suggested questions for parents and teachers at the end of the book. It considers the fishing industry and tourism as main activities of the seashore. *The Story of the Seashore* (Goodall 1990), a wordless picture book, takes a look at the English public's love affair with the seashore, beginning in the early 1800s and continuing to the present.

The Summer Sands (Garland 1995), *All Those Secrets of the World* (Yolen 1991), and *The Seashore Book* (Zolotow 1992) share the sights, sounds, and mood of the seashore with the reader. Obviously, the illustrations are of particular note. Use these books to introduce the characteristics of the shoreline in the United States. Garland's story is set on the Texas seashore (Gulf of Mexico) and focuses on the need to rebuild the dunes after storms. It might be used with *Hurricane* (Wiesner 1990) and *The Day the Hurricane Happened* (Anderson 1974) to broaden the study of the seashore to include the natural problems that exist in the southeastern region of the United States. Yolen's story is set on the Atlantic, in the Chesapeake Bay area. Zolotow's is the most generic, but the illustrations and simple text provide a very realistic and sensual description of the ocean shore. The text is rich in imagery. Both Yolen's and Zolotow's books could also contribute to a unit about the five senses. Janie, in *All Those Secrets of the World*, learns about near and far. In addition, this book, already discussed in Chapter 5 as it contributes to a study of war, it might also be used in discussing Human-Environmental Relations because the Chesapeake Bay area is also the site of the incredible Chesapeake Bay Bridge-Tunnel. Completed in 1964, this 17.5-mile structure takes the highway traveler over and under the entrance to the bay. While the four-wheeled vehicles travel along the bridge-tunnel, oceangoing vessels can continue their journey into and out of the bay.

The Caribbean

Three books set in the Caribbean provide an opportunity to introduce the political and cultural characteristics of the region. They also provide a source of contrast with what we accept as "normal." *The Day the Hurricane Happened* (Anderson 1974) is in marked contrast with *Hurricane* (Wiesner 1990). Based on a true story set on the Island of St. John in the Virgin Islands, Anderson's book tells about two children who must survive a hurricane without shelter. Wiesner's two young boys wait out the storm in the safety of their own home with their parents.

Bunting's (1990) *How Many Days to America? A Thanksgiving Story* follows a family's escape from a Caribbean country to south Florida in a small boat. Seen through the eyes of a young child, the story reminds us of the political unrest in countries quite near ours. Use this book as an "anticipatory set" for a study of the region. Ask your students to keep the book in mind as you examine the region. From what country might the family be fleeing?

Why must they get away? How far and in what direction would the boat have to travel to reach south Florida? Will the family be accepted once they arrive on American shores? The Islands of the Caribbean table included here as figure 6.2 may provide support for a study of the region.

In a much lighter story, set on Trinidad, young Rosie guides the reader through the preparations for *An Island Christmas* (Joseph 1992). The enthusiastically presented story shares the sights, sounds, and flavors of Christmas celebrated in the Caribbean. A fine contrast can be found in *Christmas on the Prairie* (Anderson 1985). You may be able to locate recordings of some of the music Rosie loves, recipes that make a Trinidad Christmas unique, and photographs that expand your students' understanding of the flora and fauna on Trinidad and Tobago.

A Unit Study of Africa

Publishers of social studies textbooks usually provide a world history or global studies text in grades five or six. Students explore the world by region, sometimes by continent. Although the abundance of visual media has broadened our understanding of cultures other than our own, we often apply one stereotypical perception to given regions. A good example is the misconceptions many Americans hold about Africa. We tend to assume it is one large continent of people who speak a common language and live in a uniform climate when, in fact, Africa is a continent of great variations in people, cultures, landforms, and language. Picture books can provide introductory and supplemental activities to enhance a social studies or interdisciplinary unit on Africa. The activities presented here are intended as stepping-stones to a unit of study. They also model ways for your students to approach new information: read, inspect, question, research. Because you best know your class and your curriculum, you will want to adapt and adopt these ideas so that the "fit" is right. I have found approximately 20 books that relate to a study of Africa (and geographic literacy) as I perceive it. There are certainly other books that might enhance your study, so please do not omit any because I did not include them here.

Introductory Activities

Conduct a brainstorming session with your students to help them access their prior knowledge about Africa and provide you with an opportunity to assess their knowledge and understanding. Ogle's (1986) "K-W-L" chart or Carr and Ogle's (1987) "K-W-L Plus" chart may provide a useful framework. The K-W-L chart presented here as figure 6.3 (on page 85) can be placed on a poster board chart or overhead transparency. Prepare three columns. The first should be titled "What I Know," the second "What I Want to Know," and the third "What I Still Want to Learn." Some of my student teachers have prepared three separate poster boards with the column titles and used appropriate decorations or shapes. For example, you might use three pieces of poster board, each cut in the shape of Africa with the column title at the top. If you laminate each one and use washable transparency markers, you can reuse the K-W-L charts for several years.

Begin with a group brainstorming activity in which everyone contributes information about Africa. Record the information under "What I Know." After you have listed everything that students can think of about Africa, have the students look at the variety of data that have been recorded. Determine into what categories the information fits. For example, you may have generated information about Animals, Landforms, and Languages Spoken. Before this activity began, you will have determined what concepts the students will encounter through the unit. The brainstorming activity will provide you with a means of assessing students' knowledge and deciding how much background information you will need to present.

The Islands of the Caribbean

	Location	Government	Capital	Industry	Cultural Characteristics
Geater Antilles					
Cuba					
Jamaica					
Haiti					
Dominican Republic					
Puerto Rico					
Lesser Antilles					
Virgin Islands					
Windward Islands					
Leeward Islands					
Netherlands Antilles					
Barbados					
Trinidad					
Tobago					
Bahama Islands					

Fig. 6.2. Caribbean Islands discussion table.

The second part of this activity, "What I Want to Know," gives your students the opportunity to set purposes for their learning and helps them see the direction in which the unit study is going. Be sure to include some of your own objectives for the unit as contributions to the list. When the unit is completed (or perhaps near the end), return to the "W" column. Contemplate which of the purposes were met.

Next, consider the "What I Still Want to Learn" column of the chart. In this activity students examine which of the purposes set in "W" were not met and, of these, which they still want to learn. Record this information. Where you go in your study from this point will be determined by your own situation. You may want to continue the study with the whole class, or perhaps some of your students will want to pursue the unanswered questions independently and then report to the whole class.

Post a map of Africa in your room—either commercial or teacher-made. Make sure this map is large enough that you can record substantial physical and political information on it. As you begin the unit, examine the map with the students. Discuss the size of Africa. Depending on the students' math abilities, determine the continent's approximate square mileage. Examine maps of Africa in encyclopedias. If you can find some older editions, note the differences in political boundaries. Let your students know that you will be returning to the map throughout the unit to add information as you learn about it. Consider placing the following information on it.

- Climatic zones: tropical rain forest, tropical savanna, steppe, arid land or desert, Mediterranean, temperate
- Significant landforms: Atlas Mountains, Ruwenzori Range, Mount Kilimanjaro, Mount Kenya, Mount Elgon, Lake Victoria, Victoria Falls, Nile River, Congo River, Zambezi River, Madagascar, Zanzibar, Saint Helena, Canary Islands, Madeira Islands

Another introductory activity involves *Ashanti to Zulu* (Musgrove 1992). Read the book to the class. Then provide several copies for the class to examine in small groups. The illustrations are very detailed, and the text offers complicated concepts. Be sure to inspect the map of Africa at the back, which indicates where the tribes are located.

Reread the book with the class, paying close attention to the clothing, landforms, and animals in the illustrations. The text will also provide clues to the similarities and differences among the various traditions. In small groups, have students fill in the Ashanti to Zulu chart (see fig. 6.4 on pages 87 and 88) to record these characteristics. Students may also want to conduct research on the traditions or tribes.

Read the book once more as the basis for a discussion about what, if any, of the traditions are similar to traditions your students know about in other cultures or their own. You should also be prepared to offer some examples.

The continent of Africa is large and contains many climatic regions: tropical rain forest, tropical savanna, steppe, arid land or desert, Mediterranean, and temperate. Indicate these regions on your classroom map. Be sure your students understand what they mean in terms of temperature and rainfall. Look at these climatic regions as you refer to the tribes you investigated on the Ashanti to Zulu chart. Draw the political lines that indicate countries. Determine what climatic regions are in each of the countries you study.

Another introductory activity that can help set the tone of study involves using *A Country Far Away* (Gray and Dupasquier 1991). This cleverly illustrated book offers side-by-side pictures of the lives of two boys, one in a Western country and one in a rural African village. The text reveals the essential similarities between the lives of the two boys. Although I have included this book as part of an introductory study of Africa, I also believe this book is a wonderful way to open discussions about the basic needs and wants of all people with students of all ages.

K-W-L

What I <u>K</u>now	What I <u>W</u>ant to Know	What I Still Want to <u>L</u>earn

Catagories of What I Know:

Fig. 6.3. K-W-L chart.

The following discussions of books are grouped as I perceive their relationship to the issues in a regional study of Africa.

Sense of Place Issue

Philippa-Alys Browne, a native of Zimbabwe, has written and illustrated *African Animals ABC* (1995). Although this is really a very simple picture book, the illustrations reflect African tribal patterns, and the informational paragraphs at the end of the book tell about the 26 insects and animals presented in the book. After you and your students read through the book you might want to assign research projects to individuals or small groups, which can be combined to create a class book of African insects and animals. Consider using a form like that found in figure 6.5, "Animal Report" on page 90, to help your students gather pertinent information.

I found I couldn't resist John Steptoe's (1993) *Mufaro's Beautiful Daughters*. It's the retelling of a folktale in fable form. You will undoubtedly find other children's books that retell African folktales. Consider including them where they are appropriate for your students. In fact, as you study Africa in social studies, consider the ways in which your whole curriculum can be integrated. Study African folktales in language arts, ask the art teacher in your building if the focus in your students' art classes can be African arts and crafts, ask the music teacher to focus on the characteristics of African music, and explore the foods of different cultural groups in Africa.

Two aspects of Steptoe's book caught my attention and imagination. First, the illustrations were influenced by the flora and fauna around an ancient city ruin in Zimbabwe. Second, Steptoe dedicated the book to the children of South Africa. Another separate, but influential, factor is John Steptoe himself. I remember when his first book, *Stevie*, was published. He was a teenager at the time, and I found myself intrigued that someone his age had accomplished something so impressive. I wondered why he dedicated this book as he did and why he used the ancient city in Zimbabwe as the subject for his artwork. Here is a place where *Talking Walls* can be pulled out for a quick look at the Great Zimbabwe, a huge structure whose purpose is unknown.

Recall that we discussed rain forests in Chapter 3. Let's return to *Panther Dream: A Story of the African Rain Forest* (Weir and Weir 1991). This is the only book I found that was specific to location other than Lynne Cherry's *The Great Kapok Tree: A Tale of the Amazon Rain Forest* (1990), which is specific to South America. The study of the African rain forest can coincide with the study of several countries located within the rain forest region. Additionally, Pygmies are inhabitants of the African rain forest. Students may wish to learn more about the Pygmy culture in Africa. The Weirs include references to specific animals found in the rain forest. Compare these with the ones profiled by Browne in *African Animals ABC* and consult *The Atlas of Endangered Animals* (Pollock 1993).

Connections with African Americans

Another mini-study that you might undertake while engaged in a study of Africa is one that seeks to understand the connections between African Americans in the United States and African cultures. Steptoe's and Browne's books may be a good place to begin. Have your students research these authors. Many of the authors and illustrators of the books cited in this chapter note the importance of trips to specific African locations to ensure the authenticity of their work. What other connections are there? Sometimes authors are willing to write to students about their work. Consider contacting the publishers for addresses and any other information they are willing and able to provide.

Ashanti to Zulu

Tribe Name	Clothing	Landform	Animals	Other
A.				
B.				
C.				
D.				
E.				
F.				
G.				
H.				
I.				
J.				
K.				
L.				
M.				

(Fig. 6.4. continues)

Fig. 6.4. Ashanti to Zulu chart.

Ashanti to Zulu

Tribe Name	Clothing	Landform	Animals	Other
N.				
O.				
P.				
Q.				
R.				
S.				
T.				
U.				
V.				
W.				
X.				
Y.				
Z.				

Fig. 6.4. Ashanti to Zulu chart.

There are a few books whose stories make the connection between Western and African cultures. In *Boundless Grace* (Hoffman 1995), a young girl living in the United States with her mother and grandmother visits her father, who is living in The Gambia with his new wife and younger children. Grace comes to terms with her atypical family situation as she spends time in this small West African country. In both of Kroll's books—*Africa Brothers and Sisters* (1993) and *Masai and I* (1992)—the characters are children living in Western environments but thinking about their connections to Africa. Young Jesse and his father discuss their African "brothers and sisters" in *Africa Brothers and Sisters*. African words are interspersed throughout their dialogue. The author's note at the end of the book provides a pronunciation key and a map of Africa locating Jesse's "brothers and sisters." In *Masai and I*, young Linda is introduced to the Masai in school. She feels such a strong connection that she continually compares her daily life with the life she would lead in East Africa if she were a Masai. The last book contributing to such a study is Tom Feelings's collection of poetry by African Americans in *Soul Looks Back in Wonder* (1993). The poems were collected as a means to project the author's and poets' positive hopes for the future of young African sisters and brothers in this country. Short biographical paragraphs about each of the 13 poets appear at the end of the book. Again, you and your students may want to learn more about the author and the poets. Perhaps you can correspond with them. Students may wish to pursue a personal study of their own "brothers and sisters" beyond the United States and share their findings in written or oral form.

Consider using the diptych project referred to at the end of Chapter 2. It would be a perfect vehicle for expressing the commonalities of life in African and Western countries. Just as *A Country Far Away* and *Masai and I* compare the two, your students can create their own comparison through the use of artwork.

Human Characteristics

As you study the various parts of Africa you will find some children's books that can expand your study. Remember to return to figure 6.4 and the map you have posted. Continuously add the physical and political information you have discovered. Muriel Feelings wrote two books, *Jambo Means Hello: Swahili Alphabet Book* (1992) and *Moja Means One: Swahili Counting Book* (1994), with the intent of sharing the importance of understanding one another's language and culture. The vocabulary used in Kroll's *Africa Brothers and Sisters* can be compared to that of Swahili. Some of your students may wish to further pursue the various languages and dialects spoken in Africa. The map Feelings includes in each book locates the areas of Africa in which Swahili is spoken. Consider using colored cellophane to indicate these areas on your classroom map.

The Old and the New

The Librarian Who Measured the Earth (Lasky 1994) is Eratosthenes. He lived more than 2,000 years ago in North Africa. He was born in what is now Libya in North Africa and was head of the library in Alexandria, Egypt. He calculated the circumference of the Earth with remarkable accuracy. Ahmed is a boy in modern North Africa. His story is told in *The Day of Ahmed's Secret* (Heide and Gilliland 1990). The ancient and the new come together in Heide's and Gilliland's unique book, set in Cairo, Egypt. We can only wonder if Eratosthenes might have traveled down some of the same narrow streets Ahmed travels delivering his butane gas canisters.

ANIMAL REPORT

ANIMAL NAME: _____

Tell about how the animal looks. Include the following information:
What size is it?   What is its most noticable feature?   What color is it?
What would it feel like if you touched it?

_____

_____

_____

Tell about where the animal lives. Include the following information:
Where in the world is it found?   Can it live in many places or only one?
Does it build a home?

_____

_____

_____

Tell about the animal's eating habits. Include the following information:
What does it eat?   (Is it a herbivore, a carnivore, or an omnivore?)
When does it eat?   Is it a hunter?   Is it dangerous to humans?

_____

_____

_____

In the space below, draw a picture of this animal or glue a picture of the animal that you
have found.

This report was written by:

Fig. 6.5. Animal report.

The Village of Round and Square Houses (Grifalconi 1986) and The Fortune-Tellers (Alexander 1992) are both set in the West African country of Cameroon. The illustrations in these texts show contrasts between the influence of Western culture on clothing (The Fortune-Tellers) and traditional native dress. Plan discussions that include exploration into fortune-telling, myths, legends, and cultural traditions. A couple of years ago I met a young couple who were preparing to go to Cameroon and Chad to help put the spoken language into written form. Your students might want to explore the challenges of not having a written language. What other countries in Africa do not have their language in a written form? What is the process by which such an undertaking happens? What is the oldest form of writing?

Bringing the Rain to Kapiti Plain (Aardema 1992) is a picture book you can use to provide your students with an opportunity to experience a tale from another culture. Have them compare the English nursery rhyme "The House That Jack Built" with this Kenyan tale. The rhyme lends itself to choral reading. Practice the poem together, then number the stanzas, assign them to individuals or small groups, and reread the poem as a group. Some children might like to model their own rhythmic poem on the common pattern. Others may be interested in finding out more about the landforms and the people. The Masai, who figure heavily in Masai and I (Kroll 1992), are a nomadic people who herd cattle in the highlands of Kenya. Check the tribes in the Ashanti to Zulu table you created earlier in the study. Which are found in Kenya?

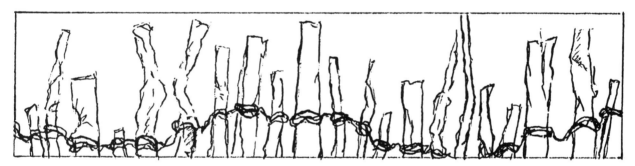

Issues in South Africa

Rachel Isadora has written two beautiful children's books set in South Africa. At the Crossroads (1991) is a joyous book about young children waiting for their fathers to return from their work far from home. The issue of the economic conditions in South Africa underlies this story but is not discussed. Depending on the age and maturity of your students, you can discuss the reasons these fathers must live away from home to earn money for the family. Brainstorm with students some parallel situations in our own country related to the decline in the number of jobs. In the background of the illustrations are shacklike structures, which may also serve to start discussions about the living conditions of the children and their families. Isadora's other book is Over the Green Hills (1992). A young boy and his mother are going to visit the boy's grandmother. The walk is many miles across the Transkei countryside on the east coast of South Africa. The flora, fauna, and human activities in this part of South Africa are the focus of the book. The author provides a note in which she talks about Transkei's political status at the time of the book's writing. Here is another place to insert Talking Walls. Nelson Mandela's prison walls in South Africa can be the catalyst for discussions about freedom, apartheid, and discrimination.

A study of the African continent can be enhanced through the use of children's literature. These books often present difficult concepts in simplified terms. I believe using children's books can help your students build concepts that avoid stereotyping.

References

Carr, E., and Ogle, D. 1987. "K-W-L Plus: A Strategy for Comprehension and Summarization." *Journal of Reading* 39: 626-31.

MacLachlan, Patricia. 1985. *Sarah, Plain and Tall*. New York: Harper & Row.

Ogle, Donna M. 1986. "K-W-L: A Teaching Model That Develops Active Reading of Expository Text." *Reading Teacher* 39 (February): 564-70.

Wilder, Laura Ingalls. 1975. *Little House on the Prairie*. New York: Harper & Row; originally published 1953.

Appendix A

ANNOTATED BIBLIOGRAPHY

This bibliography contains more than 160 books. As mentioned in Chapter 1, I examined every book included here. The vast majority of them have either been reprinted or are still in print despite their older date of publication. Those books no longer in print are preceded by an asterisk (*). Although they are no longer in print, they are available. Check the library and library book sales, garage sales, and used bookstores. You may have to search a little harder . . . but it's worth the effort. Each entry contains a summary paragraph followed by recommended activities broken down by grade levels. Content areas and geographic themes are in parentheses at the end of each activity.

Children's Literature

Aardema, Verna. 1992. **Bringing the Rain to Kapiti Plain.** New York: Puffin Books.

This tale, discovered in Kenya, Africa, more than 70 years ago, is reminiscent of "The House That Jack Built." Aardema has brought the story closer to the English nursery rhyme by putting in a cumulative refrain and giving it the nursery rhyme's rhythm, making it particularly appropriate for reading aloud. Large color illustrations enhance the text.

K - 3 The teacher can read the rhyme aloud to help students enjoy the beauty of the language. The rhyme can be read as a choral reading with a soloist reading the verses and a chorus reading the refrain. Together, the students and teacher can compare and contrast this rhyme with "The House That Jack Built." Perhaps together they can use the same rhythm to carry a new set of words to describe a story about their own locality. The illustrations of the Kenyan plains can be compared with photographs of Kenya. (Language Arts: Place)

4 - 6 Students at this age can participate in the above activity with less teacher intervention. The book fits well with a regional study of Africa. It may also be used in a unit of study on plains as a landform. (Language Arts; Social Studies: Place; Regions)

Jr/Sr High no

Alexander, Lloyd. 1992. **The Fortune-Tellers.** New York: Dutton Children's Books.

Set in Cameroon, the colorful, detailed illustrations and text tell the story of a carpenter who goes to a fortune-teller and finds the predictions about the future come true in an unusual way. The illustrator visited Cameroon to assure the accurate portrayal of the beauty and diversity of the landscape and people in this West African country.

K - 3 Students will enjoy the whimsical story. Students and teacher can locate Cameroon on an African map and compare the illustrations with photos of the same country. (Language Arts: Location; Place)

4 - 6 This book can add to a study of the African continent. Grifalconi's *The Village of Round and Square Houses* (1986) provides a look at a traditional village in Cameroon while this book represents more modern town life. (Social Studies: Location; Place; Region)

Jr/Sr High no

Anderson, Joan. 1985. **Christmas on the Prairie.** New York: Clarion Books.

This book re-creates Christmas Eve and Christmas morning in 1836 in the fictional village of Prairietown, Indiana. It shows how the holiday was celebrated in a typical frontier community. The author's text is accompanied by photographs taken at Connor Prairie Pioneer Settlement, a living history museum near Noblesville, Indiana.

K - 3 This book can be used to enhance a study of prairie regions (particularly in the United States). Several other books can accompany this study: *A Prairie Alphabet* (Bannatyne-Cugnet 1992), *My Prairie Christmas* (Harvey 1990), *My Prairie Year* (Harvey 1993), *Heartland* (Siebert 1992), and *Dakota Dugout* (Turner 1985). It can also help students understand the hardships early settlers

93

endured. Students and teacher can use maps to locate the prairies as well as Noblesville. Students may also wish to find the location of other living history museums and parks in the United States. Perhaps one will be close enough to visit as a class. (Social Studies: Location; Place; Regions)

4 - 6 In addition to the above activities, older students can explore the ways in which historians are able to create living history museums and parks. (Social Studies: Location; Place; Regions)

Jr/Sr High Students at this level may wish to create a living history event for other students or parents and community members based on their own research. (Social Studies: Location; Place; Regions)

*Anderson, Lonzo. 1974. **The Day the Hurricane Happened.** New York: Charles Scribner's Sons.

This book tells the story of a day on the island of St. John in the Virgin Islands during which a hurricane struck. Two young children, Eldra and Albie, help prepare for the storm. When it hits land, the house blows away and the family must ride out the storm without shelter. Watercolor and ink full-page illustrations accompany the text.

K - 3 This book provides a beginning point for discussing the hurricane as a type of storm particular to a specific location. It can tie in with a study of islands as a landform. Maps and globes can be used to locate St. John in the West Indies and introduce the concept of U.S. territories. (Science; Social Studies: Location; Place; Movement)

4 - 6 Again, this book provides a beginning point for discussion of hurricanes and islands. The teacher can use Wiesner's *Hurricane* (1990), set in the southeastern United States, with this book to compare and contrast the way in which the children in the two stories survive this powerful storm. In addition, this book can contribute to the study of the Carribean as a region. A more in-depth study of territories and their historical implications can also follow the reading of this book. (Science; Social Studies: Location; Place; Movement)

Jr/Sr High no

*Anno, Mitsumasa. 1980. **Anno's Italy.** New York: William Collins.

In wordless format, with detailed color drawings, Anno follows a lone traveler as he moves through Italy. Along the way he encounters famous landmarks and images from fine arts, architecture, history, and folklore.

K - 3 Small and whole group discussions based on close examination of the detailed drawings can lead to greater understanding of three geographic themes: Place, Relationships Within Places, and Movement. Children can choose a scene from the book as a source for an oral or written story. (Language Arts; Social Studies: Place; Human-Environmental Relations; Movement)

4 - 6 The teacher can conduct more in-depth discussions. Introduce into this discussion the students' search for characters and action from well-known stories, famous landmarks, and images. Students might explore which of these are out of place (either in time or location) and which belong in historic Italy. Depending on the students' background, the teacher may need to provide a "scavenger hunt"–type of list for students. (Language Arts; Social Studies: Place; Human-Environmental Relations; Movement)

Jr/Sr High Students at this level can explore the complicated issues of Human-Environmental Relations and movement as depicted in the detailed illustrations (Social Studies; Sociology: Human-Environmental Relations; Movement)

Anno, Mitsumasa. 1992. **Anno's U.S.A.** New York: Philomel Books.

In wordless format, with detailed color drawings, Anno tells the tale of a lone traveler who approaches the United States from the Hawaiian Islands in the present day and journeys across the country backward through time. The traveler departs from the East Coast just as the *Santa Maria* appears on the horizon.

K - 3 Small and whole group discussions based on close examination of the detailed drawings can help students identify specific landmarks in the United States. Children can choose a scene from the book as a source for an oral or written story. (Language Arts—Oral Fluency; Social Studies: Place; Human-Environmental Relations; Movement)

4 - 6 The teacher can conduct more in-depth discussions of the above-listed topics and introduce into this discussion the students' search for characters and action from well-known stories, famous landmarks, and images. Students might explore the way in which Anno played with time as the visitor moved from west to east. Depending on the students' background, the teacher may need to provide a "scavenger hunt"–type of list for students. Using Anno's format as a model, students may wish to depict an event in history in a similar way. (Language Arts; Social Studies: Place; Human-Environmental Relations; Movement)

Jr/Sr High In addition to the activities discussed above, students at this level can explore the complicated issues of Human-Environmental Relations and movement as depicted in the detailed illustrations. (Social Studies; Sociology: Human-Environmental Relations; Movement)

Axworthy, Anni. 1994. **Anni's Diary of France.** Boston: Whispering Coyote Press.

Preteen Anni and her parents take a self-guided tour of France. As they travel slowly by car, boat, bicycle, and on foot, Anni records in her diary the gorgeous landscapes, delicious foods, and interesting people they encounter along the way. Their leisurely journey, from beautiful Paris to the rocky coast of Brittany to the Riviera, is depicted in a collage of whimsical color drawings around the edge of each page of text. The French vocabulary words sprinkled throughout the diary entries are defined in a glossary found on the end pages.

K - 3 The diary entries in this book, like those in *Let's Go Traveling* (Krupp 1992) and *Your Best Friend, Kate* (Brisson 1992), can provide models for second- and third-grade students working in journals and diaries or writing friendly letters. Students and the teacher can locate specific destinations from Anni's trip on topographical maps of France to learn more about the landforms. (Social Studies; Language Arts: Location; Place; Movement)

4 - 6 Older students can discover more about the particular locales described in Anni's entries. Students may be interested in learning more French. They may also want to learn more about the foods Anni and her family eat along the way and why they are associated with specific regions of France. (Social Studies; Home Economics; Math; Language Arts: Location; Place; Movement)

Jr/Sr High no

Bannatyne-Cugnet, Jo. 1992. **A Prairie Alphabet.** Montreal: Tundra Books.

Detailed, full-page paintings accompany simple alliterative text describing the Canadian prairies from A to Z. A description of North American plains and prairies begins the book, and at the end of the book the author provides detailed paragraphs describing the contents of each painting.

K - 3 This book provides an interesting introduction to both alliteration and prairies. Students and the teacher can locate prairies on the North American continent. Students can explore the characteristics of the climate and vegetation on the plains. Other books that can contribute to this study are *Bringing the Rain to Kapiti Plain* (Aardema 1992), *Christmas on the Prairie* (Anderson 1985), *My Prairie Christmas* (Harvey 1990), *My Prairie Year* (Harvey 1993), *Heartland* (Siebert 1992), and *Dakota Dugout* (Turner 1985). Students can create their own alliterative sentences to describe the setting of their community. (Language Arts; Science; Social Studies: Location; Place; Regions)

4 - 6 Older students can conduct more in-depth research on prairies. (Social Studies: Location; Place; Regions; Human-Environmental Relations)

Jr/Sr High no

Bash, Barbara. 1990. **Urban Roosts.** San Francisco: Sierra Club Books.

The author explores a little-known aspect of city life with humor and imagination. Detailed watercolors illustrate the roosts of barn owls, finches, pigeons, crows, and other birds who have found ways to survive in the city. The informative text provides the reader with interesting facts about both the birds and their unusual environment.

K - 3 This book can add an unusual perspective to a study of big cities. In addition, it can provide a beginning point for a study of wildlife conservation, environmental concerns, or a unit on birds. If the school is located in a city, students might take a walking tour to discover unusual roosts close to home. (Social Studies; Science: Place; Human-Environmental Relations)

4 - 6 Students at this level can explore in more depth the problems associated with urban sprawl encroaching on the habitats of wildlife, as well as other environmental concerns. (Social Studies; Science: Place; Human-Environmental Relations)

Jr/Sr High Students at this level can further explore the issues above. Students could invite expert speakers to address local wildlife conservation and environmental concerns in which students can participate. (Social Studies; Science: Place; Human-Environmental Relations)

Baylor, Byrd. 1987. **The Desert Is Theirs.** New York: Aladdin Paperbacks.

Characteristics of the desert and the close relationships of desert people and animals to the land are expressed through simple lyric text and spare, evocative pictures. See Baylor's *Desert Voices* below.

Baylor, Byrd. 1993. **Desert Voices.** New York: Aladdin Paperbacks.

Eight desert animals and a desert person describe the beauty of their desert home. Spare, evocative pictures accompany the lyrical text.

K - 3 Young children will enjoy the lyrical descriptions of plants, animals, and humans. Together they can examine the illustrations for subtly added details that expand the text. In addition to introducing the concept of the desert as a place where life exists, this book also introduces environmental responsibility. Students and the teacher can locate the desert regions of the United States on a map. (Visual Discrimination; Social Studies; Science: Location; Place; Human-Environmental Relations)

4 - 6 Older students can explore in depth the relationship between the animals, plants, and humans in the desert environments as well as the responsibility assumed by Native Americans for the environment. (Social Studies; Science: Place; Human-Environmental Relations; Regions)

Jr/Sr High Students at this level may wish to conduct an in-depth study of Native Americans in the deserts of the United States. (Social Studies; Science: Location; Place; Human-Environmental Relations; Regions)

*Beekman, Dan. 1982. **Forest, Village, Town, City.** New York: Thomas Y. Crowell.

This book chronicles the evolution of cities from the first simple Indian villages to today's large metropolises. The illustrations are in soft black and white.

K - 3 This book can enhance a study of cities. It can also be used in a look at the "layers of history" in a given place. Companion books to such a study could include *Who Came Down That Road?* (Lyon 1992), *The Legend of New Amsterdam* (Spier 1979), *Pop! Goes the Weasel and Yankee Doodle* (Quackenbush 1976), and John Goodall's series: *The Story of a Farm* (1989), *The Story of a Main Street* (1987), and *The Story of the Seashore* (1990). (Social Studies: Place)

4 - 6 Older students can conduct more in-depth studies of the above units. Students can create a documentation of their own community's layers. (Social Studies: Place)

Jr/Sr High no

Brisson, Pat. 1992. **Your Best Friend, Kate.** New York: Aladdin Paperbacks.

Kate's letters to her best friend, Lucy, detail her family's vacation through 11 states. Kate, who has to share the backseat with her pesky brother, Brian, describes the family's visit in each state and Washington, D.C. The full-color, cartoonlike drawings provide additional information about each state, such as the state bird and flower. The map on the end pages depicts the family's stops on their whirlwind trip.

K - 3 Students and the teacher can locate the states and cities cited in Kate's letters. They can also calculate the distances traveled between stops and the total number of miles. Just as Rachel Rose in *Let's Go Traveling* (Krupp 1992) and Anni in *Anni's Diary of France* (Axworthy 1994) keep a written record of their journey, Kate also models purposeful writing. Students might create a record of their own family vacations based on memory and family photographs. (Language Arts; Math; Social Studies: Location; Place; Movement)

4 - 6 In addition to the above activities, students can create a chart of the distances and then, individually or in small groups, write word problems to be solved by the rest of the class. Students can create their own journey through a set of U.S. states. As the class studies a particular region, students might create a series of letters to describe each state as though they are traveling through it just as Kate wrote to her best friend. (Language Arts; Math; Social Studies: Location; Place; Movement)

Jr/Sr High no

Browne, Philippa-Alys. 1995. **African Animals ABC.** San Francisco: Sierra Club Books.

The author, a native of Zimbabwe, has portrayed 26 insects and mammals of Africa in vibrant paintings that celebrate the bold tribal patterns of Africa. At the end of this Sierra Club Book are informative notes about each creature for adults to share with children. Included in these notes are size, habitat, and survival status.

K - 3 This simple book can be used with young students to introduce the uniqueness of Africa and its flora and fauna. If the teacher and students use a map of Africa as they review the informational notes, they can graph locations (by country, by region), types of animals (insect, mammal), and other characteristics. Students may wish to create colorful paintings of animals native to Africa or another world region. *Boundless Grace* (Hoffman 1995) features a recurring print of an African crocodile. A printmaking process may also be an exciting way to create animal images. (Science; Math; Art: Location; Place; Regions)

> **4 - 6** Although a very unsophisticated book, it can be used to introduce a unit study of Africa. The style complements *Ashanti to Zulu* (Musgrove 1992), which is also organized by the alphabet. Students can combine the information from both books in a chart or graph. From the information they may wish to choose a country, region, tribe, or animal to investigate. They may also wish to expand the information found in each through small group or individual research. *Jambo Means Hello: Swahili Alphabet Book* (Feelings 1992), another book about Africa organized by the alphabet, introduces Swahili vocabulary words. (Science; Math; Social Studies: Location; Place; Human-Environmental Relations; Regions)

Jr/Sr High no

Bunting, Eve. 1995. **Dandelions.** San Diego: Harcourt Brace & Company.

Full-page, softly colored paintings enhance this story of a family's move from their safe, settled home in Illinois to the unsettled Nebraska territory. Zoe, the older of the two young daughters, tells the tale of her father's hopefulness and her mother's doubts. Despite the difficult journey and the unknowns that lie ahead, the family discovers the strength they have in their own unity.

> **K - 3** This book can be included in a study of regions of the United States (Midwest or prairies) or westward movement. Students and the teacher can locate Illinois and Nebraska on a map. Although the text does not provide specific geographic details, students can discover some of the obstacles to the journey by viewing the map. *Aurora Means Dawn* (Sanders 1989), *Dakota Dugout* (Turner 1985), *Going West* (Van Leeuwen 1992), and Harvey's three books—*Cassie's Journey: Going West in the 1860s* (1995), *My Prairie Christmas* (1990), and *My Prairie Year* (1993)—can contribute to this study. Students may be interested in discovering more about Nebraska. In the text, the family notes the lack of trees in the territory. The Arbor Day tradition originated in Nebraska in the late 1800s. If this book is read in the spring, students can conduct growing experiments with dandelions in the classroom. (Science; Social Studies: Place; Location; Movement; Regions)

> **4 - 6** Older students can conduct more in-depth study of the above subjects. (Science; Social Studies: Place; Location; Movement; Regions)

Jr/Sr High no

Bunting, Eve. 1990. **How Many Days to America? A Thanksgiving Story.** New York: Clarion Books.

The story, told from a child's point of view, describes a family's escape from their homeland in a boat. They encounter several adventures as they travel across the Caribbean to south Florida. The detailed color illustrations help set the mood.

> **K - 3** The issues of hiding from soldiers and escaping from one's home country require the teacher to determine this book's appropriateness for a particular class.

> **4 - 6** The time (November) in this story can contribute to a comparison and contrast study of new pilgrims with the Pilgrims of the 1600s. A book about the Pilgrims' journey that can contribute to this study is *Across the Wide Dark Sea* (Van Leeuwen 1995), which is also told from a child's point of view. Students may want to consider other places in the world where there is unrest and people are trying to leave. Other books that look at immigration are *An Ellis Island Christmas* (Leighton 1992) and *Watch the Stars Come Out* (Levinson 1995). This book can also be used in a regional study of the Caribbean. (American History; Social Studies; Current Events: Location; Place; Movement; Regions)

Jr/Sr High Students at this level can consider the issues of political unrest in greater depth. (American History; Social Studies; Current Events: Location; Place; Movement; Regions)

Bunting, Eve. 1994. **Smoky Night.** San Diego: Harcourt Brace & Company.

When the Los Angeles riots break out in the streets of their neighborhood, young Daniel and his mother learn the value of getting along with others no matter what their background or nationality. The unique illustrations are acrylic paintings placed over collages as backgrounds.

> **K - 3** This book can contribute to a study of big cities, especially Los Angeles. The teacher should determine whether the children are ready to discuss the issues of rioting and looting, which take place in the background of this story. Students and the teacher can discuss places where they feel safe, as Daniel feels safe with his mother. This might precede a discussion about class rules to

provide a safe environment for everyone. Discussions about diversity and getting along with neighbors are also appropriate. Using the illustrator's model, students can create multimedia works of art. (Social Studies; Art: Location; Place; Regions)

4 - 6 In addition to the above activities, older students can examine newspaper and magazine reports about the Los Angeles riot. Students may wish to participate in debates about the "rightness" of any of the issues. (Social Studies; Language Arts: Location; Place; Regions)

Jr/Sr High Students at this level can participate in a unit that looks at unrest in the world. Other books that might contribute to such a study are Heide and Gilliland's *Sami and the Time of the Troubles* (1992), Garland's *The Lotus Seed* (1993), and Isadora's *At the Crossroads* (1991). (Social Studies; Current Events: Location; Place; Movement)

Bunting, Eve. 1990. **The Wall.** New York: Clarion Books.

A young boy and his father come from far away to visit the Vietnam Veterans Memorial in Washington, D.C. The boy describes the people he watches visit the memorial as his father searches for the boy's grandfather's name on the wall. Soft watercolor illustrations set the mood.

K - 3 The teacher must decide whether the class has the maturity necessary to handle the issues introduced by this book.

4 - 6 This book can enhance unit studies of large cities, Washington, D.C., or the Vietnam War. Students may wish to conduct interviews with relatives or neighbors who served in Vietnam. Individual or group research can lead to discussions, and students might wish to debate the reasons for the fighting, U.S. involvement, and the results. Maps and globes can be used to locate Washington, D.C., the United States, and Southeast Asia. Other books that might be used with *The Wall* are *Grandfather's Dream* (Keller 1994), *The Lotus Seed* (Garland 1993), and *The Whispering Cloth: A Refugee's Story* (Shea 1995). (Social Studies: Place; Movement)

Jr/Sr High Older students can explore the above issues in greater depth. (American History: World History: Place; Movement)

Burleigh, Robert. 1991. **Flight.** New York: Philomel Books.

This book, based on Lindbergh's own account of his historic flight from New York to Paris in 1927, tells of the long transatlantic flight through full-color illustrations and narrative. The reader has a unique perspective because eye levels for the illustrations are in nontraditional places, such as viewing the airplane before the flight from between Lindbergh's legs. The introduction by author Jean Fritz helps the reader understand Lindbergh's status as national hero.

K - 3 This book fits well in a transportation unit because it documents the first transatlantic flight. Students and the teacher can track the flight on a world map. Other books that can contribute to a look at flight are *The Glorious Flight* (Provensen and Provensen 1983) and *Balloon Trip* (Scarry 1982). (Social Studies: Location; Human-Environmental Relations)

4 - 6 In addition to its value in adding to a transportation unit, this book can be used as a model for writing a simple, yet creative, biographical sketch of a famous person. A discussion about the position of the illustrator in each drawing can lead students to consider how their location helps to determine their perception of activities and objects. Provide opportunities for students to view the same objects or locations from several diverse vantage points, perhaps even drawing them. (Social Studies; Language Arts: Location; Human-Environmental Relations)

Jr/Sr High no

*Burningham, John. 1972. **Around the World in Eighty Days.** Norwich, England: Jarrold & Son.

In this travel book for all ages, the author re-creates Phileas Fogg's trip "around the world in eighty days." The story records his impressions of the 44,000-mile trip through 24 countries and is accompanied by color sketches based on his drawings, photographs, and tape recordings.

K - 3 Students will enjoy Burningham's illustrations. Students and the teacher can locate the sites named in the book on both a world map and a globe to compare the two- and three-dimensional representations. Burningham claims to have visited 24 countries in his 80-day trip. With the teacher's help students can verify this. Other books that document fictional journeys are *Anni's Diary of France* (Axworthy 1994), *Your Best Friend, Kate* (Brisson 1992), *The Armadillo from Amarillo* (Cherry 1994), and *Bluewater Journal: The Voyage of the Sea Tiger* (Krupinski 1995). (Social Studies; Language Arts: Location; Place)

4 - 6 Older students, in addition to the activities above, can conduct research to find out more about each of the locations Burningham notes. Some students may also wish to consider using photos, travel brochures, etc., from a trip of their own to produce a book of that trip. The teacher may choose to read Jules Verne's nineteenth-century novel to the class as a means of comparison and verification of Burningham's journey. (Social Studies; Language Arts: Location; Place)

Jr/Sr High Students at this level can read Jules Verne's classic nineteenth-century fictional journey of Phileas Fogg in *Around the World in Eighty Days* independently, charting on a map and globe the important locations. The Hollywood film can also be viewed and compared to the original text. Then, students can compare Burningham's journey to the novel and the movie. In addition to action and location comparisons, students can explore the difficulties involved in each journey and the relative costs of each. (Math; Language Arts; Social Studies: Location; Place; Human-Environmental Relations; Movement; Regions)

Carrick, Carol. 1988. **Left Behind.** New York: Clarion Books.

Young Christopher is excited about his class's field trip into the city to visit the aquarium. As the trip begins, Christopher is sure the best part of the day will be the ride on the subway. Unfortunately, it's the worst . . . Christopher becomes separated from the rest of the group in the subway. Detailed watercolor illustrations complement the text.

K - 3 This book can enhance a look at the unique characteristics of a large city, particularly those of a subway and many people in one place. The examination of subway maps can expand students' understanding of map uses. A unit study of transportation can include subways. The book also provides an opportunity for a pre–field-trip discussion about what is appropriate behavior on a class field trip to ensure everyone's safety. (Social Studies: Location; Movement; Place)

4 - 6 This book can contribute to a more in-depth study of cities or transportation. (Social Studies: Location; Movement; Place)

Jr/Sr High no

*Ceserani, Gian Paolo. 1977. **Marco Polo.** New York: G. P. Putnam's Sons.

This book follows the adventures of the thirteenth-century Venetian merchant who wrote a famous account of his travels in Asia and his life at the court of Kublai Kahn. Detailed colored drawings accompany the informative text. The book's endpapers illustrate Marco Polo's journey on a map of Europe, Asia, and North Africa.

K - 3 This book might be read to second- and third-graders to connect Marco Polo to Christopher Columbus's trip west to reach the East. Individual students may be interested in researching some of the inventions the Polos discovered in their travels. Students and the teacher can locate the places marked on the endpaper's map on a modern map. (Social Studies: Location; Place; Movement)

4 - 6 Older students can use this book more independently to enhance a study of Christopher Columbus, explorers and inventions, and world regions. Small group and individual research projects based on Chinese inventions might inspire students to hold a "fair" to share the results. (Social Studies; Science: Location; Place; Movement)

Jr/Sr High Students at this level can conduct more in-depth study of the above topics.

Cheripko, Jan. 1993. **Voices of the River: Adventures on the Delaware.** Honesdale, PA: Boyds Mills Press.

This is a photojournal chronicling a 215-mile, 10-day canoe trip on the Delaware River from Hancock, New York (the river's source), down to Philadelphia, Pennsylvania. The author, a 40-year-old writer, narrates the adventure he took part in with a 14-year-old family friend. The two discover the river's history, beauty, danger, people, and more.

K - 3 This book, although interesting, is probably too sophisticated for this age level. The teacher should review it to determine its connection with the curriculum.

4 - 6 This book models photojournalism. Students can use it to structure an account of a trip they've taken. The introduction and epilogue by Matthew Smith, the 14-year-old boy, provides students with an honest look at taking on a big project. This book can complement a study of rivers or transportation. (Social Studies; Language Arts: Location; Place; Regions)

Jr/Sr High Students at this level will appreciate Matthew Smith's honest account of the trip and the photojournalistic style of the book. (Social Studies; Language Arts: Location; Place; Regions)

Cherry, Lynne. 1994. **The Armadillo from Amarillo.** San Diego: A Gulliver Green Book.

A wandering armadillo, Sasparillo, sees some of the cities, historic sites, geographic features, and wildlife of Texas as he attempts to discover where in the world he is. Finally, aided by an eagle who soars far above the earth with Sasparillo on his back, the armadillo discovers he's in a city within a state that's one of 50 in a country that is on the North American continent on planet Earth. The story, told in verse, is accompanied by detailed, full-page watercolor drawings with postcards inset into the page, which add more information. The author's note and acknowledgments at the end of the book further expand its content.

K - 3 This delightful book can be used in many ways in a primary classroom. Sasparillo's postcard messages to his friend Brillo Armadillo model friendly writing. Other books that model communicating through letters and postcards while on a journey are *Your Best Friend, Kate* (Brisson 1992) and *Let's Go Traveling* (Krupp 1992). The four-line stanzas model rhyming couplets. The front endpapers are a topographical map of Texas, offering a way to begin a discussion of topographical maps and their uses. Students and the teacher can follow Sasparillo's progress on a map of Texas, as well as calculate the distances and time needed to complete the various sections of the journey. (Language Arts; Social Studies; Math: Location; Place; Human-Environmental Relations)

4 - 6 Older students can participate in the above activities as well as investigate more fully the subject of each of the postcards. Some of the acknowledgments by Lynne Cherry, found at the end of the book, could be used as a beginning place for other types of research. (Language Arts; Social Studies; Science; Math: Location; Place; Human-Environmental Relations)

Jr/Sr High no

Cherry, Lynne. 1990. **The Great Kapok Tree: A Tale of the Amazon Rain Forest.** San Diego: Gulliver Books.

A man with an ax comes into the rain forest with the intent of cutting down the great kapok tree. The work is so hot and tiring that he stops to rest, falling asleep. While he sleeps the inhabitants of the rain forest whisper in the man's ear. Each tells what the loss of the rain forest will mean to the world. Beautifully detailed, full-page color drawings accompany the text. The natural flora and fauna are included in the drawings as well as on the end pages. The end pages also include a world map locating the rain forests as they previously existed and as they exist today.

K - 3 The very youngest students will enjoy the many animals included in the drawings. Older students can locate the tropical regions on the globe and world maps, identifying the many countries that lie within the regions. The imaginary lines that define the region (Equator, Tropic of Cancer, Tropic of Capricorn) need to be explained by the teacher. Students can discuss why there are no rain forests outside this region. Older students will also be interested in the impact of rain forest destruction on the world. Other books that discuss the rain forests are *Nature's Green Umbrella: Tropical Rain Forest* (Gibbons 1994) and *Panther Dream: A Story of the African Rain Forest* (Weir and Weir 1991). (Social Studies; Science: Location; Place; Human-Environmental Relations; Regions)

4 - 6 Students at this level will be especially interested in the issue of rain forest destruction. Individual and small group research projects can be conducted. Students may want to pursue research about the animals found on the pages of the book. Students may want to compare the rain forests in South America with those in Africa. (Social Studies; Science: Location; Place; Human-Environmental Relations; Regions)

Jr/Sr High Students at this level can explore the worldwide repercussions of rain forest destruction. (Social Studies; Science: Location; Place; Human-Environmental Relations)

Cherry, Lynne. 1992. **A River Ran Wild.** San Diego: A Gulliver Green Book.

This book tells the environmental history of the Nashua River, from its discovery by Indians through the polluting years of the Industrial Revolution to the ambitious cleanup that revitalized it. Full-page watercolor drawings face the text pages, which are bordered by illustrations of elements associated with the narrative. The author provides detailed information about the Nashua River Valley in the author's note and on the end pages.

K - 3 This book can be used in a study of rivers. In addition, this book offers a beginning place for young students to understand the effects of industrial pollutants on rivers. Students and the teacher can locate the Nashua River on a map, trace its course, and measure its length. (Social Studies; Science: Location; Place; Human-Environmental Relations)

4 - 6   Older students can research industrial pollution problems in the United States and their own community. Field trips and outside speakers can serve to expand the study. Some students may wish to research the Nashua Indians. Perhaps the author or Marion Stoddart, who began the cleanup, would be available for correspondence with interested students. The unique small drawings surrounding the text may inspire students to create similar illustrations. (Social Studies; Science; Art; Language Arts: Location; Place; Human-Environmental Relations)

Jr/Sr High   Students at this level can conduct similar but more in-depth research. (Social Studies; Science; Art; Language Arts: Location; Place; Human-Environmental Relations)

Coerr, Eleanor. 1993. **Sadako.** New York: G. P. Putnam's Sons.

Soft-edged, full-page color illustrations accompany the true story of Sadako, a young Japanese girl who contracted leukemia, the "atom-bomb disease," in the summer of 1954. In an attempt to create a miracle that would allow her to live, Sadako began to fold 1,000 paper cranes. Unfortunately, she died before she could reach her goal.

K - 3   Unless your class is exceptionally mature, do not use this book with this age group. It has many sophisticated concepts.

4 - 6   This book can be useful in a study about the effects of war on innocent people. It would be especially well paired with *The Bracelet* (Uchida 1993). In both books, a young girl's life is directly affected by World War II and the adversarial relationship between the United States and Japan. In addition, this book can contribute to a study of the relationship between the people of the United States and Japan. Other worthwhile books for this study are *How My Parents Learned to Eat* (Friedman 1987), *The Bicycle Man* (Say 1989), and *Grandfather's Journey* (Say 1993). Students may wish to make origami cranes. (Art; Social Studies: Location; Place; Movement)

Jr/Sr High   Older students can do more in-depth research on the results of the World War II bombing of Japan, the detention camps for Japanese Americans in the United States, and the influence Sadako had on her country. Some students may want to examine the history of U.S.-Japanese relations over the centuries and particularly since the end of World War II. (Social Studies: Location; Place; Movement)

Dolphin, Laurie. 1991. **Georgia to Georgia: Making Friends in the U.S.S.R.** New York: Tambourine Books.

This book is a pictorial record of Joe Schulten's trip from Atlanta, Georgia, to the Soviet Republic of Georgia. Joe's mother began a peace project that involved a letter-writing campaign to connect children in the United States and Russia. She was invited to join a delegation to the U.S.S.R., and her family accompanied her. This book documents the journey through many photographs and fairly simple narrative text.

K - 3   This book can be used to demonstrate to students the power writing can have. It might be used to precede a letter-writing activity, especially one involving pen pals. If students have access to the Internet, daily communication with students living far away may be possible. Students and the teacher can locate Atlanta, Georgia, and the Republic of Georgia on both a map and a globe. Their relative locations, physical characteristics, weather, culture, and other aspects can be compared and contrasted. (Language Arts; Social Studies: Location; Place; Movement)

4 - 6   Older students can expand the above activities. In particular, they can conduct more in-depth research both independently and in small groups. (Language Arts; Social Studies: Location; Place; Movement)

Jr/Sr High   no

Feelings, Muriel. 1992. **Jambo Means Hello: Swahili Alphabet Book.** New York: Puffin Books.

This simple, informative book features 24 words, one for each letter of the Swahili alphabet. Author Muriel Feelings gives children a simple lesson in the language while familiarizing them with some important aspects of traditional East African life. She also advises the reader about the importance of people understanding one another's language and culture. Soft black-and-white drawings accompany the text. The foreword includes an African map showing where Swahili is spoken.

K - 3   As students learn the vocabulary in this book, the teacher can introduce the concept that different languages make use of alphabets, with Swahili as one example. The students and the teacher can compare the illustrations with actual pictures of East Africa. The map at the beginning of the book can be examined and compared to a globe to locate East Africa, determine the relative size of

Africa to the world, and estimate the distance between Africa and the United States. *Africa Brothers and Sisters* (Kroll 1993) also provides African vocabulary and a pronunciation key. (Reading; Math; Social Studies: Location; Place; Movement; Regions)

4 - 6   This book can be used to enhance a study of the various regions and customs of Africa. (Social Studies: Location; Place; Movement; Regions)

Jr/Sr High   no

Feelings, Muriel. 1994. **Moja Means One: Swahili Counting Book.** New York: Puffin Books.

The Swahili numbers for one to 10 are incorporated into a text designed to familiarize the reader with some basic aspects of East African life. Soft-edged, limited-colored drawings enhance the simple text. The foreword includes an African map showing where Swahili is spoken. The author stresses the importance of understanding others' language and culture.

K - 3   As students learn to count and match number names to their value, the teacher can introduce the concept that the same number values are called by different names in different languages, with Swahili as one example. The students and teacher can compare the illustrations with actual pictures of East Africa. The map at the beginning of the book can be examined and compared to a globe to locate East Africa, determine the relative size of Africa to the world, and estimate the distance between Africa and the United States. (Math; Social Studies: Location; Place)

4 - 6   This book can be used to enhance a study of the various regions and customs of Africa. (Social Studies: Location; Place; Regions)

Jr/Sr High   no

Feelings, Tom. 1993. **Soul Looks Back in Wonder.** New York: Dial Books.

This book of poems by African American poets, illustrated by Tom Feelings, is intended to project the author's and poets' positive hopes for the future of young African sisters and brothers. Short biographical paragraphs about each of the 13 poets are provided at the end of the book. The book is Feelings's first book published in full color.

K - 3   This book can contribute to a poetry unit or a study of the African American culture in the United States. Students might want to experiment with Feelings's model of illustrating poems. (Language Arts; Art: Place; Location)

4 - 6   This book can expand studies of slavery and the rise of the African American culture in the history of the United States. It can be used with *Nettie's Trip South* (Turner 1987), *Pink and Say* (Polacco 1994), and *Aunt Harriet's Underground Railroad in the Sky* (Ringgold 1992), which touch on the issue of slavery. Consider using this book in a unit devoted to enhancing students' self-esteem. Students may wish to write similar poetry or illustrate poetry they particularly enjoy. (Social Studies; Language Arts: Place; Location; Movement)

Jr/Sr High   no

Fisher, Leonard Everett. 1986. **The Great Wall of China.** New York: Macmillan.

The author provides a powerfully told history of the Great Wall of China in narrative form. He tells of Ch'in Shih Huang Ti, the First Supreme Emperor of China, who ordered the incredible structure built to save his people from raiding Mongols. Full-page black-and-white illustrations are accompanied by Chinese characters and the author's "chops"—Chinese artists' signatures. A map preceding the text locates the Great Wall in China, and a translation of the Chinese characters appears at the end of the book.

K - 3   This book can be used to discuss how humans have used the environment (in this case, the land) to provide the necessities of life. The Wall provided the Chinese with protection from the Mongols for more than 1,000 years. (Social Studies: Human-Environmental Relations)

4 - 6   Students will be intrigued by the huge undertaking, which took 10 years to complete and cost many their lives. Some students may wish to explore the various historical periods, while others may wish to learn more about the Chinese characters. Another book that might expand this text is *Marco Polo* (Ceserani 1977). (Social Studies; Art: Human-Environmental Relations; Movement)

Jr/Sr High   Students at this level can explore Chinese inventions and their influence on others. Some students may wish to explore Chinese art in greater depth. (Social Studies; Art: Human-Environmental Relations; Movement)

Fisher, Leonard Everett. 1990. **Prince Henry the Navigator.** New York: Macmillan.

This black-and-white picture book is the biography of Prince Henry of Portugal. His vision led to the establishment of the first school of navigation. Although he didn't participate in expeditions sent from his school, he made it possible for others to enjoy the romance of the sea.

K - 3 This book can be part of a study of Columbus as it helps set the context in which Columbus made his voyage. This book can also enhance a study of mapmaking. (Social Studies: Location; Place; Movement)

4 - 6 Students at this level can research the navigational instruments used in the fifteenth century. The maps in *Follow the Dream: The Story of Christopher Columbus* (Sis 1991) are modeled after fifteenth-century maps. They can be used to help students understand the mapmakers' perception of their world. Students can estimate the length of the trip from Portugal to India by going around the southern tip of Africa. The same trip by way of the Suez Canal can be estimated and compared. (Social Studies; Math; Science: Location; Place; Movement; Human-Environmental Relations)

Jr/Sr High Older students can conduct similar but more in-depth research. (Social Studies; Math; Science: Location; Place; Movement; Human-Environmental Relations)

Friedman, Ina R. 1987. **How My Parents Learned to Eat.** Boston: Houghton Mifflin.

An American sailor, stationed in Yokohama, courts a Japanese girl. Each tries, in secret, to learn the other's way of eating. Softly colored line drawings accompany the text.

K - 3 This book can enhance the study of basic needs: food, shelter, and clothing. The class can explore the many ways people feed themselves. The text also introduces the concept of socially acceptable behavior being relative to each culture, perhaps even each family. (Social Studies: Movement)

4 - 6 In addition to the above activities, this book might lead students to explore the development of eating utensils in various cultures. The class may wish to try some international cooking and appropriate serving. A large world map can be used to locate the various "traditions" uncovered through the students' research (Social Studies: Movement)

Jr/Sr High Students may wish to expand the research to include personal creation of eating utensils and original recipes (Social Studies; Technologies; Home Economics: Movement; Human-Environmental Relations)

Garland, Sherry. 1993. **The Lotus Seed.** San Diego: Harcourt Brace Jovanovich.

A young Vietnamese girl saves a lotus seed and carries it with her everywhere to remember a brave emperor and the homeland that she had to flee. Full-page oil paintings set the book's mood. The author's note at the end of the book expands the reader's knowledge of Vietnamese history and its connection to the United States.

K - 3 Based on the teacher's assessment of the class's ability to deal with the distress of civil war, this book can offer a look at how people continue to maintain their culture even in difficult times. Discussions can include an examination of Vietnam's location relative to the United States, its climate, and cultural elements. Other books that can be used with *The Lotus Seed* are *The Wall* (Bunting 1990), *The Whispering Cloth: A Refugee's Story* (Shea 1995), and *Grandfather's Dream* (Keller 1994). (Social Studies: Place; Location; Movement)

4 - 6 A more in-depth study of civil war can be pursued. Students may wish to interview any local Vietnamese people who have immigrated to the United States. In addition, they may find interviews with family members and neighbors who served in Vietnam to be helpful in their research and understanding. (Social Studies; Language Arts: Location; Place; Movement; Human-Environmental Relations; Regions)

Jr/Sr High Students can complete more in-depth research projects, perhaps in the form of debates about the Vietnam conflict, U.S immigration policies, the boat people, and other related topics. (American History; World History: Location; Place; Movement; Human-Environmental Relations; Regions)

Garland, Sherry. 1995. **The Summer Sands.** San Diego: A Gulliver Green Book.

Two young children vacationing at the seashore enjoy watching the native animals, running on the dunes, and roasting marshmallows on the beach. But a late summer storm sweeps the dunes away. After New Year's, the children return to join others who are placing discarded Christmas trees where the dunes used to be. In the spring the children return to the beach to discover the reformation of the dunes. Soft, full-color paintings help create a feeling of being on the beach. The author's note at the end of the book provides factual information about the ongoing task of restoring dunes destroyed by storms.

K - 3 This book, used with Zolotow's *The Seashore Book* (1992), can help students learn about the unique characteristics of the shore. *The Story of the Seashore* (Goodall 1990) provides an interesting historical note about how people have experienced the English seashore over history. In addition, *The Summer Sands* provides a wonderful introduction for a study of environmental responsibilities, especially because the children in the book are a viable part of the restoration process. (Social Studies; Science: Location; Place; Human-Environmental Relations)

4 - 6 In addition to the above activities, older students can learn more about how humans are attempting to be accountable for environmental problems. Other books appropriate for this study are *A River Ran Wild* (Cherry 1992) and *Grandfather's Dream* (Keller 1994). Some students may wish to learn more about the Texas coastline and its problems. (Social Studies; Science: Location; Place; Human-Environmental Relations)

Jr/Sr High no

George, Lindsay Barrett. 1995. **In the Snow: Who's Been Here?** New York: Greenwillow Books.

In this companion book to *In the Woods: Who's Been Here?* William and his younger sister, Cammie, take a walk in the snow-covered woods. They follow an old trail, discovering tracks, a leafy nest, a pellet of feathers and bones, and other signs of unseen animals and their activities before finding evidence of their mother's presence in a thermos of hot chocolate and doughnuts. Beautiful, full-color paintings accompany the simple text. A map drawn by William and Cammie on the front fly sheet shows the path they followed. The last page provides more information about the eight animals discussed in the story.

K - 3 Like *In the Woods: Who's Been Here?* this book provides a model for mapmaking of actual outings. However, this book allows the teacher to expand the exercise into another season. The class might take a short trip around the school grounds, stopping periodically to make observations. Then, back in the classroom, the teacher can create a map on the chalkboard or overhead with the help of the students. Cardinal directions and a key can be added, depending on the age of the students. Students can discover more about the animals introduced in this book. (Science; Social Studies: Location; Human-Environmental Relations)

4 - 6 Although a very simple book, it introduces the concept of protective coloration in the context of the woods and clearly shows that animals continue to be active during the winter months. This book may be helpful in a study of animals in their environments. (Science: Human-Environmental Relations)

Jr/Sr High no

George, Lindsay Barrett. 1995. **In the Woods: Who's Been Here?** New York: Greenwillow Books.

William and his younger sister, Cammie, take a walk in the woods. They find an empty nest, a cocoon, gnawed bark, and other signs of unseen animals and their activities. Beautiful, full-color paintings accompany the simple text. A map drawn by William and Cammie on the front fly sheet shows the path they followed. The last page provides more information about the eight animals discussed in the story.

K - 3 This book provides a model for mapmaking of actual outings. The class might take a short trip around the school grounds, stopping periodically to make observations. Then, back in the classroom, the teacher can create a map on the chalkboard or overhead with the help of the students. Cardinal directions and a key can be added, depending on the age of the students. Students can discover more about the animals introduced in this book. (Science; Social Studies: Location; Human-Environmental Relations)

4 - 6 Although a very simple book, it introduces the concept of protective coloration in the context of the woods. This book may be helpful in a study of animals in their environments. (Science: Human-Environmental Relations)

Jr/Sr High no

George, William T. 1992. **Christmas at Long Pond.** New York: Greenwillow Books.

A father and son observe the plant and animal life around Long Pond (located in the Pocono Mountains area of Pennsylvania) before finding just the right Christmas tree. The exquisitely rich, full-page color illustrations perfectly accompany the text. Other books by the same author and illustrator include *Box Turtle at Long Pond* (1989), *Beaver at Long Pond* (1988), and *Fishing at Long Pond* (1991).

K - 3   This series of books is particularly useful in examining the relationship among plants, animals, and humans in a particular location (a pond in northeastern Pennsylvania). Students and the teacher can explore issues of wildlife conservation as well as the specific characteristics of pond life. Students may also be interested in exploring the accuracy of the illustrations. (Art; Social Studies; Science: Location; Place; Human-Environmental Relations)

4 - 6   Older students can conduct research on the animals found at Long Pond. Students may be able to conduct some research on a field trip to a similar pond. Students can compare the plant and animal life in their community to pond life. (Social Studies; Science: Location; Place; Human-Environmental Relations)

Jr/Sr High   no

Gibbons, Gail. 1994. **Nature's Green Umbrella: Tropical Rain Forest.** New York: Morrow Junior Books.

This book describes the climatic conditions of the rain forest through clearly written explanations and full-color detailed drawings, diagrams, and maps. The author discusses the different layers of plants and animals that make up this complicated ecosystem. Also addressed are the destruction of the rain forests and its impact on the Earth.

K - 3   The very youngest students will enjoy looking at the many animals included in the drawings and learning incredible facts about rainfall and plant life. Older students can locate the tropical regions on a globe and world map, identifying the many countries that lie within them. The imaginary lines that define the rain forest region (Equator, Tropic of Cancer, Tropic of Capricorn) need to be explained by the teacher. Students can discuss why there are no rain forests outside this region. Older students will also be interested in the impact of rain forest destruction on the world. Other books that can contribute to this study are *The Great Kapok Tree: A Tale of he Amazon Rain Forest* (Cherry 1990) and *Panther Dream: A Story of the African Rain Forest* (Weir and Weir 1991). (Social Studies; Science: Location; Place; Human-Environmental Relations; Regions)

4 - 6   Students at this level will be especially interested in the issue of rain forest destruction. Individual and small group research projects can be conducted. Students may want to compare the rain forests in South America with those in Africa. Students may also want to research the animals and plants found on the pages of the book. (Social Studies; Science: Location; Place; Human-Environmental Relations; Regions)

Jr/Sr High   Students at this level can pursue the worldwide repercussions of rain forest destruction. (Social Studies; Science: Location; Place; Human-Environmental Relations)

Gibbons, Gail. 1991. **The Puffins Are Back!** New York: HarperCollins.

Full-page watercolor drawings enhance the telling of the true story of the return of unique birds—the puffins—to their Maine island habitat. In 1969 scientists from the National Audubon Society worked out a plan to aid the survival of Maine's puffin population. Gibbon, who owns a house on another Maine island nearby, was so captivated by the birds that she wrote the story of the successful effort to increase the puffin population.

K - 3   This book can contribute to a unit on wildlife conservation or environmental responsibility. Older students can research puffins and Maine as well as animals in their own community or region facing similar extinction. The consequences of unregulated hunting might be explored (the extinction of animals due to overkill), or the effect of changing environments might be examined (destruction of the rain forests and wetlands). *The Atlas of Endangered Animals* (Pollock 1993) and the endnotes in *African Animals ABC* (Browne 1995) provide information about the survival status of animals to aid this study. A variety of maps should be provided for students to use. *Grandfather's Dream* (Keller 1994), set in Vietnam, also addresses the topic of attracting animals to their natural habitat. The author, Holly Keller, is committed to involving children in wildlife conservation, so she may be willing to communicate with a student or class about her experiences. (Language Arts; Social Studies; Science: Location; Place; Human-Environmental Relations)

4 - 6   Older students can expand on the above activities. (Language Arts; Social Studies; Science: Location; Place; Human-Environmental Relations)

Jr/Sr High   Some students at this level may be interested in probing the issues of wildlife conservation and environmental protection. (Language Arts; Social Studies; Science: Location; Place; Human-Environmental Relations)

Goodall, John S. 1989. **The Story of a Farm.** New York: Margaret K. McElderry Books.

This wordless picture book gives a pictorial history of the development of farm life in England from the early Middle Ages to the present. The watercolor illustrations portray scenes of the farmhouse being rebuilt and the daily round of farm life. Unique half-page inserts expand each scene. A preface page provides historical information about each scene.

K - 3 This book can be used in a study of city and country. Students and the teacher can examine the changes in farming and compare the images of English farming to those of American farming. Students may take a field trip to a farm to gain a greater understanding of the relationship between humans and the land. (Social Studies; Science: Location; Place; Human-Environmental Relations)

4 - 6 In addition to the above activities, older students may wish to use this book as a model for illustrations. Students at this level can also explore the many "layers of history" in any given place as demonstrated by this book and the others in this series. Research into the specific English time periods named in this book can help students understand English history. (Social Studies; World History; Art: Place; Human-Environmental Relations; Movement)

Jr/Sr High Students at this level may conduct more in-depth research of the topics listed above. (Social Studies; World History; Art: Place; Human-Environmental Relations; Movement)

Goodall, John S. 1987. **The Story of a Main Street.** New York: Margaret K. McElderry Books.

This wordless picture history traces the evolution of an English main street from medieval times to the present. A clever half-page illustration set within each scene expands the scene's contents. The watercolor paintings, rich in authentic and colorful details, depict street and market scenes, clothing, and customs, all of which change as the time periods change. A preface page provides historical information about each illustration. The author has written several books in this format.

K - 3 This book will be more appealing to older students because of its content and the English setting. Students and the teacher can examine and discuss the changes in the same place that occurred over several hundred years. (Social Studies: Place)

4 - 6 In addition to the above activities, older students may wish to use this book as a model for illustrations. Research may uncover paintings or drawings as well as old photographs of local landmarks demonstrating the changes that have taken place over time in the students' own community. Students at this level can also explore the many "layers of history" in any given place as demonstrated by this book and the others in this series. Research into the specific English time periods named in this book can help students understand English history. (Social Studies; World History; Art: Place; Human-Environmental Relations; Movement)

Jr/Sr High Older students can conduct more in-depth research on the above subjects. (Social Studies; World History; Art: Place; Human-Environmental Relations; Movement)

Goodall, John S. 1990. **The Story of the Seashore.** New York: Margaret K. McElderry Books.

This wordless picture book shares the English public's love affair with the seashore. The detailed watercolor illustrations document changes in bathing costumes and seaside amusements from the early 1800s to the present. The author provides unique half-page inserts that extend the illustrations. A preface page provides historical settings for each illustration.

K - 3 Students and the teacher can share personal experiences of the seashore. This book can complement a study of the oceans or the seashore. *The Seashore Book* (Zolotow 1992) and *The Summer Sands* (Garland 1995) can also be used. (Social Studies: Location; Place; Regions)

4 - 6 Students at this level can also explore the many "layers of history" in any given place as demonstrated by this book and the others in this series. Research into the specific English time periods named in this book can help students understand English history. In addition to the above activities, older students may wish to use this book as a model for illustrations. (Social Studies; World History; Art: Place; Human-Environmental Relations; Movement)

Jr/Sr High Older students can conduct more in-depth research on the above subjects. (Social Studies; World History; Art: Place; Human-Environmental Relations; Movement)

Gray, Nigel, and Dupasquier, Philippe. 1991. **A Country Far Away.** New York: Orchard Books.

This book reveals the essential similarities between the lives of two boys, one in a Western country and one in a rural African village. The whimsical, detailed, full-page color illustrations are divided by a simple text running through the middle. The single text describes one day in the life of each boy as the pictures on the top show the boy in Africa and the pictures on the bottom show the boy in a Western country.

K - 3   This book can be used to enhance a unit on cultural diversity. Although the illustrations are quite different, Virginia Kroll's *Africa Brothers and Sisters* (1993) and *Masai and I* (1992) also juxtapose children from African and Western cultures to illustrate the essential similarities in their lives. (Social Studies: Location; Place; Human-Environmental Relations)

4 - 6   This book can enhance a unit on Africa. (Social Studies: Location; Place; Human-Environmental Relations; Movement; Regions)

Jr/Sr High   no

Grifalconi, Ann. 1986. **The Village of Round and Square Houses.** Boston: Little, Brown.

In this story a grandmother explains to her listeners why the men in the village live in square houses and the women live in round houses. The village and the story are inspired from the real village of Tos in the remote hills of Cameroon in West Africa. The soft-edged color illustrations enhance the text.

K - 3   This book can be used with Alexander's *The Fortune-Tellers* (1992) to provide a contrast between city and village life in Cameroon. Students and the teacher can compare the illustrations in both books with photographs of the same areas in Cameroon. (Social Studies: Location; Place)

4 - 6   This book can accompany a study of Africa. In addition to the above activities, older students can research the volcano "Old Naka" and determine when it erupted, creating the legend. (Social Studies; Science: Location; Place; Regions)

Jr/Sr High   Students at this level can conduct more in-depth research on Cameroon and volcanos. Perhaps they could explore how actual historical events lead to special legends or actions. (Social Studies; Science; Literature: Location; Place; Movement; Regions)

Harness, Cheryl. 1995. **The Amazing Impossible ERIE CANAL.** New York: Macmillan.

No one believed a canal connecting the Hudson River to the Great Lakes could be constructed. No one except DeWitt Clinton. His vision resulted in the building of the Erie Canal. In this book Cheryl Harness has presented this unique engineering feat through informative text, detailed maps, and detailed, full-page watercolor illustrations. The maps and diagrams provide additional data about how the canal was built and how the locks work, and specific details of the first trip along the fully completed canal in the fall of 1825.

K - 3   Generally, this book is a bit too sophisticated for students at this level. Older students will enjoy the story and, with the teacher's help, can trace the journey from Buffalo to New York City. A copy of the famous song about the Erie Canal, "Low Bridge, Everybody Down," appears on the back cover. Peter Spier's *The Erie Canal* (1990), a simpler version, can be used as a companion book. Students and the teacher can learn the song. (Social Studies; Music: Location; Place; Movement)

4 - 6   Older students will enjoy exploring the author's detailed diagrams and maps that accompany the traditional illustrations and text. The book can be used to enhance a study of rivers and other waterways. The diagram describing the way locks operate is clear and concise. It can be most helpful as a beginning study about the use of locks around the world to facilitate travel and the transportation of goods and services. (Social Studies; Science; Music: Location; Place; Movement; Human-Environmental Relations)

Jr/Sr High   no

Harvey, Brett. 1995. **Cassie's Journey: Going West in the 1860s.** New York: Holiday House.

The author based the fictional story of Cassie's journey on actual accounts from women's diaries. Young Cassie and her family risk the dangers and hardships of the American westward migration as they travel from Illinois to California. Black-and-white illustrations accompany the text. A map of the western half of the United States traces the trail followed by Cassie and other travelers in the 1860s.

K - 3   This book should be read aloud to younger students due to the reading level of the text. The content can contribute to a discussion of the hardships of travel in the 1860s. Another book that can contribute to this discussion is *Bluewater Journal: The Voyage of the Sea Tiger* (Krupinski

1995), which describes a journey from Boston to Hong Kong by clipper ship in this same time period. The teacher and students can calculate the distances covered by the travelers as they moved from landmark to landmark on the map. Students may wish to complete travel journals of their own. (Language Arts; Social Studies; Math: Place; Location; Human-Environmental Relations)

4 - 6 Although this book is fairly unsophisticated, it offers older students some insight into the difficulties of travel in the United States more than a century ago. Students and the teacher can compare and contrast the reasons immigrants came from Europe to the United States with those of the Americans who migrated from "civilization" to unsettled areas such as California. In addition to other activities named above, students may wish to explore diaries written during this period of time. (Language Arts; Social Studies: Location; Place; Human-Environmental Relations)

Jr/Sr High no

Harvey, Brett. 1990. **My Prairie Christmas.** New York: Holiday House.

On the first Christmas Eve after Eleanor's family moved from Maine to their new house on the prairie, everyone becomes worried when Papa goes out to cut down a Christmas tree and doesn't come back. Not only is Papa missing but it's obvious that Christmas on the prairie is going to be very different from Christmas in Maine. Color illustrations enhance the text.

K - 3 This book should be read aloud to younger students due to the reading level of the text. It can contribute to an examination of pioneer life on the plains. Other books that can enhance such a study are Harvey's other picture book about Eleanor, *My Prairie Year* (1993), and *Dakota Dugout* (Turner 1985). Students and the teacher can compare and contrast this story with Anderson's *Christmas on the Prairie* (1985). (Social Studies: Location; Place; Regions)

4 - 6 This book can be used in a regional study of the plains and the American westward movement. The author based this book on her grandmother's diary. Students can write in their own diary or create a frontier diary that tells about living on the plains. (Social Studies; Language Arts: Location; Place; Regions)

Jr/Sr High no

Harvey, Brett. 1993. **My Prairie Year.** New York: Holiday House.

The author uses her grandmother's diary to tell about homesteading life on the vast prairie of the Dakotas in the late 1880s. The black-and-white drawings appropriately illustrate the ocean of rippling prairie grass, the tornado, and the prairie fire, as well as other details of prairie life.

K - 3 This book should be read aloud to younger students due to the reading level of the text. It can contribute to an examination of pioneer life on the plains. Other books that can enhance such a study are *Christmas on the Prairie* (Anderson 1985) and *Dakota Dugout* (Turner 1985). (Social Studies: Location; Place; Regions)

4 - 6 This book can be used in a regional study of the plains and the American westward movement. The author based this book on her grandmother's diary. Students can write in their own diary or create a frontier diary that tells about living on the plains. (Social Studies; Language Arts: Location; Place; Regions)

Jr/Sr High no

Heide, Florence Perry, and Gilliland, Judith Heide. 1990. **The Day of Ahmed's Secret.** New York: Lothrop, Lee & Shepard.

Ahmed, a young boy living in Cairo, travels through this bustling ancient city on a donkey cart delivering *butagaz* (butane gas canisters used in gas stoves). As he works his way through the day and the city he loves, he hugs a special secret to himself, anxious to tell his family at the end of the day. The full-page, richly detailed watercolor illustrations enhance the text.

K - 3 This book can contribute to a study of big cities. Students can compare the buildings, traffic, and business of Cairo with those of an American big city. Ahmed discusses the location of Cairo between the desert and the Nile River. Students and the teacher can explore what effect that location has on Cairo's inhabitants. (Social Studies: Location; Place; Human-Environmental Relations)

4 - 6 This book can be included in a study of big cities or a study of Africa. Students can research the land and countries drained by the Nile River. Such a study can also contribute to directional assumptions about the flow of rivers. (The Nile flows north, which often confuses children, who think of north as "up.") (Social Studies: Location; Place; Movement; Human-Environmental Relations; Regions)

Jr/Sr High   One of the authors (Judith Heide Gilliland) and her husband are Arabists (specialists in the Arabic language and culture). Older students can explore the Arabic language and culture. Students may also find researching Cairo's thousand-year history an interesting project. (Social Studies; Language Arts: Location; Place; Human-Environmental Relations)

Heide, Florence Perry, and Gilliland, Judith Heide. 1992. **Sami and the Time of the Troubles.** New York: Clarion Books.

Ten-year-old Sami lives with his family in a basement in Beirut, the capital of Lebanon. They must live underground to remain safe from the bombings and fighting that are facts of everyday life. The full-page watercolor illustrations show Sami as he helps his mother with chores and plays with his friends despite the violence.

K - 3   I would not recommend this book for this age group.

4 - 6   This book provides an opportunity to introduce the issue of political unrest in various parts of the world. Students can collect newpaper and magazine articles as well as watch television news reports about the fighting in the Middle East. Students and the teacher can mark Beirut and Middle Eastern countries on a large world map. Further research can involve discovering the history of the political struggles, along with the landforms, culture, crops, and other characteristics of each area. Other books that touch on political unrest are *At the Crossroads* (Isadora 1991), *The Lotus Seed* (Garland 1993), *Smoky Night* (Bunting 1994), and *How Many Days to America? A Thanksgiving Story* (Bunting 1990). (Current Events; Social Studies: Place; Location; Movement)

Jr/Sr High   Older students can pursue the activities listed above at a more in-depth level. (Current Events; Social Studies: Place; Location; Movement)

Hoban, Tana. 1991. **All About Where.** New York: Greenwillow Books.

The reader is encouraged to look carefully at the colorful photographs and describe what is seen. Along the side of each page are 15 location words (e.g., *above, behind, under,* and *through*) that provide possibilities. For example: The boat is *on* the water. It is *against* the dock.

K - 3   This book provides the opportunity to help students use vocabulary to describe their own position in space or that of objects around them and the relationship between them. (Social Studies; Language Arts: Location)

4 - 6   no

Jr/Sr High   no

Hoffman, Mary. 1995. **Boundless Grace.** New York: Dial Books for Young Readers.

Young Grace, who lives with her mother and grandmother in the United States, is invited to visit her father and his new family in Africa. While she discovers more about her family in Africa, she learns firsthand about life in The Gambia. The author and illustrator traveled to The Gambia in Africa to ensure the authenticity of the text and paintings. The full-page realistic color paintings are integral to the telling of the story.

K - 3   A major focus in this book is the shape of the family unit. This book can contribute to a study or discussion of families. It can also contribute to a study of Africa, although the location is secondary to the plot. The stylized crocodiles on the cover and end pages may entice some students to create animal prints. (Social Studies; Art: Location; Place; Movement)

4 - 6   In addition to the activities suggested above, older students can learn more about The Gambia, found in the northern part of Africa with a port on the Atlantic Ocean. This book can contribute to a regional study of Africa. (Social Studies; Art: Location; Place; Movement; Regions)

Jr/Sr High   no

*Innocenti, Roberto. 1985. **Rose Blanche.** Mankato, MN: Creative Education.

Young Rose Blanche's life is changed forever by the war and the soldiers who pass through her town. Rose watches, without understanding, the movement of soldiers and the removal of whole families from her small town in Germany. This serious story of World War II is told from a child's perspective through simple text and detailed, full-page color paintings.

K - 3   The content of this book is very sad and serious. I would not use it with primary children.

4 - 6 This book would be useful in a study of World War II only with mature children. Its provocative message is one of hope in the face of horror. Be sure to read it carefully before sharing it with your class. It can be used with *Let the Celebrations BEGIN!* (Wild 1991), which deals with the concentration camps in a way children can understand. (Social Studies: Location; Movement)

Jr/Sr High Older students can explore the issue that Innocenti presents in the quote on the book cover: "In this book I wanted to illustrate how a child experiences war without really understanding it." Other books involving children and war are *Let the Celebrations BEGIN!* (Wild 1991), *The Bracelet* (Uchida 1993), and *Randolph's Dream* (Mellecker 1991). (Social Studies; World History: Location; Movement)

Isadora, Rachel. 1991. **At the Crossroads.** New York: Greenwillow Books.

Full-page watercolor paintings illustrate the not uncommon scene of children in the segregated townships of South Africa waiting for their fathers to return after many months of working in the mines far from family and home. Emphasis is on the joy of these family reunions rather than the hardship and deprivation that also accompany them.

K - 3 The maturity of the students will determine whether this book is appropriate. Although the text and illustrations appear to be simple, the concepts they carry are quite sophisticated.

4 - 6 This book can serve as an introduction to economic conditions in South Africa in a regional study of Africa. Students and the teacher can compare photographs of South Africa with the author's illustrations. Students can research the location and climate of South Africa, its history, types of mines in South Africa, and apartheid. Isadora has written another book set in South Africa, *Over the Green Hills* (1992). (Social Studies: Location; Place; Movement)

Jr/Sr High Students can research apartheid in greater depth, the international reaction to it, and its economic repercussions. (Social Studies; World History: Location; Place; Movement)

Isadora, Rachel. 1992. **Over the Green Hills.** New York: Greenwillow Books.

Young Zolani and his mother are going to visit Grandma Zindzi. The walk is many miles across the Transkei countryside on the east coast of South Africa. The story describes the flora, fauna, and human activities in this part of the country. Brilliant full-page color illustrations enhance the text.

K - 3 Young students can compare Zolani's trip to his grandmother's with their own travel experiences. Students and the teacher can locate South Africa on a map or globe. (Social Studies: Location; Place)

4 - 6 This book can be useful in a study of Africa. When combined with *At the Crossroads* (Isadora 1991), students can begin to explore the uniqueness of South Africa and its political situation. (Social Studies: Location; Place; Regions)

Jr/Sr High The author's note about Transkei's political status can trigger research into the many political issues that have led to unrest in South Africa. (World History: Location; Place)

Jakobsen, Kathy. 1993. **My New York.** New York: Little, Brown.

Becky, a young New Yorker, takes the reader and a friend from the Midwest on a tour of her favorite places in the city. Among these are Central Park, the Empire State Building, and New York Harbor. The detailed, full-color illustrations are oil paintings on canvas. The endpapers are detailed maps of Manhattan. The author provides a guide at the end of the book to the places mentioned in the text.

K - 3 The exquisitely detailed drawings and the author's explanation at the end of the book can lead to wonderful discussions about how large cities, and specifically New York City, function. Maps of New York City and its burroughs can be compared to the author's endpapers. The endpaper map can be used with Levinson's *I Go with My Family to Grandma's* (1992). (Social Studies: Location; Place; Regions)

4 - 6 This book is a good addition to a study of New York City. Many other books can also contribute to such a study. A few of them are *The Story of the Statue of Liberty* (Maestro and Maestro 1989), *Pop! Goes the Weasel and Yankee Doodle* (Quackenbush 1976), and *The Legend of New Amsterdam* (Spier 1979). Students may want to research one of the places noted at the end of the book. Correspondence with the Chamber of Commerce might glean further information about New York City. Using the author's "gimmick" of writing to a friend, students can write a letter describing their own community and its places of interest. Perhaps the class might coordinate the writing and illustrating to create a class book about their own community. (Social Studies; Language Arts: Location; Place; Regions)

Jr/Sr High Older students can explore New York City's status as an internationally known city, with special attention paid to the United Nations, the airports, and the seaport. The history of New York City can enlighten students' understanding of the importance of a city's location. (Social Studies; Language Arts: Location; Place; Human-Environmental Relations; Movement; Regions)

Jeffers, Susan. 1991. **Brother Eagle, Sister Sky: A Message from Chief Seattle.** New York: Dial Books.

Susan Jeffers, the illustrator of this book, has created detailed full-page watercolor drawings to accompany the words of Chief Seattle, a respected leader of a Northwestern Indian Nation in the mid-1850s. His words, which have been translated and rewritten more than once, remind the reader that we must care for our environment or risk losing it.

K - 3 This book can accompany a study of environmental responsibility. Other books that can enhance this study are *A River Ran Wild* (Cherry 1992), *Grandfather's Dream* (Keller 1994), and *The Summer Sands* (Garland 1995). These books can generate discussions about the need for humans to be conscious of their impact on the environment and the possible detrimental effects of irresponsibility. The book can also contribute to a study of Native American culture. Other books that can be used are *And Still the Turtle Watched* (MacGill-Callahan 1991) and *Dreamplace* (Lyon 1993). (Social Studies; Science: Location; Place; Human-Environmental Relations)

4 - 6 Students at this level can pursue the above studies in a more in-depth fashion. Some students may want to experiment with Jeffers's model of illustrating a person's words. (Social Studies; Science; Art: Location; Place; Human-Environmental Relations)

Jr/Sr High no

Joseph, Lynn. 1992. **An Island Christmas.** New York: Clarion Books.

Young Rosie's enthusiasm for the Christmas preparations on her home island of Trinidad is infectious. From the picking of red petals for the sorrel drink to the mixing of the black currant cake, through the singing with the parang band and the celebration at church on Christmas morning, the reader is treated to the sights and sounds of an island Christmas. The full-page watercolor illustrations capture the setting and enhance the text. An author's note at the end of the book provides supporting information about Trinidad and Tobago.

K - 3 This book should be read aloud to students by the teacher to model the reading of the dialect. It provides a beginning place for discussions about dialects and accents within the same language (English). It can also be used in a comparison of December holiday celebrations around the world. Two companion books are *Christmas on the Prairie* (Anderson 1985), which is set in the winter in Indiana, and *Christmas at Long Pond* (George 1992), which is set in the winter in the Pocono Mountains. (Social Studies; Language Arts: Location; Place; Regions)

4 - 6 This book can contribute to a regional study of the Caribbean. Other books set in the Caribbean are *The Day the Hurricane Happened* (Anderson 1974), *How Many Days to America? A Thanksgiving Story* (Bunting 1990), and *Encounter* (Yolen 1992). Students may also be interested in exploring the dialect and music introduced in the text. (Social Studies; Language Arts: Location; Place; Regions)

Jr/Sr High no

Kandoian, Ellen. 1992. **Molly's Seasons.** New York: Cobblehill Books.

Young Molly, who lives in Maine, observes the seasons and wonders if they are the same around the world. The four seasons Molly experiences are presented in the context of the months they include, the weather, and their effects on plants and animals. The simple text is accompanied by watercolor illustrations. The author provides a scientific explanation for the changes in seasons on Earth.

K - 3 This book can be used to begin a discussion of seasonal changes or calendars. Students and the teacher can discuss the contrasts between Maine's and New Zealand's seasons as well as their positions in relation to the equator. Joseph's *An Island Christmas* (1992) can be read and discussed in relation to the seasons and calendar, and compared with the seasons Molly experiences in Maine. *The Reasons for Seasons* (Gibbons 1995) can also be used to help explain Molly's seasons. (Social Studies; Science: Location; Place; Human-Environmental Relations)

4 - 6 no
Jr/Sr High no

*Kandoian, Ellen. 1987. **Under the Sun.** New York: Dodd, Mead.

As young Molly gets ready for bed on the East Coast of the United States, she asks her mother where the sun goes at night. Her mother explains about day and night around the world. The story follows the setting sun from a Mississippi River houseboat, to a beach in Hawaii, and, finally, to a small town in eastern Russia—watercolor illustrations depict the sun's journey.

> **K - 3**   By using a flashlight and a globe with the locations marked, the teacher can demonstrate how the Earth rotates, creating day and night. It is especially important that the teacher not reinforce Molly's phrase "Where does the sun go?" because it perpetuates the misunderstanding of many children—that the sun moves around the Earth. (Science: Human-Environmental Relations)

> **4 - 6**   no

> **Jr/Sr High**   no

Keller, Holly. 1994. **Grandfather's Dream.** New York: Greenwillow Books.

In this story, set in Vietnam after the war, a young boy's grandfather dreams of restoring the wetlands of the Mekong Delta. He particularly hopes that the Sarus cranes that once lived there will return. Classically simple full-page watercolor and pen images provide a strong sense of place. The author's preface and book cover statement add historical information about the Sarus crane and the attempt to restore the wetlands.

> **K - 3**   This book can contribute to a unit on wildlife conservation or environmental responsibility. Older students can research the Sarus crane and Vietnam as well as areas in their own community or region with similar conservation concerns. The environmental repercussions caused by war or changes in land use (e.g., cutting down the rain forests, draining the Everglades) might be explored. A variety of maps should be provided for students to use. (Social Studies; Science: Location; Place; Human-Environmental Relations; Movement)

> **4 - 6**   Older students can expand on the above activities. Closer attention can be paid to the style of the illustrations, which reflect the classic simplicity of Oriental artwork. Prints of Oriental paintings can be examined. Students may wish to create drawings in this style. Photographs of Vietnam can be compared to the author's work. Students may wish to explore the success of the environmental effort "Saving Cranes in Vietnam" and the environmental organization EARTH-WATCH. As the author is concerned about involving children in wildlife conservation, she may be willing to communicate with a student or class about her experiences in Vietnam. This book might also be used in a study of Vietnam and the war. (Social Studies; Science; Art; Language Arts: Location; Place; Human-Environmental Relations; Movement)

> **Jr/Sr High**   Students at this level may wish to complete some of the above activities but at a more in-depth level. (Social Studies; Science; Art; English: Location; Place; Human-Environmental Relations)

Knight, Margy Burns. 1992. **Talking Walls.** Gardiner, ME: Tilbury House.

This book describes walls located in different countries all around the world, from the Great Wall of China to the Berlin Wall, and discusses their significance. The author places children of the past and present at these sites, showing the effect each wall has on them. Large, full-color paintings illustrate each wall. The end of the book has an informative paragraph about each of the 14 walls found in the book. Each wall is located on a world map.

> **K - 3**   The inclusion of children of all ages at each wall makes this book appropriate for a relatively simplistic discussion of walls and their existence around the world. Second- and third-grade students may be ready to consider the psychological issues involved in the creation of walls. Students and the teacher can locate their own position on a world map and then locate the 14 walls. (Social Studies: Location)

> **4 - 6**   Students at this level will be better able to understand the psychological issues involved in the creation of walls. In addition to locating the walls on a world map, students can categorize them by such characteristics as location, date of creation, and purpose. A field trip with the intention of discovering significant local walls might lead to the creation of a class book of "talking walls." Many of the walls in this book have drawings on them that make them special. Students can create drawings using materials or techniques believed to have created the originals. This book also can be used as support for other discussions and units. For example, *Talking Walls* includes the "Great Zimbabwe," which inspired John Steptoe as he illustrated *Mufaro's Beautiful Daughters* (1993). (Art; Language Arts; Social Studies: Location; Place; Human-Environmental Relations; Movement)

Jr/Sr High   Older students may find the walls with a "mystery" particularly interesting and conduct research to uncover more information. Walls representing political separation can be researched, discussed, and debated. (Anthropology; World History: Place; Movement; Human-Environmental Relations)

Krementz, Jill. 1989. **A Visit to Washington, D.C.** New York: Scholastic.

This book features Matt Wilson, age six, who introduces the sights of his beautiful and interesting hometown, Washington, D.C. The text, written as a personal narrative, accompanies photographs of Matt as he tours the city. The endpapers are a simple map of the Washington, D.C., area, with the sights of the book identified at their location.

K - 3   This book provides a model for children to create a photo tour of their own community in addition to providing information about the U.S. capital in an easily understandable format for young children. Older students can conduct research on particular areas of interest. Maps showing Washington, D.C., as a district, not part of a state, can begin a discussion about the uniqueness of this city. (Social Studies; Language Arts: Location; Place; Movement)

4 - 6   This book can be used with others about Washington, D.C., to broaden student understanding about U.S. government and the function of a capital city. The unique status of residents of the District can be explored, especially in relation to what students understand about their own status as residents. The history of Washington, D.C., and the special landmarks can be the source of research conducted individually or in groups. If students in this age level choose to create a photographic tour of their community, they can also create an appropriate map that readers can use to follow the tour. (Social Studies; Language Arts: Location; Place; Human-Environmental Relations; Movement; Regions)

Jr/Sr High   Older students can explore the economic problems facing this city. Other topics of interest might include the special privileges enjoyed by senators and representatives who live for part of the year in the capital city but maintain residency in their own home community. (Social Studies; American Government: Location; Place; Movement)

Kroll, Virginia. 1993. **Africa Brothers and Sisters.** New York: Four Winds Press.

A small boy, Jesse, and his father play a question-and-answer game about people who live in Africa and their relationship to Jesse. Watercolor and colored pencil illustrations show Jesse and his father in the foreground while the African people they are discussing are featured in the background. The author provides additional information in an author's note at the end of the book, along with a pronunciation key and a map of Africa locating Jesse's "brothers and sisters."

K - 3   Students will enjoy the vocabulary words introduced in the context of this book. Used with Muriel Feelings's books—*Jambo Means Hello: Swahili Alphabet Book* (1992) and *Moja Means One: Swahili Counting Book* (1994)—students can examine the African words they have discovered and find where these words would be used regularly. Students and the teacher can discuss the importance of understanding one another and how to facilitate that understanding. (Social Studies; Language Arts: Location; Place; Movement)

4 - 6   This book can provide additional information about the unity and diversity within the African continent. Students involved in a regional study of Africa can use the information in this book to further expand their knowledge of African tribes and tribal life. Students may wish to pursue a personal study of their own "brothers and sisters" beyond the United States. Family trees might be constructed with close attention to *where* other family members lived. (Social Studies: Location; Place; Regions)

Jr/Sr High   no

Kroll, Virginia. 1992. **Masai and I.** New York: Four Winds Press.

When young Linda learns about the Masai in school she says she "feel[s] the tingle of kinship flowing through my veins." As she moves through her life in an American city she imagines how her life would compare if she were a Masai. Linda's life in America and her imagined Masai life in East Africa are illustrated by oil and color pencil paintings. The comparisons and contrasts of American and East African life are enhanced by the fact that the American scene is shown on one page with the East African scene on the other.

K - 3   Students and the teacher can locate Kenya in East Africa on a map. Photos of the area compared with the book's illustrations can be the source of small and large group discussions. The photos and illustrations can be further compared with those in Aardema's *Bringing the Rain to Kapiti Plain* (1992). (Visual Discrimination; Social Studies: Location; Place)

4 - 6 This book can add information about African tribes and tribal life to a unit study of Africa. The author's format might be employed by students who wish to compare life in their own community with life in another part of the world. The diptych art project described in Chapter 2 may serve as an effective vehicle for such a comparison. *A Country Far Away* (Gray and Dupasquier 1991) also compares life in a Western country to an African village. (Social Studies; Language Arts; Art: Location; Place; Human-Environmental Relations; Movement; Regions)

Jr/Sr High No

Kroll, Virginia. 1994. **The Seasons and Someone.** San Diego: Harcourt Brace & Company.

A young Eskimo girl, who refers to herself as "someone" in the old tradition, describes the changes in the seasons in Alaska. The simple text and the rich, full-page paintings tell about the effect of the seasons on everyone: plants, animals, and humans. The author's note at the beginning of the book helps explain the text.

K - 3 This book provides an interesting look at changing seasons because the area is so far north on the globe. Students and the teacher can locate Alaska on a globe and a world map, paying particular attention to the Arctic Circle. Students can compare seasons in their own community as well as living conditions with those of "someone." Older students can compare the way the young girl refers to herself with what is considered an appropriate reference in our own culture. (Social Studies; English; Science: Location; Place; Human-Environmental Relations)

4 - 6 no

Jr/Sr High no

Krupinski, Loretta. 1995. **Bluewater Journal: The Voyage of the Sea Tiger.** New York: HarperCollins.

Twelve-year-old Benjamin Slocum travels with his family from Boston to Honolulu to Hong Kong on the clipper ship *Sea Tiger*. The story, told through Benjamin's journal entries, describes the adventures and hardships of the four-month journey in 1860. Vibrant, full-page paintings enhance the descriptive text. A map of the voyage is included at the beginning of the book, with a short summary of clipper ship history and a glossary included at the end.

K - 3 This book can be used in a unit study of transportation. The details Benjamin includes in his journal entries provide many opportunities for discussion about travel. Another book worth including in such a study is *Across the Wide Dark Sea* (Van Leeuwen 1995). This book, written from the point of view of a young traveler on the *Mayflower* 200 years earlier, provides readers with the opportunity to compare and contrast ocean travel in the 1600s, 1800s, and, perhaps, using travel cruise brochures, the present day. Students can write journal entries modeled after Benjamin's. Students and the teacher can calculate the distances traveled between ports. (Social Studies; Language Arts; Math: Location; Place; Human-Environmental Relations; Movement)

4 - 6 Students at this level can participate in the activities above as well as conduct research on the ports, animals, ships, or other subjects that arise from the reading of this text. (Social Studies; Language Arts; Math: Location; Place; Human-Environmental Relations; Movement)

Jr/Sr High This book might provide an interesting and motivational introduction to a unit study of transportation or American history in the mid- to late 1800s. (Social Studies: Location; Place; Human-Environmental Relations; Movement)

Krupp, Robin Rector. 1992. **Let's Go Traveling.** New York: Morrow Junior Books.

Preteen Rachel Rose urges readers to experience the excitement, surprises, and satisfactions of traveling around the world. This book shares her trip to the prehistoric caves of France, the pyramids of Egypt, the Mayan temples of Mexico, and other ancient wonders of the world. Her impressions, diary entries, and postcards enrich each leg of the journey.

K - 3 This book can be used with young students to identify Rachel Rose's journey on both a map and a globe. The diary entries and postcards provide models for second- and third-grade students working in journals and learning to write friendly letters. *Talking Walls* (Knight 1992) can be used to compare the information about many of the places Rachel Rose visits. (Social Studies; Language Arts: Location; Place; Movement)

4 - 6 Older students can use this book as a model for planning a trip. Rachel Rose's advice about travel preparations and concerns about cost can help students organize their own trips (real or imaginary). Students might invite a travel agent to come to class to provide information about traveling. Some students may find parts of the journey interesting and worthy of research. (Social Studies; Math; Language Arts: Location; Place; Movement)

Jr/Sr High Students at this level can prepare more in-depth trip plans that include the acquisition of a passport and special regulations required for entry into foreign countries. (Social Studies; Language Arts; Math: Location; Place; Movement)

Lasky, Kathryn. 1994. **The Librarian Who Measured the Earth.** Boston: Little, Brown.

Acrylic paintings illustrate this biography of Eratosthenes. The Greek geographer and astronomer, born in Cyrene on the coast of Africa and educated in Athens, accurately measured the circumference of the Earth more than 2,000 years ago. The author offers an informational note at the beginning of the book, along with an afterword. A bibliography cites the resources used by the author and the illustrator.

K - 3 Students will enjoy learning about the accuracy of Eratosthenes's calculations from so many years ago. Because the concept of past history, especially that designated B.C., is difficult for many children to understand, creating a time line can be helpful. Make a time line that places Eratosthenes and the current year at the ends. Mark the centuries B.C. and A.D. in between. Be sure to establish several events within the nineteenth and twentieth centuries so that students can compare the time span between themselves and more current events to the time span between themselves and Eratosthenes's time. Students and the teacher can locate Greece, Libya, and Egypt on a world map. Using a grapefruit to represent Earth, the teacher can help students understand the concepts of latitude and longitude. Felt tip markings can illustrate lines of latitude and longitude as part of a map skills unit. The teacher must, however, stress to these young students that, in reality, the lines are imagined. (Social Studies; Math; Science: Location; Place)

4 - 6 Eratosthenes's model of gathering information from many sources to write a geography book can help students think about their own research methods. In addition to the activities above, this book can contribute to a unit study of Africa and a study of the angle of the sun on the Earth at various locations. (Social Studies; Math; Science: Location; Place; Regions)

Jr/Sr High Older students can examine Eratosthenes's methods and calculations, perhaps considering alternatives—especially how they might be able to complete the task. (Math; Science; Social Studies: Location; Place; Human-Environmental Relations)

*Lee, Jeanne M. 1987. **Ba-Nam.** New York: Henry Holt.

Young Nan is finally old enough to go with her family to the graveyard on Thanh-Minh Day. On Thanh-Minh Day families visit the graves of their ancestors and present them with offerings. Nan is frightened by the old graveskeeper, Ba-Nam. The author has based this book on her childhood experiences in Vietnam.

K - 3 Students will be able to identify with Nan's fear of Ba-Nam. Students and the teacher can discuss Nan's discovery that a person's outward appearance can be deceiving. A world map can be used to locate Vietnam. (Social Studies: Location; Place)

4 - 6 There are now several books available to contribute to a discussion or study of Vietnam, including *The Wall* (Bunting 1990), *The Lotus Seed* (Garland 1993), and *Grandfather's Dream* (Keller 1994). (Social Studies: Location; Place; Movement)

Jr/Sr High Older students can explore historical, cultural, and political topics related to Vietnam. (Social Studies: Location; Place; Movement)

Leigh, Nila K. 1993. **Learning to Swim in Swaziland: A Child's-Eye View of a Southern African Country.** New York: Scholastic.

Nila K. Leigh was eight when she went to live in the southern African country of Swaziland for a year. During that time she wrote to her classmates back in New York City. The book is based on her letters. The text appears to be an eight year old's manuscript. It is accompanied by photographs of Nila and the people she met in Swaziland as well as crayon drawings she created.

K - 3 Although the information Nila provides in her book is not organized in a traditional research framework, it does model sharing information in a written format. Students and the teacher can find Swaziland on a world map and check library references to confirm Nila's facts. Nila encourages readers to try new things despite their fears. This book can be used in a discussion of self-confidence. (Language Arts; Social Studies: Place; Location; Movement; Regions)

4 - 6 This book would be a delightful and informative addition to a study of Africa. Two books set in South Africa and written by Rachel Isadora, *At the Crossroads* (1991) and *Over the Green Hills* (1992), can be used with this book. *Ashanti to Zulu* (Musgrove 1992) looks at the diversity within the African continent. Nila's information about the natives of Swaziland fits very nicely with

Musgrove's work. The photographs are particularly helpful because they provide visual data. Students may wish to model their own research about an African country after the book. (Language Arts; Social Studies: Location; Place; Movement; Regions)

Jr/Sr High Older students can use Nila's book as a model for writing a book to inform readers about a particular country or culture. Students at this level can discuss the newness of the African nations' self-rule. (Social Studies; Language Arts: Place; Location; Movement; Regions)

Leighton, Maxinne Rhea. 1992. **An Ellis Island Christmas.** New York: Penguin Books.

Six-year-old Krysia tells of her family's journey from Poland to the United States to join her father, who has already emigrated. Watercolors illustrate the journey and reunion on Ellis Island. The author provides an informative historical note about Ellis Island at the end of the book.

K - 3 This book can be used in a study of New York City both to examine the significance of its port for immigration and the "layers of history." Students can identify with Krysia's fears and joys. A good companion book is *Watch the Stars Come Out* (Levinson 1995). Students and the teacher can locate Poland and New York City, establishing the approximate length, in both time and miles, of the journey across the Atlantic. (Social Studies; Math: Location; Place; Movement)

4 - 6 Older students can expand the class's knowledge about Ellis Island and immigration policies and regulations in the United States through independent and small group research. Students might keep an imaginary journal telling about the arduous journey. (Social Studies; Language Arts: Location; Place; Movement)

Jr/Sr High Current immigration issues can be explored by students at this level. More in-depth study of the Ellis Island years can also be conducted. (American History: Location; Place; Movement)

Levinson, Riki. 1992. **I Go with My Family to Grandma's.** New York: Puffin Books.

As five cousins and their families arrive by various means of transportation from the five boroughs of New York, Grandma's home in Brooklyn gets livelier and livelier. The colorful, detailed, full-page drawings whimsically present New York City in the early twentieth century.

K - 3 Young students will enjoy the humorous antics of the cousins meeting at Grandma's. The portrait of the extended family found at the end of the story may inspire students to draw a similar portrait of their own families. The book can enhance a unit on transportation. Each cousin is introduced with alliteration, for example, "Bella from Brooklyn" and "Stella from Staten Island." Students might explore ways in which they, too, could create alliterative phrases. *June 29, 1999* (Wiesner 1992) also uses alliterative phrases and could be included here. Second- and third-grade students may be interested in locating the five boroughs on a modern map of New York City. (Art; Language Arts; Social Studies: Location; Movement)

4 - 6 This simple book offers an introduction to the political boundaries drawn within cities. (Social Studies: Regions)

Jr/Sr High no

Levinson, Riki. 1992. **Our Home Is the Sea.** New York: Puffin Books.

A Chinese boy hurries home from school to his family's houseboat in Hong Kong harbor because it's the end of the school year and he'll be able to join his father and grandfather in the family profession, fishing. Subtly colored full-page paintings present the bustling streets of Hong Kong.

K - 3 This book can contribute to a study of big cities. Students and the teacher can locate Hong Kong on a world map. The teacher can provide additional information about Hong Kong's unique physical and political disposition. Another area to explore is the importance of fishing to the Hong Kong economy. (Social Studies: Location; Place)

4 - 6 Older students can conduct research about Hong Kong individually or in small groups as part of a study of big cities. (Social Studies: Location; Place)

Jr/Sr High no

Levinson, Riki. 1995. **Watch the Stars Come Out.** New York: Puffin Books.

This is a gentle good-night story told by a mother to her daughter about a long journey to America many years ago. Soft-edged, full-page color illustrations enhance the text, which conveys the joys and fears of the Atlantic crossing.

K - 3 This book can be used in a study of New York City both to examine the significance of its port for immigration and the "layers of history." A good companion book is *An Ellis Island Christmas* (Leighton 1992). Students can identify with the children's fears and joys. Students and the teacher can estimate how far the ship traveled each of the 23 days of the journey across the Atlantic. (Social Studies; Math: Location; Place; Movement)

4 - 6 Older students can expand the class's knowledge about Ellis Island and immigration policies and regulations in the United States through independent and small group research. Students might keep an imaginary journal of the arduous journey. (Social Studies; Language Arts: Location; Place; Movement)

Jr/Sr High Although the issues related to immigration are appropriate for study, this book is too simplistic for students at this level.

Locker, Thomas. 1993. **Where the River Begins.** New York: Puffin Books.

Two young boys, Josh and Aaron, watch the river that flows past their home and wonder where it begins. They and their grandfather go on a camping trip to find the river's source. Paintings reminiscent of the nineteenth-century landscape tradition document their journey.

K - 3 In a simple fictional form, the author describes the way in which a big river begins. This book can contribute to a basic study of maps and landforms, particularly rivers. Companion books include *A River Ran Wild* (Cherry 1992), *Voices of the River: Adventures on the Delaware* (Cheripko 1993), and *The Amazing Impossible ERIE CANAL* (Harness 1995). (Social Studies: Location; Place)

4 - 6 Although a rather simple story, the geographic content may make this book useful for some older students. (Social Studies: Location; Place)

Jr/Sr High no

Luenn, Nancy. 1990. **Nessa's Fish.** New York: Atheneum.

Nessa and her grandmother catch so many fish that they cannot carry them home, so they store the fish under a pile of rocks and settle in for the night. But Nessa's grandmother becomes sick, forcing Nessa to guard the fish and her grandmother from a fox, wolves, and a bear. The full-page color illustrations bring to life this authentic picture of autumn on the Arctic tundra.

K - 3 This book, used with *The Seasons and Someone* (Kroll 1994), provides an introduction to life on the Arctic tundra in North America and the Eskimo culture. The study can be expanded with a look at the characteristics of the tundra around the world. Students and the teacher can locate the Arctic tundra on a globe and determine what countries and peoples are within the region. (Social Studies; Science: Location; Place; Human-Environmental Relations; Regions)

4 - 6 Although this book is quite unsophisticated, it can be used as an introductory source. Students at this level can research tundra and Eskimo culture more closely. *A Small Tall Tale from the Far Far North* (Sis 1993) is another book that looks at Eskimo culture. Some students may wish to focus on the fragile nature of this environment. (Social Studies; Science: Location; Place; Human-Environmental Relations; Regions)

Jr/Sr High no

Lyon, George Ella. 1993. **Dreamplace.** New York: Orchard Books.

Full-page watercolor paintings contribute to the dreamlike atmosphere of this book about Mesa Verde, Colorado, "where the Anasazi sang and danced and prayed." A young girl visiting the present-day site of the pueblos envisions the way it must have looked 800 years ago when the Anasazi lived there.

K - 3 Although this book can be used to expand the study of western regions of the United States or Native Americans, the teacher needs to be aware that the illustrations depict natives wearing scant clothing and needs to consider the maturity of the students in deciding whether to use this book. (Social Studies: Location; Place)

4 - 6 Older students can research the Anasazi culture, the pueblo, and other issues raised by the simple text. Students may wish to explore the way researchers and historians learn about cultures and people who no longer exist. In a sense, this book contributes to the study of the "layers of history" in a given location. Companion books featuring Native Americans include *And Still the Turtle Watched* (MacGill-Callahan 1991) and *Brother Eagle, Sister Sky: A Message from Chief Seattle* (Jeffers 1991). (Social Studies: Location; Place; Human-Environmental Relations)

Jr/Sr High no

Lyon, George Ella. 1992. **Who Came Down That Road?** New York: Orchard Books.
   A mother and child ponder the past in discussing who might have traveled down an old, old road, looking backwards from pioneers to prehistoric animals. Full-page watercolor paintings illustrate the text.

   K - 3 The simple text in this book can be used to introduce the concept of the "layers of history" particular to a given locality. Second- and third-grade students often study local history, thus discovering the "layers" in their own community. Other books that contribute to such a study include John Goodall's books and *Dreamplace* (Lyon 1993). (Social Studies: Place)

   4 - 6 Students can uncover more local history by interviewing older citizens, reading old newpapers, examining diaries, and visiting local history museums. (Social Studies: Place)

   Jr/Sr High no

MacGill-Callahan, Sheila. 1991. **And Still the Turtle Watched.** New York: Dial Books for Young Readers.
   Long ago an old Indian carved a turtle into a rock on the bluff overlooking the river to watch over the Delaware people. Indeed, with great sadness, the turtle watches destructive changes humans bring as the years pass. Finally, a wise man with a knowing eye and loving heart comes to move the rock with the turtle on the top to a botanical garden in New York City. Full-page, detailed watercolor illustrations enhance the text.

   K - 3 This book can be used with others in a study of Human-Environmental Relations, a study of rivers, or a study of Native Americans. Other useful books include *Grandfather's Dream* (Keller 1994) and *A River Ran Wild* (Cherry 1992). This book might also contribute to a study of the "layers of history" in a given place. (Social Studies; Science: Location; Place; Human-Environmental Relations)

   4 - 6 Older students can conduct more in-depth research of the above topics. If the class lives near New York City, perhaps a field trip that includes a visit to see the turtle can be included. (Social Studies; Science: Location; Place; Human-Environmental Relations)

   Jr/Sr High no

Maestro, Betsy, and DelVecchio, Ellen. 1991. **Big City Port.** New York: Four Winds Press.
   Clear, informative text and colorful, full-page illustrations describe the unceasing activity at a busy seaport. Readers are introduced to all kinds of boats, the wide variety of equipment used to load and unload them, and the police boats and fireboats available to keep the port running smoothly and productively.

   K - 3 Despite the generic nature of the book, it can contribute to a study of specific big cities such as New York City, a general study of big cities, or a study of transportation. (Social Studies: Location; Place; Human-Environmental Relations; Movement)

   4 - 6 The book is very basic but may be helpful, depending on the maturity of the class. (Social Studies: Location; Place; Human-Environmental Relations; Movement)

   Jr/Sr High no

Maestro, Betsy, and Maestro, Guilio. 1990. **Delivery Van: Words for Town and Country.** New York: Clarion Books.
   The reader is introduced to typical town and country words such as *roadside stand, village, dairy farm,* and *marina* as a delivery van and its driver travel through a busy workday. Detailed color drawings enhance the text.

   K - 3 This book can contribute to vocabulary development and group discussions about both town and country. The simplicity of the text and concepts developed make this book best for the youngest children. (Social Studies: Place)

   4 - 6 no

   Jr/Sr High no

Maestro, Betsy, and Maestro, Guilio. 1991. **The Discovery of the Americas.** New York: Lothrop, Lee & Shepard.
   This book discusses both hypothetical and historical voyages of discovery to America by the Phoenicians, Saint Brendan of Ireland, the Vikings, and such later European navigators as Columbus. Additional information at the end of the book includes a table of dates, people of the ancient and early Americas, and interesting voyages. Detailed, panoramic color illustrations enhance the text.

   K - 3 The teacher needs to decide whether this book is too sophisticated for the class. (Social Studies: Location; Movement)

4 - 6 In addition to supporting a study of the Americas, this book can contribute to a study of travel and transportation, the development of exploration, and the interaction of cultures. (Social Studies: Location; Place; Movement; Regions)

Jr/Sr High This book can serve as a springboard to a large unit study of the "discovery of the Americas." Individually and in small groups, students can research the many topics raised in this book and contribute to a broader understanding of what discovery and exploration have meant to the world. (World History; Social Studies; Science: Location; Place; Movement; Regions)

Maestro, Betsy, and Maestro, Guilio. 1986. **Ferryboat.** New York: Thomas Y. Crowell.

The Maestros tell the story of a family who crosses a river on a ferryboat and observes how the ferry operates. Detailed watercolor drawings depict the crossing. The authors' historical note at the end of the book tells the reader about this Connecticut ferry, which has been in operation since 1769.

K - 3 This book can be used in a study of transportation. It also opens a discussion of how humans cross bodies of water. Small groups can research particular ways of crossing water or discover whether ferries are in use in their home state. If so, a field trip might be possible. Other books that can contribute to such studies include *Bridges* (Robbins 1991), *The Amazing Impossible ERIE CANAL* (Harness 1995), *The Random House Book of How Things Are Built* (Brown 1992), and *Stone and Steel* (Billout 1980). (Social Studies: Location; Place; Human-Environmental Relations; Movement)

4 - 6 Older students can conduct more independent and in-depth studies as described above. Students can expand the study of ferries to include those around the world, some of which carry people from one country to another (e.g., across the English Channel). (Social Studies: Location; Place; Human-Environmental Relations; Movement)

Jr/Sr High This book is most likely too simplistic for this age group, but it does offer an introduction to ferry use. (Social Studies: Location; Place; Human-Environmental Relations; Movement)

Maestro, Betsy, and Maestro, Guilio. 1989. **The Story of the Statue of Liberty.** New York: Morrow.

Full-page watercolor illustrations help tell the story of the world's most famous symbol of liberty. This book tells how the statue was conceived by Frederic Auguste Bartholdi and built twice before its dedication in 1886. The authors provide six pages of interesting facts about the statue and its history.

K - 3 This book can contribute to a study of New York City, particularly the harbor area. This book can also expand the use of *An Ellis Island Christmas* (Leighton 1992) and *Watch the Stars Come Out* (Levinson 1995), both of which describe the journey and arrival of immigrant children to America after a long ocean voyage. (Social Studies: Location; Place; Movement)

4 - 6 Older students can conduct more in-depth research on Bartholdi and the Statue of Liberty. An examination of Bartholdi's building methods can enable students to create their own sculptures. Students may also wish to explore the multitude of events undertaken in the United States in 1976 to celebrate the country's 200th birthday. (Social Studies; Art: Location; Place; Human-Environmental Relations)

Jr/Sr High no

Maestro, Betsy, and Maestro, Guilio. 1990. **Taxi: A Book of City Words.** New York: Clarion Books.

The reader is introduced to such typical city words as *theatre, museum, office building,* and *train station* as a taxi travels through a hectic workday in and around the city. Detailed color drawings enliven the text.

K - 3 This book can contribute to vocabulary development and group discussions about big cities. The simplicity of the text and concepts developed make this best for the youngest children. A companion book is *Delivery Van: Words for Town and Country* (1990), also written by the Maestros. (Language Arts; Social Studies: Place; Movement)

4 - 6 no

Jr/Sr High no

Mellecker, Judith. 1991. **Randolph's Dream.** New York: Alfred A. Knopf.

In the summer of 1940, seven-year-old Randolph Pearce misses his father and dreams of flying away. In full-page color illustrations he soars out of his bedroom window and flies over the English village where he's staying to avoid the dangers of London. One night he flies farther than before and visits his father, who is stationed with the British forces in North Africa.

K - 3 Older students will enjoy the mix of fact and fantasy in this book. When Randolph flies for the first time, he gets a bird's-eye view of the town. The students can imagine their own flight above their classroom, home, school, neighborhood, or town and draw it in map form. On a map of Europe and the Mediterranean Sea the students and the teacher can trace Randolph's flight from England to North Africa. A discussion about the contrast between the climates of England and North Africa can be helpful. Ringgold's two books, *Aunt Harriet's Underground Railroad in the Sky* (1992) and *Tar Beach* (1991), both contain main characters who fly. (Social Studies: Location; Place; Movement)

4 - 6 In addition to the above activities, this book can be used in a study of World War II. It provides an introduction to the war in North Africa, which caused special difficulty for the Allied troops, as well as introduces the way the British attempted to protect their children during the war. Two of John Goodall's books, *The Story of a Farm* (1989) and *The Story of the Seashore* (1990), also show some of the impact the war had on England. The effect of World War II on children can be discussed through the use of this book, as well as *Rose Blanche* (Innocenti 1985) and *Sadako* (Coerr 1993). *The Whispering Cloth: A Refugee's Story* (Shea 1995) is also about war's effects on children. (Social Studies: Location; Place; Movement; Human-Environmental Relations)

Jr/Sr High Students can pursue the above activities in greater depth. (Social Studies: Location; Place; Movement; Human-Environmental Relations)

Munro, Roxie. 1994. **Christmastime in New York City.** New York: Puffin Books.

This book presents panoramic drawings of various sights in New York City during the Christmas season. The detailed, color, full-page illustrations include the Thanksgiving Day Parade, decorated shop windows, and the New Year's Eve celebration in Times Square. Paragraphs included at the end of the book provide historical information.

K - 3 This book can be a part of a study of big cities or New York City in particular. Used in conjunction with Jakobsen's *My New York* (1993) or Munro's *The Inside-Outside Book of New York City* (1994), students can get a clearer look at special sights in New York City. (Social Studies: Location; Place)

4 - 6 This book can be used as part of a study of big cities or New York City in particular. Students can explore the question of why merchants create such expansive displays at this time of year. (Social Studies: Location; Place)

Jr/Sr High no

Munro, Roxie. 1989. **The Inside-Outside Book of London.** New York: E. P. Dutton.

Detailed, full-page, color drawings of sights in London are seen from the outside and inside. Among the sights are the Houses of Parliament, the Tower of London, and Waterloo Station. The author has included a section at the back of the text that provides information about each of the sights.

K - 3 This book offers the reader an unusual tour of London, looking at the outside of the building, then the inside. It provides the teacher of younger children with the opportunity to introduce a discussion of their position in space (location) using relative terms: *above, below, near, far,* etc. Older students can use this book as a model for drawing the inside-outside views of locations with which they are familiar. (Social Studies; Art: Location; Place)

4 - 6 This book can contribute to a study of big cities, or London specifically. Students at this level may also wish to create their own inside-outside drawings. (Social Studies; Art: Location; Place; Regions)

Jr/Sr High no

Munro, Roxie. 1994. **The Inside-Outside Book of New York City.** New York: Puffin Books.

This book offers detailed, full-page, color drawings of famous New York City sights. Each sight is presented from both the inside and outside. Explanatory paragraphs, found at the end of the book, provide interesting historical and statistical information about each sight.

K - 3 This book offers the reader an unusual tour of New York City, looking at the outside of the building, then the inside. It provides the teacher of younger children with the opportunity to introduce a discussion of their position in space (location) using relative terms: *above, below, near, far,* etc. Older students can use this book as a model for drawing the inside-outside views of locations with which they are familiar. (Social Studies; Art: Location; Place)

4 - 6   This book can contribute to a study of big cities, or New York City specifically. Students at this level may also wish to create their own inside-outside drawings. (Social Studies; Art: Location; Place; Regions)

Jr/Sr High   no

Munro, Roxie. 1993. **The Inside-Outside Book of Washington, D.C.** New York: Puffin Books.

This book offers detailed, full-page, color drawings of famous Washington, D.C., sights. Each sight is presented from both the inside and outside. Explanatory paragraphs, found at the end of the book, provide interesting historical and statistical information about each sight.

K - 3   This book offers the reader an unusual tour of our nation's capital, looking at the outside of the building, then the inside. It provides the teacher of younger children with the opportunity to introduce a discussion of their position in space (location) using relative terms: *above, below, near, far,* etc. Older students can use this book as a model for drawing the inside-outside views of locations with which they are familiar. (Social Studies; Art: Location; Place)

4 - 6   This book can contribute to a study of big cities, or Washington, D.C., specifically. Students at this level may also wish to create their own inside-outside drawings. (Social Studies; Art: Location; Place; Regions)

Jr/Sr High   no

Musgrove, Margaret. 1992. **Ashanti to Zulu.** New York: Puffin Books.

This collection of vignettes, accompanied by detailed color drawings, introduces the reader to 26 African tribes through the depiction of a custom important to each. The 26 tribes are located on an African map at the end of the book.

K - 3   This book would be a good secondary source of information when sharing Virginia Kroll's two books, *Africa Brothers and Sisters* (1993) and *Masai and I* (1992). Students may want to learn more about specific African people through research and then share their discoveries in oral or written form. (Language Arts; Social Studies: Location; Place; Human-Environmental Relations; Movement; Regions)

4 - 6   This book can provide a wonderful introduction to a unit on Africa, particularly its rich diversity, which we often miss. Among the books that can contribute to such a study are *The Fortune-Tellers* (Alexander 1992), *At the Crossroads* (Isadora 1991), *Over the Green Hills* (Isadora 1992), and *Panther Dream: A Story of the African Rain Forest* (Weir and Weir 1991). (Social Studies; Language Arts: Location; Place; Human-Environmental Relations; Movement; Regions)

Jr/Sr High   Older students may wish to conduct more in-depth research into one or many of the tribes. Crafts created in the tradition of a given tribe can help expand the understanding of cultural traditions. (Art; Social Studies; World History: Location; Place; Human-Environmental Relations; Movement; Regions)

Polacco, Patricia. 1994. **Pink and Say.** New York: Philomel Books.

Sheldon Russell Curtis, "Say," was wounded in a fierce battle in Georgia during the Civil War. Pinkus ("Pink") Aylee, a Black Union soldier, found him and took him home to be nursed back to health. On their way back to their own companies, the two teens were captured by the Confederates and taken to the Andersonville prison. This true story has been passed from great-grandfather to grandmother, to son, and finally to the author-artist, who passes it on to the reader and dedicates it to the memory of Pinkus Aylee.

K - 3   This book can be used in a regional study of the southeastern states. Students and the teacher can locate the state of Georgia and the infamous Andersonville prison. The book provides beginning places for discussions about various aspects of the Civil War, particularly the young age of many of the soldiers. Students can discuss oral history, sharing some of their own family stories passed down through generations. Other books to use in this study are *Aunt Harriet's Underground Railroad in the Sky* (Ringgold 1992) and *Nettie's Trip South* (Turner 1987). (Language Arts; Social Studies: Location; Place; Movement)

4 - 6   Older students, in addition to the activities above, may wish to research the role of Black soldiers in the Civil War (they can view the movie *Glory*), Abraham Lincoln, the states involved in the conflict, the many reasons for the war, as well as Andersonville and other war prisons. (Social Studies; Language Arts: Location; Place; Movement)

Jr/Sr High Students at this level can explore the role of Black soldiers in U.S. conflicts at home and abroad. Students might compare prison camps written about in past history with those associated with more recent conflicts in the world. Two books dealing with children and World War II prison camps are *Rose Blanche* (Innocenti 1985) and *Let the Celebrations BEGIN!* (Wild 1991). *The Bracelet* (Uchida 1993) focuses on the Japanese internment camps in the United States during World War II. (American History; World History; Current Events: Location; Place; Movement)

Provensen, Alice, and Provensen, Martin. 1983. **The Glorious Flight.** New York: Viking.

This book tells of Louis Bleriot's obsession with flying and his daring flight across the English Channel in 1909. The story is told through simple text and detailed color paintings.

K - 3 Students and the teacher can locate Cambrai, France; the English Channel; and the "white cliffs of Dover" on a map or globe. Older students can calculate the distance of the flight and, with the teacher's help, calculate the rate of speed. *Flight* (Burleigh 1991), which documents Lindbergh's flight 18 years later, can be examined and compared with Bleriot's flight. (Social Studies; Math: Location; Place; Human-Environmental Relations; Movement)

4 - 6 In addition to the above activities, students at this level can learn more about Bleriot and his other inventions, the phenomenon of the Dover cliffs, and the history of aviation. (Social Studies; Math; Science: Location; Place; Human-Environmental Relations; Movement)

Jr/Sr High no

Provensen, Alice, and Provensen, Martin. 1987. **Shaker Lane.** New York: Viking Kestrel.

This book tells the story of how a rural community begins by chance and is changed by the construction of a new reservoir. The Provensens introduce the reader to the houses and their inhabitants along Shaker Lane through descriptive text and detailed, full-color illustrations.

K - 3 This book provides a look at how communities develop and change. It can be used with John Goodall's series of books, each of which covers a longer time period, as well as Beekman's *Forest, Village, Town, City* (1982) and Spier's *The Legend of New Amsterdam* (1979). The map at the beginning of the book helps the reader "see" how the houses in the community are related. This book can be used in a map skill study. Students can create a map of the area immediately surrounding their school. (Social Studies: Place; Location)

4 - 6 In addition to the above activities, older students can research reservoirs and their function. Students living in a community in which there is a reservoir may be able to visit it as a class or invite a guest speaker to explain how it functions in the community. (Social Studies: Place; Location)

Jr/Sr High no

Provensen, Alice, and Provensen, Martin. 1994. **Town and Country.** Orlando, FL: Harcourt Brace.

Detailed illustrations accompany text that describes a bustling town with its restaurants, stores, museums, and ports. The book concludes with scenes of the farmhouses, general stores, lush fields, and winding roads. The authors have cleverly arranged the text physically to suit the place: vertically in the city, horizontally in the country.

K - 3 This book can be an important part of a class study of where people live. It offers strong contrasts and opens the door to discussions about where students live, particularly if they live in either the city or country as described by the Provensens. Companion books for a study of city and country include *Forest, Village, Town, City* (Beekman 1982), *Big City Port* (Maestro and DelVecchio 1991), *Delivery Van: Words for Town and Country* (Maestro and Maestro 1990), and *Taxi: A Book of City Words* (Maestro and Maestro 1990). (Social Studies: Place)

4 - 6 Older students might explore why the text uses the term "Western world" to qualify the description of the city and country and what its alternative is. Books that contrast Western life with African life are *A Country Far Away* (Gray and Dupasquier 1991), *Africa Brothers and Sisters* (Kroll 1993), and *Masai and I* (Kroll 1992). (Social Studies: Place)

Jr/Sr High no

*Quackenbush, Robert. 1976. **Pop! Goes the Weasel and Yankee Doodle.** Philadelphia: J. B. Lippincott.

This book illustrates the two popular songs of the Revolutionary era. The author provides a historical note about the songs' origins in a preface. In the book he provides illustrations of historical sites in New York City in 1776 and 1976 as accompaniment to the songs' words. Two maps at the end of the book locate the sites, and short paragraphs describe them.

K - 3 Students will enjoy learning the songs and their historical background. Students and the teacher can compare the author's illustrations with photos of the same landmarks. (Social Studies; Music: Location; Place)

4 - 6 This book can be used as a part of a study of big cities or New York City specifically. Older students may enjoy the political nature of the songs' words and attempt to create additional verses that reflect current politics. (Social Studies; Music: Location; Place)

Jr/Sr High Students at this level may enjoy watching videotapes of Mark Russell, the political satirist, who creates new lyrics for familar tunes. Individually or in small groups, students can create political songs. (Music; Current Events; Social Studies: Location; Place; Movement)

Ringgold, Faith. 1992. **Aunt Harriet's Underground Railroad in the Sky.** New York: Crown.

Fictional characters Cassie and her brother, Be Be, encounter historical figure Harriet Tubman as they soar through the skies. Within this fantasy adventure, the author shares information about the Underground Railroad and Harriet Tubman's life. Rich, full-page, color paintings enhance the text. The author provides a biographical profile of Tubman at the end of the book, along with a map of the Underground Railroad routes and sources for further reading.

K - 3 This book can be included in a regional study of the United States. It provides a beginning place for a discussion of slavery, civil rights, or the Civil War. Students living in areas where there were Underground Railroad stations might discover more about the local stop. (Social Studies: Location; Place; Movement)

4 - 6 In addition to the above activities, students can write diary entries to document imaginary trips on the Underground Railroad or the life of a conductor. Some students may wish to discover more about Harriet Tubman. Other books that deal with the Civil War or slavery are *Pink and Say* (Polacco 1994) and *Nettie's Trip South* (Turner 1987). (Social Studies; Language Arts: Location; Place; Movement)

Jr/Sr High Students at this level can conduct more in-depth research on the above topics. (Social Studies; Language Arts: Location; Place; Movement)

Ringgold, Faith. 1991. **Tar Beach.** New York: Crown.

Based on her own childhood memories of Harlem and her story quilt, *Tar Beach,* the author-artist tells the story of eight-year-old Cassie Louise Lightfoot, who dreams of flying over New York City. As the adults play cards, Cassie and her younger brother, Be Be, lie on a mattress on their apartment building's rooftop and "fly" over the important places in the city. Full-page color paintings are integral to the story.

K - 3 Students will enjoy Cassie's flights over the city. They may enjoy envisioning their own flight in their local community. In *Randolph's Dream* (Mellecker 1991), Randolph also makes flights, which eventually become heroic. The book can be used in a study of big cities or New York City in particular. Students can use a map of New York City to locate Harlem and the important landmarks Cassie visits on her flight, particularly the George Washington Bridge. Companion books for this study include *My New York* (Jakobsen 1993), *I Go with My Family to Grandma's* (Levinson 1992), *An Ellis Island Christmas* (Leighton 1992), and *The Inside-Outside Book of New York City* (Munro 1994). (Social Studies; Art: Location; Place; Movement; Regions)

4 - 6 Older students can explore the author's unique story quilt. A page at the end of the book provides biographical and artistic information that the teacher and students can use to begin their own study of quilts, the African-American folktale motif of "flying" to freedom, or the whole issue of slavery. Ringgold's other book, *Aunt Harriet's Underground Railroad in the Sky* (1992), also involves flight, both real and imagined. The author may be willing to communicate with students via letters, or students may wish to learn more about Ringgold and her artwork. (Social Studies; Art: Location; Place; Movement; Regions)

Jr/Sr High Although this book is quite unsophisticated, the informational page at the end of it raises some very interesting topics worth exploring. Of particular interest is the introduction of the "flying" motif seen in African American folktales. Students may wish to undertake the study of folktales, comparing and contrasting motifs and other characteristics. (English; Social Studies: Location; Place; Movement; Regions)

*Rius, Maria, and Parramon, J. M. 1986. **Let's Discover the City.** New York: Childrens Press/Choice.

Very simplistic descriptions of the elements of a city are presented, along with colorful drawings. A guide for parents and teachers appears at the end of the text. The evolution of cities and their good and bad aspects are the guide's focus.

> **K - 3** This book is appropriate for the very youngest students as they are introduced to the characteristics of cities. (Social Studies: Place)

> **4 - 6** no

Jr/Sr High no

*Rius, Maria, and Parramon, J. M. 1986. **Let's Discover the Countryside.** New York: Childrens Press/Choice.

This book presents very elementary descriptions of the fields, gardens, crops, and livestock of the country. A guide for parents and teachers appears at the end of the text. The guide explores the often unseen work involved in farming.

> **K - 3** This book is appropriate for the very youngest students as they are introduced to the country. (Social Studies: Place)

> **4 - 6** no

Jr/Sr High no

*Rius, Maria, and Parramon, J. M. 1986. **Let's Discover the Mountains.** New York: Childrens Press/Choice.

This book describes, in very elementary text, mountains, the plants and animals that live on them, and the many pleasures they offer. A guide for parents and teachers appears at the end of the book. The focus of the guide is the ways mountains have influenced human life.

> **K - 3** This book is appropriate for the very youngest students as they are introduced to mountains. (Social Studies: Place; Human-Environmental Relations)

> **4 - 6** no

Jr/Sr High no

*Rius, Maria, and Parramon, J. M. 1986. **Let's Discover the Seaside.** New York: Childrens Press/Choice.

This book describes, in very elementary terms, the seaside, including the physical characteristics, plants, animals, and activities located there. A guide for parents and teachers appears at the end of the book. The focus of the guide is the fishing industry and tourism, which are the main activities of the seaside.

> **K - 3** This book is appropriate for the very youngest students as they are introduced to the seaside. (Social Studies: Place; Human-Environmental Relations)

> **4 - 6** no

Jr/Sr High no

Robbins, Ken. 1991. **Bridges.** New York: Dial Books.

Fourteen bridges, from the simple log bridge to long suspension bridges, are described in this book. The author includes both the physical description and the purpose of each bridge. The illustrations are hand-tinted photographs. A list at the end of the book gives the location of the bridges, all of which are in Connecticut, Massachusetts, New York, or New Jersey.

> **K - 3** This book can contribute to a study of transportation. Students can conduct a community search for the various types of bridges found in the text. Students and the teacher can use state maps to locate the bridges identified in the book to determine how long they are and what body of water they span. (Social Studies; Math: Location; Human-Environmental Relations; Movement)

> **4 - 6** In addition to the above activities, older students can build bridges using toothpicks, craft sticks, or other construction materials according to the information given in the text. Some bridges may require further research. Other books to complement this project are *Stone and Steel* (Billout 1980) and *The Random House Book of How Things Are Built* (Brown 1992). Students can duplicate the author's technique in producing the illustrations by coloring photocopies of photographs with colored pencils. (Social Studies; Science; Art: Location; Place; Human-Environmental Relations; Movement)

Jr/Sr High Physics students often participate in bridge-building contests. This book can be used to introduce and enhance a study preceeding such as a contest. Students in art or photography courses can explore the author's technique of hand-tinting photographs. (Physics; Art; Photography: Location; Place; Human-Environmental Relations; Movement)

Sanders, Scott Russell. 1989. **Aurora Means Dawn.** New York: Bradbury Press.

After traveling from Connecticut to Ohio in 1800 to start a new life in the settlement of Aurora, the Sheldons find that they are the first family to arrive. They realize they will be starting a new community by themselves, with the help of the residents in the nearby village of Hudson. Rich, full-page, watercolor paintings capture the story's mood.

K - 3 This book can be used in a study of the westward movement in the United States. The difficulties encountered by pioneers are also seen in Brett Harvey's books, *Cassie's Journey: Going West in the 1860s* (1995), *My Prairie Christmas* (1990), and *My Prairie Year* (1993), and Turner's *Dakota Dugout* (1985). Students and the teacher can locate Aurora and Hudson, Ohio, on a map of Ohio. The author has written a collection of 50 brief tales about the settling of the Ohio River Valley, called *Wilderness Plots,* which includes this text. The teacher can secure a copy of the book and read it to the class. (Social Studies; Language Arts: Location; Place; Movement)

4 - 6 In addition to the above activities, older students can explore the way the author created the stories (see the author's note at the end of the book). If there is a local historical museum, either the class could take a field trip to look a memorabilia or a representative from the museum could visit the class. Based on the experience, students, like the author, can create a tale about the settling of the local community. (Social Studies; Language Arts: Location; Place; Movement)

Jr/Sr High no

Say, Allen. 1989. **The Bicycle Man.** Boston: Houghton Mifflin.

In this autobiographical book, Allen Say tells about a special day in his school in post–World War II Japan. Two American soldiers stationed nearby add an exciting finale to the children's Sportsday. Delicate pen drawings complement the text.

K - 3 This book connects the past and present as well as American and Japanese culture as the reader learns about "Sportsday," which is similar to typical "field day" activities. Students and the teacher can locate Japan and the city of Yokohama on a map. They can use a topographical map to discover the position of the mountains in relation to the coast in Japan. Students can find other parts of the story in which they can compare and contrast the two cultures. Students might consider what school experience they have had that would be worth telling to their children or writing about in a book. Another book that is set in Yokohama and tells about Japanese-American relationships is *How My Parents Learned to Eat* (Friedman 1987). (Language Arts; Social Studies: Location; Place; Movement)

4 - 6 Older students can discuss why the students in the book had never seen Americans before, what the author's apprenticeship at age 12 meant, and how the Japanese were able to farm on the mountainside. *The Bracelet* (Uchida 1993) tells of a young Japanese American girl who is placed in an internment camp in the United States during World War II. Students can discover what events led to formation of such camps. (History; Social Studies: Location; Place; Human-Environmental Relations; Movement)

Jr/Sr High no

Say, Allen. 1993. **Grandfather's Journey.** Boston: Houghton Mifflin.

Using full-page color paintings and limited text, Say, a Japanese American, shares reminiscences of his grandfather's life in the United States and Japan. Say, too, loves both countries and describes the strong and constant desire to be in the two places at once.

K - 3 Used with Friedman's *How My Parents Learned to Eat* (1987) and Say's *The Bicycle Man* (1989), this book can provide an introduction to a unit about diversity and cross-cultural experiences. Students and the teacher can use a map to discover how far apart Say's two countries are located. (Social Studies: Location; Place; Movement)

4 - 6 The time period covered by this book would be a good focus in studying it: determining just when Grandfather came to the United States, returned to Japan, and when Allan Say came to the United States. Using this book with Say's *The Bicycle Man* (1989), students can begin to see the effects of World War II on the two countries. *The Bracelet* (Uchida 1993) can be used to introduce discussion of the Japanese internment camps established in the United States during World War II. Interestingly, Say actually refers to the war only fleetingly in both books. (Social Studies; Math: Location; Place; Movement)

Jr/Sr High Students at this level can explore the complicated relationship between the Japanese and American cultures over the centuries. Some students may be interested in learning more about the internment camps set up during World War II to detain Japanese Americans. Uchida's *The Bracelet* (1993) can be used in such a study. Recently, artwork produced in these camps has been exhibited. Students may wish to locate photographs or newspaper and magazine accounts of the artwork. (Social Studies; World History; Art: Location; Place; Movement)

*Scarry, Huck. 1982. **Balloon Trip.** Englewood Cliffs, NJ: Prentice-Hall.

The author describes the history and techniques of ballooning while on a hot-air balloon trip in Europe. Detailed black-and-white drawings offer a bird's-eye view of the world while airborne on moving currents in the balloon.

K - 3 Students will enjoy listening to Scarry's adventures in a hot-air balloon as well as all the information he provides in a whimsical style. The drawings and diagrams help to make the text all the more interesting. Students can attempt to draw from a bird's-eye view perspective. Topographic maps of the area of Scarry's trip can be consulted to verify his drawings. Students and the teacher may want to try constructing and flying their own hot-air balloons, as described by Scarry. This book can help demonstrate the scientific principles that cause a balloon to ascend and descend. A member of a local ballooning club may be invited to speak to the class, or a field trip to a hot-air balloon company or launch site might be possible. (Social Studies; Science; Art: Location; Place; Human-Environmental Relations; Movement)

4 - 6 In addition to the above activities, older students can work independently in small groups to construct hot-air balloons to be flown outside later. (Social Studies; Science: Location; Place; Human-Environmental Relations; Movement)

Jr/Sr High Students at this level can conduct similar experiments. (Social Studies; Science: Location; Place; Human-Environmental Relations; Movement)

Schmid, Eleonore. 1994. **The Water's Journey.** New York: North-South Books.

Softly colored, full-page illustrations accompany a simple explanation of the water cycle. The text connects the water cycle with landforms and the important role water plays in supporting life on Earth.

K - 3 This book can contribute to a study of the water cycle, a unit on rivers, or even pollution. Students and the teacher can examine local maps to determine the source of water in local streams and rivers. (Science; Social Studies: Place; Human-Enviornmental Relations)

4 - 6 no

Jr/Sr High no

Scott, Ann Herbert. 1993. **Cowboy Country.** New York: Clarion Books.

Beautifully detailed, full-page watercolor illustrations accompany the lyrical text in this book about the life of the cowboy. A young boy has the opportunity to find out what it's like to be a cowboy (or buckaroo) on a pack trip to Devil's Canyon. The text of this book is actually the monologue of the old-timer who guides and protects the boy. He provides the reader with a glimpse of current practices and a look back at what it meant to be a cowboy years ago.

K - 3 This book can be used in a comparison study of town and country. It may also contribute to a look at the "layers of history" in a given place because the narrator of the book tells about how the same land was used in the past. (Social Studies: Location; Place; Human-Environmental Relations)

4 - 6 no

Jr/Sr High no

Shea, Pegi Deitz. 1995. **The Whispering Cloth: A Refugee's Story.** Honesdale, PA: Boyds Mills Press.

Little Mai loves to sit with the older women as they stitch and talk, talk and stitch. They tell stories of their past lives in Laos and the past lives of their grandmothers in China 100 years ago. The *pa'ndau* story cloths they are stitching tell these stories as well. Mai's grandmother teaches her to stitch, and she, too, creates a *pa'ndau* story cloth that tells her story. The author has provided a map to locate the real refugee camp where the fictional Mai lives and a limited glossary to aid the reader in understanding the Laotian words included in the text.

K - 3 The story is most enchanting and can provide a model for interested students to tell a story in illustration form and then translate it into embroidery. Depending on the maturity of your students, this book can be used to discuss the effect wars have on children and their families. Locate the map found in the book on a world map to allow students to see where this story takes place in relation to where they live. Other books that may contribute to such a study are *The Bracelet* (Uchida 1993), *Randolph's Dream* (Mellecker 1991), and *Let the Celebrations BEGIN!* (Wild 1991). (Language Arts; Art; Social Studies: Location; Place; Movement)

4 - 6 In addition to the above activities, older students can include this book in a study of the Vietnam War. Mai and her family are Hmong people who were forced by Laotian Communists to flee their homeland in Laos because they fought alongside the Americans in Vietnam and Laos. Other books to accompany this story are *The Wall* (Bunting 1990), *Grandfather's Dream* (Keller 1994), and *The Lotus Seed* (Garland 1993). (Social Studies: Location; Place; Movement)

Jr/Sr High Students at this level can conduct more in-depth studies of the above topics. (Social Studies: Location; Place; Movement)

Siebert, Diane. 1992. **Heartland.** New York: HarperCollins.

The simple, poetic text evokes the land, animals, and people of the Midwest. Rich, detailed, full-page color paintings enhance the text.

K - 3 This book can contribute to a study of the plains and prairie. Students can compare the paintings to photographs of the Midwest and their own community. The paintings all show vast expanses of space. Students and the teacher can discuss how the illustrator was able to create this illusion. (Social Studies; Visual Discrimination: Place)

4 - 6 In addition to the above activities, the teacher can introduce older students to the use of linear perspective to express spatial relations. Students may wish to create an illustration, using linear perspective, of their own community and write a poem to accompany the illustration. (Social Studies; Language Arts; Art: Place)

Jr/Sr High no

Siebert, Diane. 1993. **Plane Song.** New York: HarperCollins.

The author's lyrical poem is accompanied by full-page, realistic oil paintings. The deceptively simple poetic text introduces the many types of airplanes and their purposes.

K - 3 This book can contribute to a transportation unit, particularly one related to flight. Companion books that focus on flight are *Flight* (Burleigh 1991), *The Glorious Flight* (Provensen and Provensen 1983), and *Balloon Trip* (Scarry 1982). Students can list various types of planes and their purposes. The teacher and students can create a list of important vocabulary words to be researched, such as *girth, Mach 1, turbo props,* and *cockpit.* The paintings place the viewer in a variety of places. Students and the teacher can discuss where the viewer is, using relational terms. (Science; Social Studies; Language Arts; Visual Discrimination: Location; Human-Environmental Relations; Movement)

4 - 6 This book is too simplistic for most students at this level.

Jr/Sr High no

Siebert, Diane. 1991. **Sierra.** New York: Thomas Y. Crowell.

One of the Sierra Nevada Mountains speaks of the beauty and timelessness of herself and her sister peaks. Full-page acrylic paintings accompany the poetic text.

K - 3 The book can contribute to a study of mountains, particularly the Sierra Nevada. Students and the teacher can locate the mountains on a map of California. The physical characteristics of this mountain range can be compared to others in the United States or the world. (Social Studies: Location; Place)

4 - 6 Older students can make the above comparisons independently. Students may wish to create poetic text and illustrations about their own region. (Social Studies: Location; Place)

Jr/Sr High no

Siebert, Diane. 1993. **Train Song.** New York: HarperCollins.

Simple poetic text is enhanced by full-page, softly colored paintings in this book that tells about the journeys of a variety of transcontinental trains. The trains are viewed from the inside and outside.

K - 3   This book can contribute to a transportation unit. The poetic text lends itself to dramatic reading, using the rhythm of the train, speeding and slowing as it passes through town and country. Students and the teacher can locate the specific towns named in the text, determining the direction the train is traveling and the distances between the towns. (Language Arts; Social Studies: Location; Place; Movement)

4 - 6   no

Jr/Sr High   no

Siebert, Diane. 1984. **Truck Song.** New York: Thomas Y. Crowell.
   The very simple rhyming text about transcontinental trucks is enhanced by equally simple, cartoonlike color illustrations.

K - 3   This very simple rhyming text will be useful with the youngest students in a transportation unit. Young students can also look and listen for rhyming words. (Language Arts; Social Studies: Movement)

4 - 6   no

Jr/Sr High   no

Sis, Peter. 1991. **Follow the Dream: The Story of Christopher Columbus.** New York: Alfred A. Knopf.
   A "traditional" look at the life of Christopher Columbus, who overcomes a number of obstacles to fulfill his dream of sailing west to find a new route to the Orient. The unique full-page illustrations done in oil, ink, and watercolor, reflect the fifteenth-century maps that inspired Sis.

K - 3   This is a good book for commemorating Columbus's voyage each Columbus Day. The maps Sis has drawn provide students with a look at early mapmaking and the fifteenth-century concept of the world. Students and the teacher can discuss the problems and rewards in trying new things and making new discoveries. (Social Studies; Science: Location; Movement)

4 - 6   In addition to reflecting on the Columbus voyage, Sis's text provides the opportunity to consider two assumptions of fifteenth-century life: that a son would assume his father's occupation and that the world was flat. Students can create a globe to represent Columbus's vision of the world in which he could sail west from Italy to reach Japan. This book, paired with *Encounter* (Yolen 1992), can lead to discussion and debate about the ethics of "discovering the new world." Ceserani's *Marco Polo* (1977) can be used to introduce Marco Polo's contribution to and influence on European society. Sis reminds the reader that Columbus was influenced by Marco Polo's travels. The author's foreword discusses "walls" in the minds of the fifteenth-century travelers as well as the Iron Curtain, which enclosed his home country of Czechoslovakia. *Talking Walls* (Knight 1992) can be included here to expand a study of "walls." (Social Studies; World History: Location; Place; Movement)

Jr/Sr High   Students at this level can consider the concepts discussed above in greater depth. (Social Studies; World History: Location; Place; Movement)

Sis, Peter. 1993. **Komodo!** New York: Greenwillow Books.
   A young boy who loves dragons goes to the Indonesian island of Komodo in hopes of seeing a real dragon. Full-page illustrations accompany the simple text. Factual information about the Komodo dragon is incorporated into the illustrations as well as in an author's note at the end of the book.

K - 3   After the teacher reads this book to the class, students can be invited to determine what part(s) of the story they believe are fact and which are fiction. Together, students and the teacher can verify the information in encyclopedias and other reference books. Perhaps the librarian can join in an information "scavenger hunt." Students and the teacher can locate the island of Komodo in Indonesia. (Social Studies; Language Arts; Library Skills: Location; Place; Human-Environmental Relationships)

4 - 6   Students at this level can, individually or in small groups, conduct the research listed above. (Social Studies; Language Arts; Library Skills: Location; Place; Human-Environmental Relations)

Jr/Sr High   no

Sis, Peter. 1993. **A Small Tall Tale from the Far Far North.** New York: Alfred A. Knopf.
   Sis tells the tale of Jan Welzl, a folk hero of Czechoslovakia. There is some debate about whether Welzl really existed, but Sis, asserting that he did, recounts Welzl's breathtaking journeys from central Europe to the Arctic regions. Very detailed, full-page color illustrations enhance the text.

K - 3   Students at the higher end of this grade range can use maps and a globe to trace Welzl's route. As he goes up and over the Arctic region, he moves to the south to arrive in Alaska. This is a challenging concept for beginning geographers. Other, simpler books that take place in the Arctic region are *Nessa's Fish* (Luenn 1990) and *The Seasons and Someone* (Kroll 1994). (Social Studies; Science: Place; Location; Human-Environmental Relations; Movement; Regions)

4 - 6   The finely detailed drawings introduce some thought-provoking concepts. As Welzl talks about the arrival of the gold diggers, Sis creates drawings that dramatize the cultural clash between the Eskimos and Western civilization. Students may want to use Sis's illustrations as models for telling a story in thumbnail sketches with captions or adding information to minimal text through detailed drawings. (Social Studies; Science; Art: Place; Location; Human-Environmental Relations; Movement; Regions)

Jr/Sr High   Students at this level can participate in discussions of what exploration meant for the explorer and the "discovered." Yolen's *Encounter* (1992) is another book that introduces this issue. (Social Studies: Place; Location; Movement)

Sorensen, Henri. 1995. **New Hope.** New York: Lothrop, Lee & Shepard.

Young Jimmy loves visiting his grandfather. Each time they visit a statue in the park Jimmy asks, "Who is that man?" His grandfather tells the same story—the story of how Jimmy's great-great-great-grandfather started the town of New Hope because his axle broke. Beautiful full-page acrylic paintings enhance the text.

K - 3   This lovely book provides a look at the growth of a community. Among other books to use in this study are John Goodall's *The Story of . . .* titles, Beekman's *Forest, Village, Town, City* (1982), and Spier's *The Legend of New Amsterdam* (1979). Students and the teacher can gather photographs of their own community "then and now" and learn about the first settlers and other interesting facts about the community's history. (Social Studies; Language Arts: Location; Place; Human-Environmental Relations)

4 - 6   Older students can participate in the above activities. They may also wish to prepare a similar book, based on individual or small group work. (Social Studies; Language Arts: Location; Place; Human-Environmental Relations)

Jr/Sr High   no

Spier, Peter. 1990. **The Erie Canal.** Garden City, NY: Doubleday.

In this illustrated version of the well-loved folk song, set in the early 1850s, the reader travels along the Erie Canal from Albany to Buffalo. Detailed color drawings accompany the text. The author includes a short history of the Erie Canal and the musical score for the song at the end of the book.

K - 3   Students will enjoy learning the song. This book can contribute to a study of transportation. The canal can be located on a New York State map, using the map at the end of the book to help. Students can examine the details to find clues to where the barge is located in each drawing. (Music; Social Studies: Location; Place)

4 - 6   Older students can extend the above activities to include a discussion of why the canal was built, how barges were moved along the canal, and where other canals were built in the United States or other countries. A more recent and more complex treatment of the Erie Canal and its creation is *The Amazing Impossible ERIE CANAL* (Harness 1995). (Music; Social Studies: Location; Place; Movement)

Jr/Sr High · no

Spier, Peter. 1979. **The Legend of New Amsterdam.** Garden City, NY: Doubleday.

Wonderfully detailed color illustrations and humor highlight Spier's portrait of city life on Manhattan Island more than 300 years ago, when it was called New Amsterdam. Readers visit specific places, such as the schoolhouse, the sawmill, and the shipyards, as well as important residents, such as the smith, the carpenter, and the miller.

K - 3   The humorous illustrations belie the sophistication of the text. This book can be useful in a study of big cities or New York City. Second- and third-grade students may enjoy learning more about historic New Amsterdam (New York City). Good companion books to use are *My New York* (Jakobsen 1993) and *I Go with My Family to Grandma's* (Levinson 1992). Students and the teacher can compare the books' maps and illustrations. (Social Studies: Location; Place)

4 - 6   In addition to the above activities, older students may wish to confirm whether Spier's characters are real and how he was able to provide the map of New Amsterdam at the back of the book. This book provides another example of the "layers of history" in a particular locale. (Social Studies; Language Arts; Library Skills: Location; Place; Human-Environmental Relations)

Jr/Sr High   Students at this level can conduct more in-depth research into the history of New York City, including its leading citizens. (Social Studies; Language Arts: Location; Place; Human-Environmental Relations)

Spier, Peter. 1988. **People.** Garden City, NY: Doubleday.

This book celebrates the diversity of the 5 billion people in the world with descriptive text and detailed color illustrations. Spier groups thumbnail drawings to show variations on a theme (such as games, feasts, and religions) and the specific geographic location where each is found.

K - 3   This book can serve as a reference or support source in a unit about diversity. The class can create a class version of this book by creating thumbnail drawings that show the variations on a theme (favorite food, family pet, type of home) that each student represents. (Social Studies; Language Arts: Place)

4 - 6   Older students can discover more about the various types of transportation, rules for games, and clothing introduced in the book. (Social Studies: Place)

Jr/Sr High   no

Spier, Peter. 1992. **The Star-Spangled Banner.** New York: Dell.

To the words of the national anthem, Peter Spier presents a series of detailed color illustrations representing our nation's regions, history, heritage, and historical landmarks of Washington, D.C. Also included is a historical note about how " The Star-Spangled Banner" came to be written.

K - 3   Although the tune is difficult for anyone to master, students can learn to sing the first verse. The map at the end of the book describes the battle that inspired Key. Students and the teacher can locate Baltimore on a map. (Social Studies; Music: Location; Place; Movement)

4 - 6   Again, students can learn to sing the first verse. Students can discuss the reasons why the song's status as our national anthem is reconsidered from time to time. Students may want to survey their peers or adults to discover who would want to change the anthem, to what song, and why. (Social Studies; Music: Location; Place; Movement)

Jr/Sr High   no

Steptoe, John. 1993. **Mufaro's Beautiful Daughters.** New York: Morrow.

The author has created a modern fable of pride before the fall, in keeping with the moral of the folktale that was its inspiration. Mufaro's two daughters, one bad-tempered, one kind and sweet, go before the king, who is choosing a wife. Details of the paintings illustrating the tale were inspired by the ruins of an ancient city in Zimbabwe and the flora and fauna of that region.

K - 3   The universal nature of the story's moral can help students recognize the ways in which humans everywhere are connected. The teacher can provide other examples of the same moral but set in other cultures. Students and the teacher can locate Zimbabwe and South Africa on an African map and a world map as well as a globe. The Great Zimbabwe is one of the walls included in *Talking Walls* (Knight 1992). Students can use it as a cross-reference. (Language Arts; Social Studies: Location; Place; Regions)

4 - 6   This book can be included in a regional study of Africa. Older students can research Zimbabwe and South Africa. The author, who had his first book published when he was quite young, can also be the focus of a study. Students may wish to write Steptoe to discover why he dedicated his book to the children of South Africa. The many issues involved in apartheid can be explored. Isadora has written two books set in South Africa: *At the Crossroads* (1991) and *Over the Green Hills* (1992). (Language Arts; Social Studies; Current Events: Location; Place; Regions)

Jr/Sr High   In addition to the above activities, students can independently gather examples of literature from other cultures that contain this moral. (Language Arts; Social Studies; Current Events: Location; Place; Regions)

Turner, Ann. 1985. **Dakota Dugout.** New York: Macmillan.

A woman tells her granddaughter what it was like to live in a sod house on the Dakota prairie a century ago. The lyrical text tells how she grew accustomed to living in difficult circumstances. Black-and-white line drawings set the mood.

K - 3   Students can imagine the difficulties associated with living on the U.S. plains in the nineteenth century. Other books depicting the plains and prairies include Brett Harvey's *My Prairie Christmas* (1990) and *My Prairie Year* (1993) as well as *Dandelions* (Bunting 1995) and *Going West* (Van Leeuwen 1992). Students and the teacher can locate the Great Plains and the Dakota territory on a map. (Social Studies: Location; Place)

4 - 6   Other texts about the plains can be explored to expand student understanding of how life is influenced by the landform. *A Prairie Alphabet* (Bannatyne-Cugnet 1992) describes the modern Canadian prairies. If possible, students may create a sod wall or other sod structure. (Social Studies: Location; Place; Human-Environmental Relations)

Jr/Sr High   no

Turner, Ann. 1989. **Heron Street.** New York: Harper & Row.

This very simple text cleverly tells the tale of progress. The marsh, the home of the herons, gradually changes as humans farm the land and fill in the wetlands to build homes. Full-page, dreamlike color paintings illustrate the text.

K - 3   This book can best be used as a companion to other books dealing with the issue of humans changing the environment with problematic results. The content of this book is more subtle as it portrays the destruction of the wetlands. Other books to accompany this study are *Grandfather's Dream* (Keller 1994), *A River Ran Wild* (Cherry 1992), and *Everglades: Buffalo Tiger and the River of Grass* (Lourie 1994). (Science; Social Studies: Place; Location; Human-Environmental Relations)

4 - 6   no

Jr/Sr High   no

Turner, Ann. 1987. **Nettie's Trip South.** New York: Macmillan.

Ten-year-old Nettie writes to her friend Addie in Albany, New York, about her trip to Richmond, Virginia, telling her of the sights, smells, and sounds of the pre–Civil War South. She also relates her surprise and distress as she encounters the ugly realities of slavery when she sees a slave auction. This story was inspired by the author's great-grandmother's diary of her trip south in 1859. The soft pencil drawings accompanying the text help set the tone of this book.

K - 3   This book can be used in a study of the southeastern part of the United States. It provides a means of introducing some of the issues of the Civil War to younger students. Students and the teacher can also locate Albany and Richmond on a map. They can then calculate the distance between the two and the time required to travel that distance in 1859 and today. (Social Studies: Location; Place)

4 - 6   Students at this grade level can benefit from the above activities as well as more in-depth study of the Civil War and its complicated issues. *Pink and Say* (Polacco 1994) and *Aunt Harriet's Underground Railroad in the Sky* (Ringgold 1992) are other books to be used. (Social Studies: Location; Place; Movement)

Jr/Sr High   no

Uchida, Yoshiko. 1993. **The Bracelet.** New York: Philomel Books.

This is the story of Emi, a Japanese American girl in the second grade, who is sent with her family to an internment camp during World War II. Following the loss of the bracelet her best friend gave her, Emi proves to herself that she does not need a physical reminder of friendship. Full-page watercolor illustrations capture the poignant story.

K - 3   Students can recall their own memories of past friendships or occasions when they had to part from loved ones. Students and the teacher can locate Japan, San Francisco, Montana, and Utah on a world map or globe. Older students can further discuss the reasons that Japanese Americans were sent to internment camps. (Social Studies: Location; Movement)

4 - 6   Older students can examine the internment camps in greater detail. The author based this book on her personal experience as a Japanese American. Students can write to her to ask about her experiences. Other books that would contribute to a study of Japanese-American relationships include *The Bicycle Man* (Say 1989) and *Grandfather's Journey* (Say 1993). (Social Studies; Language Arts: Location; Movement)

Jr/Sr High   Students at this level can consider the issue of Japanese American internment camps in the larger context of racial prejudice and war hysteria. (Social Studies; Sociology: Location; Movement)

Van Allsburg, Chris. 1982. **Ben's Dream.** Boston: Houghton Mifflin.

One rainy afternoon, young Ben falls asleep with a geography book on his lap. In his dream, the great monuments of the world, which were pictured on the pages of his book, float by Ben's house. Black-and-white line drawings show 10 monuments, including the Statue of Liberty, the Leaning Tower of Pisa, and the Eiffel Tower.

K - 3   Students can participate in a "scavenger hunt" to discover the names and locations of the 10 monuments shown in the drawings. The teacher or librarian might assemble books for use in the classroom, or the students can work in the library during class time. (Social Studies; Library Skills: Location; Place)

4 - 6   Individually or in small groups, students can conduct research into the identity of the monuments and then provide text for the wordless section of the book. (Social Studies; Language Arts: Location; Place)

Jr/Sr High   no

Van Leeuwen, Jean. 1995. **Across the Wide Dark Sea.** New York: Dial Books for Young Readers.

The author retells the story of the *Mayflower*'s journey and the Pilgrims' first year in America from the point of view of nine-year-old Love Brewster, son of William Brewster. Using primary sources for her research, Van Leeuwen's fictionalized account depicts the joys and struggles of this momentous undertaking. Full-page, softly colored illustrations help to set the mood of this book.

K - 3   Young students will enjoy hearing the Pilgrims' story told by a young boy. Older students might welcome the opportunity to write an account of this journey either in diary or journal form. Both groups can trace the Pilgrim journey on maps and globes. (Language Arts; Social Studies: Location; Movement)

4 - 6   Students at this level can consult reference materials to examine the accuracy of Van Leeuwen's text. This book can be used in a more global study of immigration. Other books that enhance this study are *How Many Days to America? A Thanksgiving Story* (Bunting 1990), *An Ellis Island Christmas* (Leighton 1992), and *Watch the Stars Come Out* (Levinson 1995). (Language Arts; Social Studies: Location; Movement)

Jr/Sr High   no

Van Leeuwen, Jean. 1992. **Going West.** New York: Dial Books for Young Readers.

Seven-year-old Hannah and her family leave their home and friends to travel west in a covered wagon. Softly colored, full-page drawings illustrate the text. The story of the family's long journey and first hard winter in the American West is told from Hannah's point of view.

K - 3   This book can be included in a study of regions of the United States (Midwest or prairies), westward movement, or the difficulties of life on the American plains or prairie in the 1800s. Other books that support this study are *Dandelions* (Bunting 1995), *My Prairie Christmas* (Harvey 1990), *Dakota Dugout* (Turner 1985), *Aurora Means Dawn* (Sanders 1989), and *My Prairie Year* (Harvey 1993). *Cassie's Journey: Going West in the 1860s* (Harvey 1995) focuses on the long journey across the continent. Students and the teacher can use maps to locate the states that are part of the plains. Older students can determine where wagon trains began and ended. (Social Studies: Location; Place; Movement)

4 - 6   Students may wish to create a sod wall or other sod structure. Small groups can conduct research to discover what physical difficulties pioneers had to overcome and if these varied from location to location. (Social Studies; Science: Location; Place; Movement)

Jr/Sr High   no

*Ventura, Piero. 1975. **Piero Ventura's Book of Cities.** New York: Random House.

In words and detailed drawings, the author shows how people live, work, travel, and have fun in cities around the world. Included in the tour of cities are Paris, Amsterdam, London, Venice, Stockholm, and Milwaukee.

K - 3   The book can be used as a beginning place for a study of big cities in general or as a source of information about specific world cities. The teacher should read the text aloud to most students at this level and conduct discussions about the concepts and cities presented. Students and the teacher can create a chart of general characteristics of a big city and then identify unique qualities of specific world cities. Books that focus on specific world cities include *The Inside-Outside Book of London* (Munro 1989), *My New York* (Jakobsen 1993), *The Day of Ahmed's Secret* (Heide and Gilliland 1990), *Sami and the Time of the Troubles* (Heide and Gilliland 1992), *Our Home Is the Sea* (Levinson 1992), and *The Moon Was the Best* (Zolotow 1993). The cities discussed in the book can be located on both a globe and a world map to help students recognize the relationship between the two- and three-dimensional representations. (Social Studies: Location; Place)

4 - 6   Older students can participate in the same types of activities as those listed above but with greater independence. Students may wish to tell someone else about their favorite world city by creating a tour of the city's special sites and landmarks through a brochure or friendly letter. (Social Studies: Location; Place)

Jr/Sr High   no

vonTscharner, Renata, and Fleming, Ronald Lee. 1992. **New Providence.** Swedesboro, NJ: Preservation Press.

Six full-color, double-page spreads intricately detail the imaginary but typical American city, New Providence, as it changes over a period of nearly 80 years. The text points out the changes and why they have occurred.

K - 3   This interesting book provides a way to look at the history of one location. Among other books to use in this study are John Goodall's *The Story of . . .* titles, Beekman's *Forest, Village, Town, City* (1982), and Spier's *The Legend of New Amsterdam* (1979). Students and the teacher can gather photographs of their own community "then and now," learn about the first settlers, and research other interesting facts about the community's history. (Social Studies; Language Arts: Location; Place; Human-Environmental Relations)

4 - 6   Older students can participate in the above activities. They may also wish to prepare a similar book, based on individual or small group work. (Social Studies; Language Arts: Location; Place; Human-Environmental Relations)

Jr/Sr High   Students at this level, particularly in drafting and art classes, can combine the "then and now" aspect of the study above with book preparation to prepare an illustrated book about their own community's history. (Social Studies; Language Arts; Drafting; Art: Location; Place; Human-Environmental Relations)

Ward, Lynd. 1992. **The Silver Pony.** Boston: Houghton Mifflin.

In black-and-white illustrations, this wordless book tells the story of a lonely boy living on a Midwestern farm who escapes on the back of a winged pony to faraway places. He visits various regions of the United States, including Alaska, the New England coast, and the American Southwest.

K - 3   As the teacher shows the illustrations, students can tell what is happening. Together, they may wish to create a chart that includes the divisions within the story, the actions within each time period, and the specific locations the illustrations represent. They can also use a map to locate the regions. Students and the teacher can explore the reasons and visual clues they used as they identified the particular locations. Students can also pay close attention to the reader's visual point of view. In many of the illustrations, the reader has a bird's-eye view of the location. (Language Arts; Social Studies: Place; Location; Regions)

4 - 6   In addition to the above activities, younger students may wish to write, in prose or verse, the story told by Ward's illustrations. The boy's flight can be compared to the flight taken by the characters in *Randolph's Dream* (Mellecker 1991) and Ringgold's two books, *Aunt Harriet's Underground Railroad in the Sky* (1992) and *Tar Beach* (1991). (Language Arts; Social Studies: Place; Location; Regions)

Jr/Sr High   no

Weir, Bob, and Weir, Wendy. 1991. **Panther Dream: A Story of the African Rain Forest.** New York: Hyperion Paperbacks for Children.

A young boy, Lokuli, who lives with his family in a village on the edge of the rain forest, breaks a village rule and risks his own life by going into the rain forest to search for meat. This fictional account contains many facts about the African rain forest. Detailed acrylic paintings accompany the text. A key to the illustrations at the end of the book provides the names of plants and animals. A large map of Africa identifies the location of rain forests on the continent. The authors also provide a glossary of terms used in the book.

    K - 3 This book should be read aloud by the teacher and discussed. Complementary books include *Nature's Green Umbrella: Tropical Rain Forest* (Gibbons 1994), which provides a more factual approach to the subject and is less location specific, and *The Great Kapok Tree: A Tale of the Amazon Rain Forest* (Cherry 1990) and *Welcome to the Green House* (Yolen 1993), which are more lyrical in their approach. Together, these books can introduce the uniqueness of rain forests. Students and the teacher can use a world map or globe to find the imaginary lines that help locate rain forests (Equator, Tropic of Cancer, Tropic of Capricorn). Students can discuss why no rain forests are found outside this region. (Social Studies; Science: Location; Place; Human-Environmental Relations; Movement; Regions)

    4 - 6 Students at this level may wish to explore the Pygmy culture of Africa and the specific animals named in the book. Students can also research the changing condition of the rain forests in the world, particularly their destruction. (Social Studies; Science: Location; Place; Human-Environmental Relations; Movement; Regions)

  Jr/Sr High Older students can participate in the activities listed above in greater depth. (Social Studies; Science: Location; Place; Human-Environmental Relations; Movement; Regions)

Wiesner, David. 1990. **Hurricane.** New York: Clarion Books.

Two young boys weather a hurricane in the safety of their home. The next day they have wonderful imaginary adventures in an uprooted tree. Although the main focus of the story is the boys' adventures in the tree, the full-page watercolor illustrations and the text provide limited information about hurricanes and their effects on humans and the environment.

    K - 3 This book can contribute to a study of weather. *The Day the Hurricane Happened* (Anderson 1974) is a marked contrast to this book. Rather than being safely enclosed in their home, the children on the island of St. John are without shelter during the storm. Students can locate this island as well as discover what other parts of the world experience hurricanes. (Science; Social Studies: Place; Location; Human-Environmental Relations; Regions)

    4 - 6 In addition to the above activities, students can determine how location influences the likelihood that hurricanes will occur, what causes hurricanes, and how hurricanes are predicted. (Science; Social Studies: Place; Location; Human-Environmental Relations; Regions)

  Jr/Sr High no

Wiesner, David. 1992. **June 29, 1999.** New York: Clarion Books.

Holly Evans sends seedlings aloft into the ionosphere for her science project. On June 29, 1999, gigantic vegetables start falling from the sky: "Cucumbers circle Kalamazoo," "artichokes advance on Anchorage," "arugula covers Ashtabula." Detailed watercolor illustrations expand the whimsical text.

    K - 3 Children will enjoy listening to this imaginative tale of a science experiment gone awry. Students and the teacher can locate the specific U.S. towns and cities named in the alliterative text. Students might like to try their hand at creating alliterative phrases about their own local communities. In reading the book aloud to the class, the teacher will end with Holly's question, "And whose broccoli is in my backyard?" Students can tell or write their own ending to the story before the teacher completes the story. (Language Arts: Location; Place)

    4 - 6 In addition to the above activities, this book can be used to introduce the idea of scientific process. Students can determine what Holly did as she set up her experiment and carried it out. (Language Arts; Science: Location; Place)

  Jr/Sr High no

Wild, Margaret. 1991. **Let the Celebrations BEGIN!** New York: Orchard Books.

Miriam, who lives in hut 18, bed 22 in a concentration camp during World War II, tells about how she and the women of the camp plan a very special party for the children. They make toys from scraps of material, rags, torn pockets, and yarn from unraveled sweaters. The full-page, color illustrations accompany a very celebratory text, which is based on a reference to a small collection of stuffed toys made by Polish women in Belsen for the first children's party held after the liberation.

    K - 3 This book, although celebratory in nature, embraces a difficult and sophisticated subject. I would not use this book at this level.

4 - 6 This book can be used in a study of wars in general, or specifically World War II. Other books that involve World War II are *Rose Blanche* (Innocenti 1985), *Randolph's Dream* (Mellecker 1991), *The Bracelet* (Uchida 1993), and *The Bicycle Man* (Say 1989). Some students might enjoy the challenge of creating toys similar to those described by Miriam. (Social Studies; Home Economics: Location; Movement)

Jr/Sr High This book can be used to introduce the subject of concentration camps or detention camps used by enemies during war. Other books to accompany this study are *The Bracelet* (Uchida 1993) and *Pink and Say* (Polacco 1994). Students in home economics classes can make toys from materials noted in the book, creating their own patterns and directions. (Social Studies; Home Economics: Location; Movement)

Yolen, Jane. 1991. **All Those Secrets of the World.** Boston: Little, Brown.

When four-year-old Janie's father goes off to war, she and her mother and infant brother move into her grandparents' home on the Chesapeake Bay. Playing on the beach with her older cousin, Michael, she discovers a secret about near and far and big and little. Beautiful watercolors set the tone for this warm family drama.

K - 3 The concepts of near and far are clearly explained in this text, which can be used to help young children work with relational concepts: *near, far, up, down, above, below,* etc. (Social Studies: Location)

4 - 6 At this level the near and far concept can be expanded to an understanding of linear perspective. Students can be given instructions about how artists create perspective and how they can create perspective in their own drawings. Clues in the text help the reader discover the time period of this story. Students can learn more about how families like Janie's changed during wartime. They can also research the communities around Chesapeake Bay and the reason why soldiers disembarked from that location. (Social Studies; Art: Location; Place; Human-Environmental Relations; Movement)

Jr/Sr High no

Yolen, Jane. 1992. **Encounter.** San Diego: Harcourt Brace Jovanovich.

Set in 1492 in the New World, this story details Christopher Colombus's first meeting with the Taino tribespeople who lived on San Salvador, as seen through the eyes of a Taino boy. Full-page acrylic paintings illustrate the limited text, which nonetheless carries complex ideas.

K - 3 I would not use this book at this level.

4 - 6 This book can contribute to a study of Christopher Columbus's discovery of the New World. It provides an unsettling picture of the discovery and sets the stage for discussions about human rights and the impact of cultural interaction. This book can also be used in a study of the Caribbean region. Sis's book, *A Small Tall Tale from the Far Far North* (1993) looks at European influence on another cultural group—Eskimos. (Social Studies: Location; Place; Movement; Regions)

Jr/Sr High Students can explore other peoples who feel their "discovery" has been detrimental rather than helpful. (Social Studies: Location; Place; Movement; Regions)

Yolen, Jane. 1992. **Letting Swift River Go.** Boston: Little, Brown.

Sally Jane tells about the changing times in her rural community in western Massachusetts. In the mid-1900s the government purchased the Swift River area and flooded it to create a reservoir that would provide good, clear, clean water for the city of Boston. Award-winning artist Barbara Cooney has created large, full-color watercolors to illustrate this experience from the author's childhood.

K - 3 This book can provide another piece of information about big cities. In this instance it's the loss of homes in rural areas to provide water to a big city (Boston). Students can discover the source of water for their own homes or community. Students and the teacher can locate on a map the Quabbin Reservoir in Hatfield, Massachusetts. (Social Studies; Science: Location; Place; Human-Environmental Relations)

4 - 6 Older students can learn more about how water is supplied to homes and communities. The topic of reservoirs can also be researched. Students can read *Shaker Lane* (Provensen and Provensen 1987), another book that focuses on the changes brought about by the construction of a reservoir in a community. Students may wish to debate the issues of whose rights should be observed in these situations. (Social Studies; Science: Location; Place; Human-Environmental Relations)

Jr/Sr High no

Yolen, Jane. 1993. **Welcome to the Green House.** New York: G. P. Putnam's Sons.

Through the simple, lyrical text and full-page, color illustrations, this book provides a picture of the flora and fauna of the rain forest. A note at the end of the book encourages the reader to learn more about the rain forest and ways to preserve it.

> **K - 3** This book can provide an introduction to a rain forest study. Although the text is quite simple, it introduces the names of many animals found in the rain forest. Students may enjoy becoming classroom "experts" on one or more of the animals. Other, more informative books about the rain forest include *The Great Kapok Tree: A Tale of the Amazon Rain Forest* (Cherry 1990), *Nature's Green Umbrella: Tropical Rain Forest* (Gibbons 1994), and *Panther Dream: A Story of the African Rain Forest* (Weir and Weir 1991). (Language Arts; Social Studies: Location; Place; Human-Environmental Relations; Regions)

> **4 - 6** no

> **Jr/Sr High** no

Zolotow, Charlotte. 1993. **The Moon Was the Best.** New York: Greenwillow Books.

A mother visiting Paris brings back to her daughter all her best memories of beautiful fountains, the sparkling Seine, parks like paintings, and paintings like parks. The simple text is accompanied by full-page photographs by Tana Hoban.

> **K - 3** This book can contribute to a study of big cities. Students can compare and contrast the photographs of Paris with those of other large cities. Students and the teacher can speculate about the places the mother chose not to remember. Books that focus on other, specific world cities include *The Inside-Outside Book of London* (Munro 1989), *My New York* (Jakobsen 1993), *The Day of Ahmed's Secret* (Heide and Gilliland 1990), *Sami and the Time of the Troubles* (Heide and Gilliland 1992), and *Our Home Is the Sea* (Levinson 1992). (Social Studies: Location; Place)

> **4 - 6** In a study of big cities, students can create brochures designed to draw visitors to their community. Using this book as a model, students can then create a brochure that highlights the places within their community that they personally find significant. (Social Studies; Language Arts: Location; Place; Human-Environmental Relations)

> **Jr/Sr High** no

Zolotow, Charlotte. 1992. **The Seashore Book.** New York: HarperCollins.

In answer to her son's question, "What is a seashore like?," a mother describes the sights and sounds of the seashore as if she and her son were there to experience them. Full-page watercolors accompany the simple but descriptive text.

> **K - 3** This simple book provides a very realistic and sensual description of the ocean shore. The illustrations also contribute to its realism and tone. The book can be used with other books about the seashore, such as *Let's Discover the Seaside* (Rius and Parramon 1986), *The Summer Sands* (Garland 1995), and *The Story of the Seashore* (Goodall 1990). It can also contribute to a study of the five senses as the text contains many sense-related phrases and sentences: "washed smooth by the sea," "the swishswashing sound," and "the setting sun is a huge orange ball." (Science; Social Studies: Location; Place)

> **4 - 6** no

> **Jr/Sr High** no

Geography Reference Books for Children

The books in this section are recommended as classroom reference books to be made available regularly to students as well as part of specific classroom studies and activities.

*Anno, Mitsumasa. 1987. **Anno's Sundial.** New York: Philomel Books.

In this unique pop-up picture book, Anno provides the reader with a three-dimensional view of time. The complex relationship between the motions of the sun and the Earth is presented clearly. Readers are encouraged to interact with the pop-ups as well as create their own sundials.

> **K - 3** no

> **4 - 6** Appropriate for more mature students. (Math; Science: Location)

Jr/Sr High   A very useful and usable resource for this grade range. (Math; Science: Location)

Berger, Melvin, and Berger, Guilda. 1993. **The Whole World in Your Hands: Looking at Maps.** Nashville, TN: Ideals Children's Books.

This book introduces children to maps, beginning in the home of Sammy and Jane, and progressing through their town, state, country, and the world. The text offers information on directional clues and symbols found on maps, as well as geographic terms. Small, colorful, cartoonlike illustrations accompany the text.

      K - 3   This book provides a good basis for a beginning map skills unit in the primary classroom. With the teacher's guidance, students can create floor plans of the classroom, their bedroom, and their home. Later they can make maps of the school and local neighborhood. (Social Studies: Location)

      4 - 6   Although this book is very simply written, some students at this level can benefit from the presentation of mapping skills and geographic terms. (Social Studies: Location)

Jr/Sr High   no

*Billout, Guy. 1980. **Stone and Steel.** Englewood Cliffs, NJ: Prentice-Hall.

The author uses line drawings, watercolors, and text to describe bridges and buildings of historical interest. The text includes facts about the construction and use of each structure. Included in the book are the Chesapeake Bay Bridge and Tunnel, Minot's Ledge Lighthouse, and the Cathedral of St. John the Divine.

      K - 3   Second- and third-graders will find this book intriguing because of the illustrations and the uniqueness of the subjects the author chose to depict. Students and the teacher can locate each site on a world map as well as explore the specifics of the locality. Some students may want to try to duplicate Billout's method of drawing and painting the same subject. (Social Studies; Art: Location; Place)

      4 - 6   In addition to the above activities, older students might want to research some of the book's subjects. (Social Studies; Art: Location; Place; Human-Environmental Relations)

Jr/Sr High   Older students, particularly in drafting classes, may want to attempt creating similar types of drawings of local subjects. (Social Studies; Art: Location; Place; Human-Environmental Relations)

*Branley, Franklyn M. 1986. **What Makes Day and Night.** New York: Thomas Y. Crowell.

This book provides a beginning look at how the Earth's rotation creates day and night. Cartoonlike illustrations enhance the text.

      K - 3   This very elementary book can be used to begin a study of the concept of rotation and Earth's day and night. (Social Studies; Science: Location)

      4 - 6   no

Jr/Sr High   no

Brown, David J. 1992. **The Random House Book of How Things Are Built.** New York: Random House.

This is an illustrated history of the most notable structures of the world located on the five most densely populated continents. The buildings are presented in four sections: The Ancient World, The Age of Discovery, The "New" Technology, and The Modern World. Included among the more than 60 detailed pen-and-ink diagrams are the Parthenon, the Tower of London, the Eiffel Tower, the Hong Kong Bank, the Channel Tunnel, and the Golden Gate Bridge.

      K - 3   Although students will enjoy this book's illustrations, the explanations are quite sophisticated. (Social Studies: Location; Place)

      4 - 6   Older students will enjoy using this book to expand their knowledge about the famous landmarks described in this text. Included are several structures mentioned in other books, such as the Great Wall of China, featured in *Talking Walls* (Knight 1992); *Let's Go Traveling* (Krupp 1992); and *Ben's Dream* (Van Allsburg 1982). This book can contribute to a study of Human-Environmental Relations. (Social Studies: Location; Place; Human-Environmental Relations)

Jr/Sr High   Students at this level can complete the above activities in more depth. (Social Studies; Science: Location; Place; Human-Environmental Relations)

Bulla, Clyde Robert. 1994. **What Makes a Shadow?** New York: HarperCollins.

This delightful little 30-page book, with bright, cheerful illustrations, provides a clearly written, logical explanation of what makes a shadow. The book also touches briefly on the concepts of day and night.

K - 3 This book can introduce very young students to basic scientific concepts about the relationship of the Earth and the sun. (Science; Social Studies: Location)

4 - 6 no

Jr/Sr High no

Chapman, Gillian, and Robson, Pam. 1993. **Maps and Mazes.** Brookfield, CT: Millbrook Press.

This text provides a visual introduction to the principles of maps and mazes. Among the principles covered are 3D and 2D, direction, scale, contours and coasts, and latitude and longitude. Colorful illustrations enhance the text, which also includes projects for children to complete independently.

K - 3 The book can be a helpful reference tool as the teacher introduces the principles included in the text. It can also be a useful resource for more mature students to use independently. (Language Arts; Social Studies: Location)

4 - 6 A useful resource for students to use independently. (Language Arts; Social Studies: Location)

Jr/Sr High no

Fowler, Allan. 1993. **North, South, East, and West.** Chicago: Childrens Press.

Using photographs, the author gives a simple explanation of the four main directions and tells how to use the sun to determine directions.

K - 3 This very elementary book can be used to begin a study of the concept of ordinal directions. Students can go outside on a sunny day and, using the author's instructions, practice finding north, south, east, and west. (Social Studies: Location)

4 - 6 no

Jr/Sr High no

Gerberg, Mort. 1991. **Geographunny.** New York: Clarion Books.

This is a collection of riddles about four world areas: the United States and Canada; Mexico, South America, and Antarctica; Europe, the Middle East, and Africa; and Asia and the Pacific Islands. A map introduces each section. A riddle example: "Why would you wear lots of sweaters in a certain South American country? Because it's Chile."

K - 3 Second- and third-graders who delight in riddles will enjoy this silly introduction to world areas. Students can identify the seven continents. Students and the teacher can compare the maps in the book to the same world areas on a globe. (Social Studies; Language Arts: Location; Place)

4 - 6 Gerberg's humor can serve as a model for students as they study particular regions of the world. Students can then create their own geography riddles. (Social Studies; Language Arts: Location; Place)

Jr/Sr High no

Gibbons, Gail. 1995. **Planet Earth/Inside Out.** New York: Morrow Junior Books.

Full-page color illustrations and diagrams provide visual information to accompany written descriptions of how scientists believe the Earth was formed and how it has changed over billions of years. Descriptions of rocks in the Earth's crust and various "Earth Facts" are found at the end of the book.

K - 3 This book provides a clear explanation of scientific theory describing the Earth's formation and related geology facts. It offers basic information about plate tectonics, volcanoes, and earthquakes. (Science: Movement)

4 - 6 This book may be helpful for some students at this level. (Science: Movement)

Jr/Sr High no

Gibbons, Gail. 1995. **The Reasons for Seasons.** New York: Holiday House.

Full-page, color illustrations and diagrams explain how the position of the Earth in relation to the sun causes the seasons. The characteristics of each season and the activities humans engage in are also described.

K - 3 This book provides a clear explanation of how the relationship between the Earth and the sun causes the seasons. It can be very helpful in a science unit about seasons, revolution and rotation of the Earth, and the contrast between hemispheres. (Social Studies; Science: Human-Environmental Relations)

4 - 6 This book may be useful in helping students confused by the concepts of seasons and the revolution and rotation of the Earth. (Social Studies; Science: Human-Environmental Relations)

Jr/Sr High no

Hartman, Gail. 1991. **As the Crow Flies: A First Book of Maps.** New York: Bradbury Press.
This introductory map book begins by showing the reader five mini-maps from the perspectives of an eagle, a rabbit, a crow, a horse, and a gull. The five maps are then combined into one large map. The whimsical illustrations are pen and ink and watercolor.

K - 3 This book provides an introduction to connecting parts to make a whole. Older students can each make a map of their own neighborhood or a map illustrating their trip from home to school. Then, with the teacher's help, all of the maps can be combined to illustrate the school's neighborhood and the relationship between individual homes and school and the relationship among the students' homes. (Social Studies: Location; Place)

4 - 6 no

Jr/Sr High no

Hartman, Gail. 1994. **As the Roadrunner Runs: A First Book of Maps.** New York: Bradbury Press.
This introductory map book, set in the Southwest, begins by showing the reader five mini-maps from the perspectives of a lizard, a jackrabbit, a roadrunner, a mule, and a deer. The five maps are then combined into one large map. The whimsical illustrations are pen and ink and watercolor.

K - 3 This book provides an introduction to connecting parts to make a whole. Older students can each make a map of their own neighborhood or a map illustrating their trip from home to school. Then, with the teacher's help, all of the maps can be combined to illustrate the school's neighborhood and the relationship between individual homes and school and the relationship among the students' homes. (Social Studies: Location; Place)

4 - 6 no

Jr/Sr High no

Knowlton, Jack. 1988. **Geography from A to Z: A Picture Glossary.** New York: Thomas Y. Crowell.
This book is a glossary of geographic terms, from *archipelago* to *zone,* with 63 definitions and descriptions of the Earth's features. The text is accompanied by colorful, cartoonlike drawings.

K - 3 This book is a good classroom reference for this level. (Social Studies: Location)

4 - 6 no

Jr/Sr High no

Knowlton, Jack. 1985. **Maps and Globes.** New York: Thomas Y. Crowell.
The author begins with a simple, brief history of mapmaking. He then offers a clear explanation of how to read and use maps and globes. Also included is an introduction to the many kinds of maps and an explanation for more than two dozen important geographic terms. The text is enhanced by colorful, cartoonlike drawings.

K - 3 This book can be useful to expand older students' understanding of maps and globes. It is probably too complicated for the younger end of this age level. (Social Studies: Location; Place)

4 - 6 This book will provide a good review for more knowledgeable students. It provides good basic facts and information for students with limited map and globe skills. (Social Studies: Location; Place)

Jr/Sr High Of limited use for this level. (Social Studies: Location)

Lourie, Peter. 1994. **Everglades: Buffalo Tiger and the River of Grass.** Honesdale, PA: Boyds Mills Press.
The author and photographer, Peter Lourie, takes the reader on a trip through the Florida Everglades. The guide, Buffalo Tiger, is a Native American and former chief of the Miccosukees. Buffalo Tiger provides Lourie and his readers with a tour of the Everglades' flora and fauna, along with a historical look at this endangered region.

K - 3 The text in this book is too sophisticated for this level.

4 - 6 The text in this book is quite complex, so it would be best used by more mature students or with the teacher's help. The book can contribute to a look at endangered regions, the conflict between cultures, and a regional study of the U.S. Southeast. *The Atlas of Endangered Animals* (Pollock 1993) could be used in conjunction with this book. (Social Studies; Science: Location; Place; Human-Environmental Relations; Regions)

Jr/Sr High This book would be especially useful for students at this level who are studying human influence on the environment. The problems that modern society have brought to the Everglades can be researched by students. They may wish to explore the sacred beliefs of Native Americans, which Lourie asserts might help us save this endangered region. (Social Studies; Science: Location; Place; Human-Environmental Relations; Regions)

Morris, Neil. 1993. **The Student's Activity Atlas.** Milwaukee, WI: Gareth Stevens.
Maps, photographs, and charts accompany clearly written, informative text that introduces regions and countries of the world. The author also provides activities for students to complete to practice reading the maps and interpreting the atlas symbols.

K - 3 This book can serve as a good classroom reference book for student study of locations and map skills. (Social Studies: Location)

4 - 6 This book can be useful as a reference book at this level. (Social Studies: Location)

Jr/Sr High This book can be useful at the junior high level. (Social Studies: Location)

Pollock, Steve. 1993. **The Atlas of Endangered Animals.** New York: Facts on File.
The text and maps in this book focus on areas of the world in which human activity is threatening to destroy endangered species of animals. Nineteen regions, including the United States, South America, central and southern Africa, and the Commonwealth of Independent States (CIS—the former USSR), are the focus of coverage. Each regional study features a topographical map, which includes animal locales and photographs of the locales, as well as a mileage scale and a small insert map showing the region's location relative to the world. Symbols indicate the condition of the endangered animal: extinct, vulnerable, or commercially threatened.

K - 3 Older students will enjoy reading this text for the information it supplies. This book can accompany the rain forest picture books *Nature's Green Umbrella: Tropical Rain Forest* (Gibbons 1994), *Welcome to the Green House* (Yolen 1993), *The Great Kapok Tree: A Tale of the Amazon Rain Forest* (Cherry 1990), and *Panther Dream: A Story of the African Rain Forest* (Weir and Weir 1991). (Social Studies; Science: Human-Environmental Relations)

4 - 6 This book can provide important references for students at this level as they consider the relationship of humans to the environment. (Social Studies; Science: Human-Environmental Relations)

Jr/Sr High This book would be suitable for the younger students at this level. (Social Studies; Science: Human-Environmental Relations)

Rosenthal, Paul. 1992. **Where on Earth: A Geografunny Guide to the Globe.** New York: Alfred A. Knopf.
This book offers a humorous introduction to geographic concepts and how they affect life on the continents. Interesting facts about each continent are woven through traditional text and colored cartoon drawings. The international date line, specific mountain ranges, the Great Lakes, the Panama Canal, and plants and animals indigenous to each continent are among the subjects discussed.

K - 3 Of limited use at this level.

4 - 6 This text can be useful as students study the seven continents. The illustrations are cleverly constructed cartoons that express a concept contained in the text. They offer models for cartoons or posters that students can create based on factual information they wish to share. The humor may be too sophisticated for some students to understand. (Social Studies: Location)

Jr/Sr High Students at this level can use this text as a resource. (Social Studies: Location)

Sipiera, Paul P. 1991. **Globes.** Chicago: Childrens Press.
This book describes the usefulness of globes to show the roundness of the Earth and various consequences of that roundness. Photographs and diagrams accompany historical information and conceptual explanations.

K - 3 This book can be a useful classroom reference and support source for map skills study. (Social Studies: Location)

4 - 6 This book can be useful at this level. (Social Studies: Location)

Jr/Sr High no

Taylor, Barbara. 1993. **Maps and Mapping.** New York: Kingfisher Books.

Through simple text and colored drawings, this book explains what maps are and why they are used. Map symbols are introduced as well as cartographers' skills. Do-it-yourself activities are included.

K - 3 This book can be useful as a reference and support tool for map skills study by more mature students. (Social Studies: Location)

4 - 6 This book can be useful at this level. (Social Studies: Location)

Jr/Sr High This book can be useful as a reference and support tool for junior high students. (Social Studies: Location)

Appendix B

TEACHER RESOURCES

Professional Journals and Books

Abler, R. F. 1987. "What Shall We Say? To Whom Shall We Speak?" *Annals of the Association of American Geographers* 77: 511-24.

Audet, T. I., Gibson, K., and Flag, A. 1995. "A Treasure Chest of Life." *The Mailbox* 17, no. 2: 26-30.

Boehm, R. G., and Petersen, J. F. 1994. "An Elaboration of the Fundamental Themes in Geography." *Social Education* 58, no. 4: 211-18.

Gardner, D. P. 1986. "Geography in the School Curriculum." *Annals of the Association of American Geographers* 76: 1-4.

Grosvenor, G. M. 1985. "Geographic Ignorance: Time for a Turnaround." *National Geographic* 167, no. 6.

Hill, A. D., and LaPrairie, L. A. 1989. "Geography in American Education. In *Geography in America,* edited by G. L. Gaile and C. J. Willmott, 1-26. Columbus, OH: Merrill.

Jenness, D. 1990. *Making Sense of Social Studies.* New York: Macmillan.

Kimball, W. 1987. *K-6 Geography: Themes, Key Ideas, and Learning Opportunities.* New York: American Geographical Society.

Lawton, M. 1995. "Students Fall Short in NAEP Geography Test." *Education Week* 15, no. 8: 1, 23.

Natoli, S. J. 1994. "Guidelands for Geographic Education and the Fundamental Themes in Geography." *Journal of Geography* 93, no. 1: 2-6.

Ogle, D. M. "K-W-L: A Teaching Model That Develops Active Reading of Expository Text." *Reading Teacher* 39 (February 1986): 564-70.

———. "K-W-L Plus." *Journal of Reading* 30 (1988): 628-29.

Rogers, L. and Bromley, K. "Children's Literature: A Vehicle for Developing Geographic Literacy." *Social Studies and the Young Learner* 8 (November-December 1995): Pull-out feature II.

Salter, C. L. 1987. "The Nature and Potential of a Geographic Alliance. *Journal of Geography* 86, no. 5: 211-15.

Salter, K. 1991. "The University and the Alliance: A Study in Contradictions." *Journal of Geography* 90, no. 2: 55-59.

Salter, K., and Salter, C. 1995. "Significant New Materials for the Geography Classroom." *Journal of Geography* 94, no. 4: 444-52.

Saveland, R. N. 1993. "School Geography." In *Teaching Social Studies*, edited by V. S. Wilson, J. A. Litle, and G. L. Wilson, 131-46. Westport, CT: Greenwood Press.

Schmudde, T. H. 1987. "The Image of Geography Equals the Structure of Its Curriculum and Courses." *Journal of Geography* 86, no. 2: 46-47.

Other Useful Resources

The Children's Rainforest, P.O. Box 936, Lewiston, ME 04240. Contact this organization for information about purchasing acres of rain forest.

Geography for Life: National Geography Standards 1994. To order, send a check and a written request with your name, institution, address, and product number [#01775-12160] to National Geographic Society, P.O. Box 1640, Washington, DC 20013-1640. Single copy: $9. Discount for multiple copies.

K-6 Geography: Themes, Key Ideas, and Learning Opportunities. To order, send a check and a written request with your name, institution, and address to National Council for Geographic Education, Western Illinois University, Macomb, IL 61455. Single copy: approx. $6.

Key to the National Geography Standards. To order, send a check with your name, institution, and address to Ms. Connie McCardle, National Council for Geographic Education, NCGE Central Office, Indiana University of Pennsylvania, Indiana, PA 15705. (412) 357-6290; (412) 357-7708 (fax). Single copy: approx. $3.

Geographic Alliance Network - Alliance Coordinators

Alabama

Howard G. Johnson
Department of Geography
Jacksonville State University
Jacksonville, AL 36265
(205) 782-5813

David Weaver
Department of Geography
University of Alabama
Tuscaloosa, AL 35487-1982
(205) 348-5047

Alaska

Roger W. Pearson
Department of Geography
University of Alaska
Fairbanks, AK 99775-0780
(907) 474-9474

Arkansas

D. Brooks Green
Department of Geography
University of Central Arkansas
Conway, AR 72032
(501) 450-3164

Gerald T. Hanson
Department of Geography
University of Arkansas at Little Rock
2801 South University
Little Rock, AR 72204
(501) 569-8730

California

Northern

Jerry R. Williams
Department of Geography
California State University
Chico, CA 95929-0425
(906) 898-6219

Southern

John Brierley
Venice High School
13000 Venice Boulevard
Los Angeles, CA 90066
(213) 306-7981

Gail L. Hobbs
Department of Earth Sciences/Geography
Pierce College
6201 Winnetka Avenue
Woodland Hills, CA 91371
(818) 992-0359

Colorado

David Cole
Department of Geography
University of Northern Colorado
Greeley, CO 80639
(303) 351-2346

A. David Hill
Department of Geography
Campus Box 260
University of Colorado
Boulder, CO 80309-0260
(303) 492-6854

Connecticut

Daniel W. Gregg
Social Studies Consultant
Connecticut State Department of Education
165 Capitol Avenue, Room 373
Hartford, CT 06106
(203) 566-5223

Judith W. Meyer
Department of Geography, U-148
University of Connecticut
Storrs, CT 06269-2148
(203) 486-0374

Delaware

Lewis Huffman
Social Studies Coordinator
Department of Public Instruction
Townsend Building
Dover, DE 19903
(302) 739-4629

Peter W. Rees
Department of Geography
University of Delaware
Newark, DE 19716
(302) 831-2294

Florida

Edward A. Fernald
Laurie Molina
Institute of Science and Public Affairs
Florida State University
Tallahassee, FL 32306
(904) 644-2007

Georgia

Truman A. Hartshorn
Department of Geography
Georgia State University
Atlanta, GA 30303
(404) 651-3232

Robert R. Myers
Department of Geography
West Georgia College
Carrollton, GA 30118
(404) 836-6457

Hawaii

Mary Frances Higuchi
Thomas Ohta
Department of Geography
University of Hawaii at Manoa
Portcus 407, 2424 Maile Way
Honolulu, HI 96822
(808) 956-7445 or 956-7698

Idaho

Elton Bentley
Boise State University
Department of Geography
1910 University Drive
Boise, ID 83725
(208) 385-1561

Katherine A. Young
Department of Teacher Education
Boise State University
1910 University Drive
Boise, ID 83725
(208) 385-3593

Illinois

Norman C. Bettis
Department of Curriculum and Instruction
Illinois State University
Normal, IL 61761-6901
(309) 438-2669

Indiana

Frederick Bein
Department of Geography
Indiana University/Purdue University at Indianapolis
425 University Boulevard
Indianapolis, IN 46202
(317) 274-8879

Iowa

James N. Hantula
Department of Teaching
Price Lab School
University of Northern Iowa
Cedar Falls, IA 50614-3593
(319) 273-2055

C. Murray Austin
Department of Geography
University of Northern Iowa
Cedar Falls, IA 50614-0406
(319) 273-2016

Kansas

M. Duane Nellis
Department of Geography
Dickens Hall
Kansas State University
Manhattan, KS 66506-0801
(913) 532-6727

Paul E. Phillips
Earth Sciences Department
Fort Hays State University
600 Park Street
Hays, KS 67601-4099
(913) 628-5821

Kentucky

Dennis Spetz
Department of Geography
University of Louisville
Louisville, KY 40292
(502) 588-6444

Albert J. Petersen, Jr.
Department of Geography
336 Environmental Science Building
Western Kentucky University
Bowling Green, KY 42101
(502) 745-5977 or 745-4555

Louisiana

Philip Larimore
Louisiana State University
Department of Geography
    and Anthropology
Room 227, Geology Building
Baton Rouge, LA 70803-4105
(504) 388-5942

William J. Miller
Louisiana State Department of Education
P.O. Box 94064
Baton Rouge, LA 70804-9064
(504) 342-1136

Maine

Robert French
University of Southern Maine
Department of Geography
    and Anthropology
37 College Avenue
Gorham, ME 04038
(207) 780-5570

Connie Manter
Maine Department of Education
State House 23
Augusta, ME 04333
(207) 287-5925

Maryland

Sari Bennett
Department of Geography
University of Maryland-
    Baltimore County
5401 Wilkens Avenue
Catonsville, MD 21228-5398
(410) 455-3148

Massachusetts

Richard T. Anderson
Department of Geography
Salem State College
Salem, MA 01970
(508) 741-6486

Paul Mulloy
Winchester Public Schools
154 Horn Pond Brook Road
Winchester, MA 01890
(617) 721-1257

Michigan

Michael Libbee
Department of Geography
Central Michigan University
Mount Pleasant, MI 48859
(517) 774-3723

Joseph P. Stoltman
Department of Geography
Western Michigan University
Kalamazoo, MI 49008
(616) 387-3429

Minnesota

David A. Lanegran
Department of Geography
Macalester College
St. Paul, MN 55105
(612) 696-6504

Mississippi

Jesse McKee
University of Southern Mississippi
Geography and Area Department
Southern Station, Box 5051
Hattiesburg, MS 39406-5051
(601) 266-4729

Missouri

Gail S. Ludwig
Department of Geography
University of Missouri
Columbia, MO 65211
(314) 882-3233 or 882-3993

Nebraska

Charles R. Gildersleeve
Department of Geography
University of Nebraska-Omaha
60th and Dodge Streets
Omaha, NE 68182-0199
(402) 554-4803

Robert H. Stoddard
Department of Geography
University of Nebraska-Lincoln
313 Avery Hall
Lincoln, NE 68588-0135
(402) 472-3573 or 472-2865

Nevada

Gary Hausladen
University of Nevada-Reno
Department of Geography, 154
Reno, NV 89557-0048
(702) 784-6965

Robert S. Amblad
Greenspun Junior High School
140 N. Valle Verde
Hendersen, NV 89014
(702) 799-0920

New Hampshire

Carter B. Hart
New Hampshire Department of Education
State Office Park South
101 Pleasant Street
Concord, NH 03301
(603) 271-2632

Thomas Havill
Department of Geography
Keene State College
229 Main Street
Keene, NH 03431
(603) 358-2511

New Mexico

Peggy J. Blackwell
University of New Mexico
College of Education
Albuquerque, NM 87109
(505) 277-3637

New York

John Crawford
Lake Shore Central Schools
8855 Erie Road
Angola, NY 14006
(716) 549-2300

Robert M. Pierce
Department of Geography
SUNY-Cortland
Cortland, NY 13045
(607) 753-2995

North Carolina

William Imperatore
Department of Geography
Appalachian State University
Boone, NC 28608
(704) 262-2652

Douglas C. Wilms
Department of Geography
East Carolina University
Greenville, NC 27858
(919) 757-1463

North Dakota

Curt Eriksmoen
Social Studies Curriculum Coordinator
North Dakota Department
    of Public Instruction
State Capitol
600 East Boulevard Avenue, 9th Floor
Bismarck, ND 58505-0440
(701) 224-4568

Douglas C. Munski
Department of Geography
Box 8275, University Station
University of North Dakota
Grand Forks, ND 58202
(701) 777-4246

Ohio

W. Randy Smith
Department of Geography
Ohio State University
Mershon Center
199 W. 10th Avenue
Columbus, OH 43201
(614) 292-1681

Oklahoma

James M. Goodman
Department of Geography
University of Oklahoma
Norman, OK 73019-0535
(405) 325-6524

Oregon

Gil Latz
International Trade Institute
One World Trade Center
121 Southwest Salmon Street,
    Suite 203
Portland, OR 97204
(503) 725-3246

Joanne Flint
Dayton High School
801 Ferry Street
Dayton, OR 97114
(503) 864-2273 or 864-2331

Pennsylvania

Ruth Shirey
Department of Geography
    and Regional Planning
Indiana University of Pennsylvania
Indiana, PA 15705
(412) 357-5098

James J. Wetzler
Social Studies Coordinator
Pennsylvania Department of Education
333 Market Street, 8th Floor
Harrisburg, PA 17126-0333
(717) 783-1832

Puerto Rico

Jose Molinelli
Environmental Science Program
University of Puerto Rico
Rio Piedras Campus
P.O. Box 22540, UPR Station
Rio Piedras, PR 00931
(809) 764-0000, ext. 2550

Lillian Bird
Department of Chemistry
University of Puerto Rico
Rio Piedras Campus
P.O. Box 23346, UPR Station
Rio Piedras, PR 00931
(809) 763-3599

Rhode Island

Anne K. Petry
Rhode Island College
Providence, RI 02908
(401) 456-0816

Chester E. Smolski
Rhode Island College
Providence, RI 02908
(401) 456-8486

South Carolina

Richard Silvernail
Department of Geography
University of South Carolina,
    CSSC 114
Columbia, SC 29208
(803) 777-5234

South Dakota

Charles F. Gritzner
South Dakota State University
Department of Geography
Brookings, SD 57007-0648
(605) 688-4613

Tennessee

Sidney R. Jumper
Ted Schmuddee
Department of Geography
University of Tennessee
Knoxville, TN 37996-1420
(615) 974-2418

Texas

Sarah Bednarz
Department of Geography
Texas A&M University
College Station, TX 77843-3147
(409) 845-7141

Richard Boehm
Department of Geography
Southwest Texas State University
San Marcos, TX 78666
(512) 245-2170

Utah

Cliff Craig
Department of Geography
Natural Resources Building
Room 201
Utah State University
Logan, UT 84322-5240
(801) 750-1370

Wayne Wahlquist
Department of Geography
Weber State College
Ogden, UT 84408
(801) 626-6207

Vermont
> Aulis Lind
> University of Vermont
> Department of Geography
> 112 Old Mill Building
> Burlington, VT 05405-0114
> (802) 656-3060

Robert Churchill
Middlebury College
Department of Geography
Middlebury, VT 05753
(802) 388-3711

Virginia
> Steven K. Pontius
> P.O. Box 6940
> College of Arts and Sciences
> Radford University
> Radford, VA 24142
> (540) 831-5338

Robert Morrill
Department of Geography
301 Patton Hall
Virginia Polytechnic Institute & State University
Blacksburg, VA 24061
(540) 231-5790

West Virginia
> Barbara Jones
> Office of Instructional Services
> West Virginia Department of Education
> B-330, Building 6
> 1900 Kanawha Boulevard East
> Charleston, WV 25305-0330
> (304) 558-7805

Joseph T. Manzo
Concord College
Department of Geography
P.O. Box 68
Athens, WV 24712
(304) 384-5208

Wisconsin
> Michael Hartoonian
> Wisconsin Department
>   of Public Instruction
> 125 S. Webster Street
> P.O. Box 7841
> Madison, WI 53707
> (608) 267-9273

Richard S. Palm
Department of Geography
University of Wisconsin, Eau Claire
Eau Claire, WI 54701
(715) 836-5166 or 836-3244

Wyoming
> William J. Gribb
> Linda Marston
> University of Wyoming
> Department of Geography
> Box 3371
> Laramie, WY 82071
> (307) 766-3311

Author/Title Index

Authors' names are in roman type; titles are in italic. Bold page numbers indicate entries in "Appendix A: Annotated Bibliography."

Subject Index

Bold page numbers indicate works in "Appendix A: Annotated Bibliography."

ABOUT THE AUTHOR

Linda K. Rogers was born and raised in Springfield, Illinois. She has a B.A. in Elementary Education from Blackburn College, an M.S. in Reading from the University of Scranton, and will complete an Ed.D. in Educational Theory and Practice from Binghamton University in 1997.

Linda's career began in Illinois as an elementary classroom teacher. She worked with children in small groups as a Title I/Chapter I reading teacher and provided enrichment activities to all of the students (K-6) as the school's Resource teacher. After the family moved to Pennsylvania, Linda became involved in teacher education and Christian education. She was Coordinator of Christian Education for 10 years in her own parish and continues to serve on the Diocesan Christian Education Committee. She edits the Diocesan Christian Education newsletter, *Our Staff*. Linda has taught methods courses and supervised undergraduate student teachers at the University of Scranton, supervised master's students at Binghamton University, and is a full-time supervisor for East Stroudsburg University. Throughout her career in education, Linda has seen herself as a resource person, catalyst, and advocate for teachers.

Linda and her husband, John ("Jack"), live in Clarks Summit, Pennsylvania. They have three children: John, Sarah, and Hallie.

From **Teacher Ideas Press**

U.S. HISTORY THROUGH CHILDREN'S LITERATURE:
From the Colonial Period to World War II
Wanda J. Miller

Enhance the study of U.S. history with historical fiction and nonfiction. Stepping back in time to experience a character's dilemmas, thoughts, feelings, and actions helps students easily grasp and retain a true understanding of an era. Here is all the material you need to begin a literature-based history program. **Grades 4–8**.
xiv, 229p. 8½x11 paper ISBN 1-56308-440-6

APPRECIATING DIVERSITY THROUGH CHILDREN'S LITERATURE: Teaching Activities for the Primary Grades
Meredith McGowan, Patricia J. Wheeler, and Tom McGowan

Incorporating literature about diverse people into the curriculum encourages students to comprehend and value diversity. In this resource, stories that focus on four areas of diversity—age, gender, physical abilities, and ethnicity—provide the basis for activities that encourage children to think, empathize, and take action. **Grades 1–3**.
xvii, 135p. 8½x11 paper ISBN 1-56308-117-2

SOCIAL STUDIES THROUGH CHILDREN'S LITERATURE: An Integrated Approach
Anthony D. Fredericks

This activity-centered approach to elementary social studies features children's picture books that illustrate important social studies concepts. Fredericks shows you how to make connections between social studies and literature and how to use book webbing. **Grades K–5**.
xviii, 192p. 8½x11 paper ISBN 0-87287-970-4

MATH THROUGH CHILDREN'S LITERATURE: Making the NCTM Standards Come Alive
Kathryn L. Braddon, Nancy J. Hall, and Dale Taylor

Launch children into the world of mathematical literacy with books that give them the opportunity to experience the joy of math through their **own** understanding. Following the NCTM Standards, these literature activities are designed around an integrated reading process that captures a child's interest and brings math to life. **Grades 1–6**.
xviii, 218p. 8½x11 paper ISBN 0-87287-932-1

SCIENCE THROUGH CHILDREN'S LITERATURE: An Integrated Approach
Carol M. Butzow and John W. Butzow

This best-seller provides instructional units that integrate all areas of the curriculum and serve as models to educators at all levels. Adopted by schools of education nationwide, it features more than 30 outstanding children's fiction books that are rich in scientific concepts yet equally well known for their strong story lines and universal appeal. **Grades K–3**.
xviii, 234p. 8½x11 paper ISBN 0-87287-667-5

ART THROUGH CHILDREN'S LITERATURE: Creative Art Lessons for Caldecott Books
Debi Englebaugh

With this book, your students can create art with qualities similar to the award-winning illustrations of 57 Caldecott books. Myriad lessons focus on such principles and elements as line, color, texture, shape, value, and space with step-by-step instructions, materials lists, and detailed illustrations. **Grades K–6**.
xii, 199p. 8½x11 paper ISBN 1-56308-154-7

For a FREE catalog or to place an order, please contact:

Teacher Ideas Press
Dept. B37 · P.O. Box 6633 · Englewood, CO 80155-6633
1-800-237-6124, ext. 1 · Fax: 303-220-8843 · E-mail: lu-books@lu.com

 Check out the TIP Web site!
www.lu.com/tip